1996

an introduction to

Dynamics of Group Leadership

and

Organizational Change

Also by Russell D. Robinson:

An Introduction to Helping Adults Learn and Change
Revised Edition (1994)

Available from Omnibook Co.
1171 Decorah Rd
West Bend, WI 53095

Teaching the Scriptures: A Study Guide for Bible Students and Teachers
Sixth Edition, Revised (1993)

Available from Bible Study Aids,
9017 N. 70th Street
Milwaukee, WI 53223

an introduction to

DYNAMICS
of
GROUP
LEADERSHIP
and
ORGANIZATIONAL
CHANGE

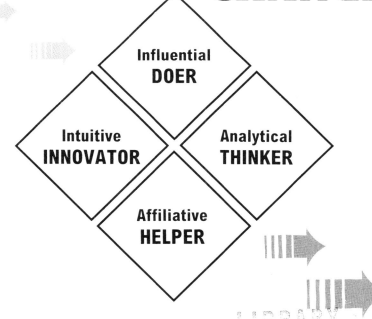

Influential
DOER

Intuitive
INNOVATOR

Analytical
THINKER

Affiliative
HELPER

by
Russell D. Robinson, Ph.D
Professor of Administrative Leadership
University of Wisconsin-Milwaukee

Revised Edition

OMNIBOOK CO.
West Bend, Wisconsin, U.S.A.

Fifth Edition, Revised and Expanded
Copyright, 1995
by
Russell D. Robinson

First Edition, 1977

Second Edition
Copyright, 1979

Third Edition, 1982

Fourth Edition, 1989

ISBN 1-877837-02-4

Printed in the United States of America

1171 Decorah Road   ●   West Bend, Wisconsin 53095-9509   U.S.A.
Phone: (414) 675-2760   ●   FAX: (414) 675-2340

to my father and mother,

> Dean D. Robinson and Dorothea Carter Robinson
> whose examples of effective community leadership
> shaped my youth and young adulthood

to my children,

> my sons, Dean and Daniel
> and my daughter, Lynn
> who are providing leadership in many ways
> at home and in the workplace

to my grandchildren,

> Steven, Heather, Jennifer, Brittany, and Hannah
> budding leaders though they may not yet realize it

to my wife, Helen

> doer, thinker, helper, innovator,
> partner in leadership and change

THE CALF-PATH

One day, thru the primeval wood,
A calf walked home, as good calves should,
But made a trail all bent askew,
A crooked trail as all calves do.

Since then two hundred years have fled,
And, I infer, the calf is dead.
But still he left behind his trail,
And thereby hangs my moral tale.

The trail was taken up next day
By a lone dog that passed that way;
And then a wise bellwether sheep
Pursued the trail o'er vale and steep,

And drew the flock behind him, too,
As good bellwethers always do.
And from that day, o'er hill and glade,
Through those old woods, a path was made;

And many men wound in and out,
And dodged, and turned, and bent about
And uttered words of righteous wrath
Because 'twas such a crooked path.

But still they followed—do not laugh—
The first migrations of that calf,
And through this winding wood-way stalked,
Because he wobbled when he walked.

This forest path became a lane,
That bent, and turned, and turned again;
This crooked lane became a road,
Where many a poor horse with his load

Toiled on beneath the burning sun,
And traveled some three miles in one.
And thus a century and a half
They trod the footsteps of that calf.

The years passed on in swiftness fleet,
The road became a village street;
And thus, before men were aware,
A city's crowded thoroughfare;

And soon the central street was this
Of a renowned metropolis;
And men two centuries and a half
Trod in the footsteps of that calf.

Each day a hundred thousand rout,
Followed the zigzag calf about;
And o'er his crooked journey went
The traffic of a continent.

A hundred thousand men were led
By one calf near three centuries dead.
They followed still his crooked way,
And lost one hundred years a day;

For thus such reverence is lent
To well-established precedent.
A moral lesson this might teach,
Were I ordained and called to preach;

For men are prone to go it blind
Along the calf-paths of the mind,
And work away from sun to sun
To do what other men have done.

They follow in the beaten track,
And out and in, and forth and back,
And still their devious course pursue,
To keep the path that others do.

But how the wise old woods-gods laugh,
Who saw the first primeval calf!
Ah! many things this tale might teach,—
But I am not ordained to preach.

                    -Sam Walter Foss

> *Ye are the salt of the earth:*
> *Ye are the light of the world.*
> — *Christ Jesus*

> *Men at some time are masters of their fates:*
> *The fault, dear Brutus, is not in our stars*
> *But in ourselves, that we are underlings.*
> *-William Shakespeare*

> *If whatever trees are in the earth were pens, and He*
> *should after that swell the seas into seven seas of*
> *ink, the Words of God would not be exhausted.*
> *-The Koran*

> *Those things which one has been accustomed to for*
> *a long time, although worse than things which one*
> *is not accustomed to, usually give less disturbance;*
> *but a change must sometimes be made to things one*
> *is not accustomed to.*
> *-Hippocrates*

Contents
dynamics of group leadership and organizational change

> *The real magic of discovery lies not in seeking new landscapes but in having new eyes.*
> *-Marcel Proust*

Appendixes

> *Pray thee, take care, that tak'st my book in hand,*
> *To read it well; that is, to understand.*
> *-Ben Jonson*

> *Management is about human beings. Its task is to*
> *make people capable of joint performance, to make*
> *their strengths effective and their weaknesses irrele-*
> *vant.*
> *-Peter Drucker*

> *A leader is best*
> *When people hardly know that he exists,*
> *Not so good when people obey and acclaim him,*
> *Worst when they despise him.*
> *"Fail to honor people, They fail to honor you."*
> *But of a good leader, who talks little,*
> *When his work is done, his aim fulfilled,*
> *They will say, "We did this ourselves. "*
> *-Ancient Chinese Poem*

INTRODUCTORY NOTE

This book is about the dynamics of group leadership and organizational change. The Greek word **dynamis** represents ability, capacity, competence. The word carries with it a sense of "power"—ability to lead with competence, and a sense of "possibility"—capacity to change. This book looks at leadership in terms of group dynamics, leadership skill dynamics, and leadership style dynamics.

Chapter 1 is about joining together—the dynamics of groups. Chapters 2, 3, 4, and 5 expand and develop four essential elements of group formation and leadership: purpose, structure, communication, and acceptance. The chapters deal with such issues as decision making, organization, helping and culture. Chapters 6 and 7 summarize underlying theoretical conceptions of human behavior, motivation, and perspectives of leadership practice. Chapters 8, 9, 10, and 11 revisit the four elements of group formation and focus on the dynamics of leadership skills involved in action, excellence, collaboration, and creativity, and they include such areas as visioning and planning, quality improvement, conflict and problem solving, innovation and change.

Chapter 12 looks at systems as learning organizations undergoing continuing change. Finally, Chapter 13 describes the dynamics of leadership styles and the desirability of developing a synergistic balance of one's personal competence as influential doer, analytical thinker, affiliative helper, and intuitive innovator. A transformative leadership model helps in assessing one's own group participation and leadership styles. An accompanying inventory provides a way to identify one's capacities and skills needing improvement for effective leadership for change.

This book draws on and summarizes the work of scores of authorities, researchers, theorists, and practitioners who have written on the subjects of leadership, groups, organization, systems, and change. Throughout the book, names are boldfaced in the text pointing to sources in the hundreds of bibliographic references listed for further study. The appendix includes instruments, worksheets, and exercises for group activity and practice.

This book grew out of a need for concise introductory materials for workshops and classes. The popularity of the first and subsequent editions shows that the book was found useful beyond its original purpose. This newest revision has more than doubled the amount of material included and the whole book is thoroughly revised and updated. The original outline format, suitable for workshops, is maintained as well as expanded. My thanks to Omnibook Company for making this and earlier editions possible.

We all possess leadership abilities, capacities, competence, possibilities, potential that we have barely tapped. I hope this book will help its readers continue to develop their own dynamic theory and practice of leadership as they participate in workplace groups, management teams, administrative councils, associations, communities, governmental bodies, wherever people work with people and interact for the common good.

Milwaukee, Wisconsin, 1995   Russell D. Robinson

> *Perhaps the most promising trend in our thinking about leadership is the growing conviction that the purposes of the group are best served when the leader helps followers to develop their own initiative, strengthens them in the use of their own judgment, and enables them to grow and to become better contributors.*
>
> *-John W. Gardner*

> *The credit belongs to those who are actually in the arena, who strive valiantly; who know the great enthusiasm, the great devotions, and spend themselves in a worthy cause; who at the best, know the triumph of high achievement; and who, at the worst, if they fail, fail while daring greatly, so that their place shall never be with those cold and timid souls who know neither victory nor defeat.*
>
> *-Theodore Roosevelt*

> *Whether we lead only a family or a handful of friends, and where and how we will lead, is up to us, our views and our talents. But the hour will come for each of us, and, because we know this, we surely must also know that the very nature of humanity and society, regardless of its size or complexity, will always turn on the act of the individual and, therefore on the quality of the individual.*
>
> *-Sandra Day O'Connor*

1 Joining Together
groups, teams, and roles

> *Never doubt that a small group of thoughtful, committed citizens can change the world. Indeed, it's the only thing that ever has.*
>
> *-Margaret Mead*

What makes a group or team

A. A distinction should be made between a "group" and a mere collection or aggregate of people with a wide variety of individual goals, values and skills, such as might be found on a bus, in a theater or in a shopping area.

   1. For our purpose, a group is: **a number of people who are thought of together and who are consciously or unconsciously directed toward a common goal.**

B. Essential elements required for the formation of a stable group are listed below followed by a statement of optimal conditions for an effective group.

   1. *Purpose: A common goal to attain or task to accomplish.*

      ● With a well-understood, shared vision and common purpose, the interests and motivation of all members are readily tapped, goals turned into plans for action, and progress toward selected goals is attained.

   2. *Structure: Some form of structure or organization.*

      ● The group is organized and structured for accomplishment of goals. Roles are selected, differentiated and responsibilities shared by group members who accept some degree of interdependence and control.

   3. *Communication: Some system of communication and interaction.*

      ● A system of open communication permits persons to collaborate and communicate their hopes, beliefs, and knowledge to secure basic understandings. Disagreements and frustrations may be expressed and resolved without threatening group cooperation.

   4. *Acceptance: A culture of mutual acceptance and meaning.*

      ● Group members share a culture or community where they feel secure, wanted and needed. They are able to accept fellow members and know they themselves are accepted. They feel free to question, be creative, express new ideas and risk innovation.

C. **Types of "teams"**

1. Just as there are many types of groups (work groups, task groups, social groups, project groups, planning groups, etc.), so there are many types of **teams**. **Peter Drucker** has identified three types of teams, each very different.

    ● Each type of team has its own unique characteristics, requirements, strengths, limitations.
    ● Compromising or combining team types will not work. They cannot be made into hybrids.
    ● Each type of team can play as a team in a prescribed way.
    ● To change from one type of team to another requires a complete break with the past. Gradual change will not work.

2. **Team Type I**

    ● Examples: baseball team, surgical team, assembly line, traditional design team.
    ● Players play on the team; they do not play as a team.
    ● Players have fixed positions, fixed roles. Players play their roles in turn.
    ● The traditional boss is clearly in charge.
    ● Roles are inflexible. Works best when sequence of actions is well practiced and known to everyone.
    ● Each member can be evaluated separately, can have clear and specific goals, can be held accountable, can be measured.
    ● Each member can be trained and developed to the fullest extent of the individual's strengths.
    ● Every team member can be a "star" because members don't have to adjust to anybody else.

3. **Team Type II**

    ● Examples: football team, symphony orchestra, hospital emergency unit, Japanese design teams.
    ● Players have fixed positions, but play as they have learned to play.
    ● Team members work in parallel, along side each other.
    ● There is flexibility, but there is a score to follow, stringent details to be adhered to, and the word of the coach or conductor or leader is law.
    ● Each member is evaluated on individual performance as well as in terms of how well they play as a team.
    ● Players are beholden to one boss (the team leader) for orders, rewards, appraisals, promotions.

> *The good news is we're beginning to recognize that education is a team sport. The bad news is we haven't all realized we're on the same team.*
> *-a school superintendent*

4. **Team Type III**

- Examples: tennis doubles, jazz combo, president's office, "skunk works," innovation-development team.
- Players have a primary rather than a fixed position.
- They cover for teammate strengths and weaknesses and to changing demands of the game.
- Team must be small—not more than 5 to 7 members.
- Members are trained together and need to work together for some time to fully function as a team.
- There must be one clear goal for the entire team but considerable flexibility with respect to each individual member's work and performance.
- Only the team "performs"; individual member's "contribute."
- Rewards are to the team on its performance.

5. Type III is representative of the team model considered the ideal to be emulated in the workplace and other contexts. **Type III most approximates the optimum conditions for an effective group as described above.**

> *It's easy to get the players. Gettin' them to play together, that's the hard part.*
> -Casey Stengel

How a group or team develops

A. Just as an individual goes through stages of development, a group (or team) may be thought of as developing through stages or phases. The four stages of group development (or team building) may be denominated *groping, griping, grasping* and *grouping.* All groups, however, may not develop in this sequential order, nor are the stages found in all groups under all conditions.

1. **Groping Stage.**

- There is lack of "group feeling."
- Each individual tries to find a place in the group and engages in "testing behavior"; tentative exploring of boundaries of acceptable behavior.
- There are feelings of excitement, anticipation and optimism, along with suspicion, fear and anxiety of what lies ahead.
- There are concerns about "safety"—is it safe to be here?
- The group may be characterized as "individual centered."

3

2. **Griping Stage**.

- This is often the most difficult stage, a period of discouragement, discomfort, power struggles, conflict, arguing, impatience, competition, doubt, resistance, blaming and frustration.
- Not sure of what to do or how to make decisions, or where others are "coming from", group members resist collaboration and find it difficult to adjust to a place in the group.

3. **Grasping Stage**.

- Group members begin to "grasp" the idea of becoming a group, that is, begin to accept each other.
- Efforts are made toward group cohesion and consolidation, to develop group harmony, modify or avoid conflicts, establish norms, seek conciliation and common goals, develop confidence and trust in each other.
- Members begin to be more comfortable with each other and begin to "fit" in place.
- They begin to think of themselves as members of a group.

4. **Grouping Stage**.

- Members collectively develop a sense of common purpose, a feeling of acceptance of each other's strengths and weaknesses, a system of communication, and a structure to enable them to work together.
- They are ready as a group to diagnose and solve problems and implement change.
- They identify themselves as a group.

B. The group may return to some of the earlier stages from time to time as individuals themselves change or membership changes (new persons join the group or members leave).

Those who have used music metaphors in describing leadership, particularly jazz metaphors, are on a quantum track. Improvisation is the saving skill. As leaders, we play a crucial role in selecting the melody, setting the tempo, establishing the key, and inviting the players. But that is all we can do. The music comes from something we cannot direct, from a unified whole created among the players—a relational holism that transcends separateness. In the end, when it works, we sit back, amazed and grateful.

-Margaret J. Wheatley

4

C. Comparison of team development models

	Groping	Griping	Grasping	Grouping
Tuckman	Forming	Storming	Norming	Performing
Drexler, Sibbet and Forester	Step 1: Why am I here?	Step 2: Who are you?	Step 3: What shall we do?	Step 4: How?
Schuk	Phase 1: Inclusion	Phase 2: Control	Phase 3: Affection	
Bion	Stage 1: Flight	Stage 2: Fight	Stage 3: Unite	

D. Group size for efficient teamwork

1. Optimum group size: 5 to 9 members

2. Outer limits of group size: 3 to 12 members

3. Groups of 12 or more persons almost inevitably break into two or more smaller groups.

4. All organizations (no matter how large) may be conceived of operationally as essentially a collection of interlocking and overlapping small groups.

Group characteristics

A. Characteristics of any group depend largely on the individuals who make up the group. But as the members of the group continue to interact, the group begins to take on a "personality" of its own, which will tend to persist even as the membership changes. Some of these persisting group characteristics are:

1. *Atmosphere/Climate*

   ● Group atmosphere may be permissive or restrictive, cold or friendly, formal or informal.
   ● In an atmosphere of freedom, members feel free to speak when they have something to say.

2. *Communication Patterns*

   ● This refers to what people say, how they say it, and what effect it has on other group members.
   ● Much communication is also non-verbal and involves posture, facial expressions and gestures.

3. *Participation Patterns*

- In every group situation people participate and interact with one another in many different ways.
- Participation involves who is talking to whom and whether all or only a few members of the group are participating.
- Participation is usually described in terms of amount and direction of communications and ratio of listeners to talkers.

4. *Leadership Patterns*

- Every group develops its own unique leadership patterns, ranging from essentially authoritarian leadership, where decisions are made by the designated "leader," to more "democratic" patterns, where the group membership is involved.

5. *Cohesiveness*

- This characteristic relates to the attractiveness of the group to its members, and how effectively the group sticks together or functions in a crisis situation.

6. *Sub-groups*

- Cliques may be formed or determined on the basis of friendships, common agreement and interests, or even opposition to the direction of the group.
- The development of sub-groups is a normal thing, but should be understood and diagnosed to develop effective group relations.

7. *Norms*

- Norms, or standards, have reference to the uniform manner in which the group carries out its work and the methods established for working together, as well as the guidelines for the individual in adjusting his behavior to that acceptable by the group.
- Norms may be written, codified, and formalized, but often the "most important" norms are not written at all; they are "understood."

8. *History and Traditions of the Group*

- Every group over time develops its own traditions, its particular structures and procedures which, whether written or unwritten, become "the way the group is."

> *Healthy companies are about shared ideals, shared goals, shared respect, and a shared sense of values and mission.*
>
> *-Max DePree*

9. *Group Goals*

- **Goals or Ends**
  These are statements of the objectives group members wish to accomplish, "short term" or "long term."

- **Program or Activities**
  Programs are developed to achieve the goals or ends. Ideally, all activities should meet the test: Is this in keeping with our goals?

- **Evaluation**
  Evaluation is asking: To what extent are the objectives or goals actually being accomplished?

10. *Group Pressure to Conform*

- The power of a group to make its members conform is well known. In fact, members must give up something of their own individual desires in order to be a part of a group.

- When a member fails to conform, cr go along with a group decision, the group will take a series of steps to bring the member back into line, and if these fail, will effectively expel the person from the group.

  1) **Try reason and logic one more time.** Go over all the arguments in favor of action the member opposes.
  2) **Appeal to fellowship.** "You're a great member, and we all like you."
  3) **Attack.** "You never have been any help to our group . . ."
  4) **Amputate.** Go on as if the member is no longer present.

- Obviously, it is easiest to capitulate immediately. The progressive pressure is less effective the more allies the non-conforming member has.

> *The paradox of modern man is that only as the individual joins with his fellows in groups and organizations can he hope to control the political, economic, and social forces which threaten his individual freedom. This is especially true now that massive social groupings—in nations and combinations of nations—are the order of the day. Only as the individual in society struggles to preserve his individuality in common cause with his fellows can he hope to remain an individual.*
> *-Kretch, Crutchfield, and Ballachey, 1962*

7

B. **Fourteen characteristics for an effective group or team:**

1. Has a clear understanding of its purposes and goals.

2. Is flexible in selecting its procedures as it works toward its goals.

3. Is able to initiate and carry on effective decision-making, carefully considering minority viewpoints and various alternatives, arriving at decisions by consensus, thus securing the commitment of members.

4. Provides for sharing of leadership responsibilities by group members, so that all members are concerned about contributing ideas, elaborating and clarifying the ideas of others, giving opinions, testing the feasibility of potential decisions, and in other ways helping the group to work on its task and maintain itself as an effective working unit.

5. Achieves an appropriate balance between group productivity and the satisfaction of individual needs of members.

6. Has achieved a high degree of communication and understanding among its members. Communication of personal feelings and attitudes, as well as ideas, occurs in a direct and open fashion because they are considered important to the work of the group.

7. Maintains a balance between emotional and rational behavior, channeling emotionality into productive group effort.

8. Has a high degree of cohesiveness (attractiveness for the members) but not to the point of stifling individual freedom.

9. Makes intelligent use of the differing abilities of its members.

10. Is not dominated by its leader or by any of its members.

11. Allows members to disagree and has an effective way to resolve problems and intergroup conflict.

12. Expresses ideas fully and frankly so that everyone has all relevant information, and "hidden agendas" are minimized.

13. Attaches high value to new, creative approaches to problems.

14. Can be objective about reviewing its own processes. It can face its problems and adjust to needed modifications in its operation.

> *If we did all the things we are capable of doing, we would literally astonish ourselves.*
> *-Thomas Edison*

> *Leadership begins where management ends, where the systems of rewards and punishments, control and scrutiny, give way to innovation, individual character, and the courage of convictions. Your challenge is to lead your staff to get extraordinary things done. This requires inspiring and motivating your staff toward a common purpose and building a cohesive and spirited team.*
> *-David and Roger Johnson*

Team building

A. **Opening up group communication and acceptance**

1. A group functions in the open "public" area, shown below by the Johari window (developed by **Joe Luft and Harry Ingham**):

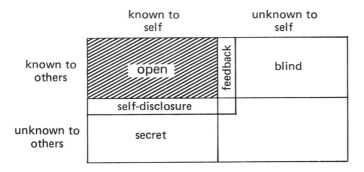

2. This open area is enlarged through self-disclosure and feedback.

3. *Self-disclosure is* sharing something about yourself with the group.

4. *Feedback is* letting group members give you information about your behavior as they perceive it.

    ● *Rules for giving feedback:*

    1) Be descriptive rather than judgmental.
    2) Be specific rather than general.
    3) Deal with things that can be changed.
    4) Give feedback when it is desired.
    5) Consider your motives for giving feedback.
    6) Give feedback at the time the behavior takes place.
    7) Give feedback (in a group) when its accuracy can be checked with others.

B. **Managing the team process**

1. **Peter Russell and Roger Evans** provide recommendations for facilitation of the ongoing process of team building.

    ● Set aside time at the beginning of a meeting for people to talk.
      ‣ how they are, what they are feeling, concerns
      ‣ do not force disclosure but concentrate on creating an environment where this is possible

    ● Do not rush straight into the agenda.
      ‣ people need some time to "come together," settle in, feel at ease and accepted as part of the group
      ‣ the less often they meet and the less well they know each other, the longer the time this takes

    ● Get the hidden human agendas on the table.
      ‣ this is a time investment that pays off in a climate within which the team will work far more smoothly and tackle more effectively the "official" issues on the table
      ‣ if this is "opening a can of worms", the sooner it is opened and the worms released the better—they can do far more harm hidden

    ● The best way to encourage others to talk about personal issues is to talk about any concerns and feelings you may have.
      ‣ put your own hidden agenda on the table

    ● Handle other people's personal feelings and concerns with the sensitivity, care, and compassion you would like your own feelings to be handled.

C. Listening in Groups

1. Learning to listen is an imperative for smooth group functioning.

2. Some points to consider:

    ● Listen to understand what is meant, not to ready for a reply.
    ● Don't interpret too quickly what speaker is trying to say.
    ● Put yourself in speaker's shoes; how does the world look to him?
    ● Put aside your own views and opinions for the moment.
    ● We think faster than another speaks; keep thought on what the other is saying.
    ● Expect the speaker to say what he means in different words than you would use.
    ● Before you answer, sum up what you understand the speaker to be saying.

10

> *In the conventional mode, people want to know whether the followers believe in the leader; a more searching question is whether the leader believes in the followers.*
>
> *-John W. Gardner*

Success of teams

A. Success of teams is related to characteristics and commitment of team members, and how the team is structured for facilitation and leadership.

1. A team has been defined as a small number of people with complementary skills who are committed to a common purpose, an accepted set of performance goals, and an approach for which they hold themselves mutually accountable.

2. Not all work groups are teams. The two may be contrasted as follows: (**Jon Katzenbach and Douglas Smith**)

CHARACTERISTICS OF TEAM	CHARACTERISTICS OF GROUP
Shared leadership roles	Strong, clearly focused leader
Specific team purpose that the team agrees on and works to deliver	Group's purpose is same as the broader organizational mission
Open-ended discussion and active, problem-solving meetings.	Efficiently run meetings
Discusses, decides, and does real work together	Discusses, decides and delegates
Individual and mutual accountability	Individual accountability
Collective work-products	Individual work-products
Measures performance directly by assessing collective work-products	Measures effectiveness indirectly (e.g., financial performance of business)

3. **Leaders of teams** are expected to lead team meetings, be knowledgeable of group process, design agendas, design action plans, maintain team momentum, teach and lead the team through the process, and to communicate and coordinate with related units or areas affected or involved.

11

4. **Members of teams** are expected to attend and participate in all meetings, gather data, analyze root causes, participate in presentations, recommend solutions, and establish on-going monitoring (quality control).

5. A **team facilitator** (someone outside the process and/or department and not the leader of the team) may serve the team as process helper, particularly during early stages of the team. The facilitator should be skilled in data-based problem-solving, knowledgeable about group process, a skilled communicator who can serve as an outside resource attending meetings as helper, coach and instructor in process issues as needed.

B. Essential elements of effective work teams

1. **David and Frank Johnson** define a team as a set interpersonal relationships structured to achieve established goals.

2. They identify five essential conditions for ensuring that teams function productively:

   - **Positive Interdependence**—the perception that one is linked with others, that you cannot succeed unless the others do (and vice versa), and their work benefits you and your work benefits them.

   - **Individual Accountability**—the performance of each individual group member is assessed to inform the group which members need more assistance or encouragement in completing the work and to increase members' perceptions that their contributions to the group effort are identifiable and that they must fulfill their responsibilities in order for the group (and themselves) to be successful.

   - **Face-to-Face Interaction**—the interaction pattern among members is fostered by the positive interdependence that most powerfully influences productivity, morale, and effectiveness.

   - **Collaborative Skills**—groups cannot function effectively without having and using collaborative skills such as conflict resolution, and problem solving.

   - **Group Processing**—groups need specific time to discuss how well they are doing in achieving their goals, and in maintaining effective working relationships among members.

> *Two are better than one, because they have a good reward for their toil. For if they fall, one will lift up his fellow; but woe to him who is alone when he falls and has not another to lift him up. . . . And though a man might prevail against one who is alone, two will withstand him. A threefold cord is not quickly broken.*
>
> *-Ecclesiastes*

What each individual brings to a group

A. Each person brings to the group unique interests, abilities, attitudes and feelings, individual experiences, expectations and "mental set."

B. Contributions to the group by individual members may sometimes help to build up and maintain the group and/or may help the group to get group tasks accomplished. These are often referred to as **functional** behaviors. Or members, in trying to satisfy individual needs, may block progress or even do something destructive to the group. Such behavior is considered **non-functional** in terms of the group or even dysfunctional.

C. Behaviors occurring in groups are often referred to as roles people play in groups. Whether a particular role is functional for the group at a particular time or nonfunctional is dependent on the context. Typically people play more than one role in the course of meetings.

D. Examples of role behaviors in groups

   1. **Group Maintenance Behaviors**

      ● Behaviors which alter or maintain the group's patterns of interaction and strengthen or perpetuate the group as a group.

      1) Encouraging: Responding to others and being friendly.

      2) Compromising: Seeking to resolve conflict by yielding status or admitting error.

      3) Harmonizing: Making efforts to reconcile or mediate divergent ideas or points of view.

      4) Gate Keeping: Regulating participation by limiting excessive talkers and encouraging others, giving all members chance to talk.

      5) Regulating: Helping groups stay on the topic, making "ground rules."

13

6) *Energizing:* Stimulating the group to respond and to maintain group cohesion. "Come on, y'all."

7) *Protecting:* Maintaining group norms and traditions.

8) *Following:* Going along so group stays together.

9) *Expressing* Group *Feeling:* Speaking on behalf of others in the group.

10) *Consensus Taking:* Seeking an action acceptable to all.

11) *Tension Relieving:* Telling a joke or getting a laugh to relieve tension, or putting a tense situation in a larger context

12) *Supporting.* Agreeing and commending contributions of others

> *Leadership is always dependent on the context, but the context is established by the relationships we value. We cannot hope to influence any situation without respect for the complex network of people who contribute to our organizations.*
> *-Margaret J. Wheatley*

2. Group Task Behaviors

- Behaviors which advance the group in doing its tasks and accomplishing its goals.

   1) *Initiating Action:* Starting the ball rolling, suggesting procedures to follow.

   2) *Setting Goals:* Helping decide just what should be done.

   3) *Assessing Resources:* Establishing what the group has to work with.

   4) *Information Seeking:* Requesting information, facts, or suggestions pertinent to problem being discussed.

   5) *Information Giving:* Offering facts and providing relevant information.

   6) *Summarizing:* Pulling related ideas together and restating suggestions after the group has discussed them.

7) *Elaborating:* Sharing by giving examples from experience or reading.

8) *Clarifying:* Clarifying to help group understand various suggestions being discussed.

9) *Testing Feasibility:* "Trying out" possible solutions by discussing possible ramifications.

10) *Diagnosing:* Helping to collect and analyze data, determine sources of difficulties.

11) *Dissenting:* Opposing on basis of anticipated consequences to group or program.

12) *Evaluating:* Critically considering courses of action, measuring accomplishments against goals.

3. **Individual Need-filling Behaviors**

● Behaviors which serve to satisfy individual needs but are not functional for the group.

1) *Horsing around:* Making efforts to distract other group members with inappropriate behavior, clowning, joking, disrupting

2) *Blocking:* Disagreeing and opposing anything that is brought up.

3) *Seeking Recognition:* Calling attention to one's self, talking to be heard and/or boasting.

4) *Dominating:* Seeking to take over by subordinating or downgrading contributions made by other group members, or by flattery or asserting superior status.

5) *Pulling Into Own Shell:* Refusing to take active part, day dreaming, doodling.

6) *Making Irrelevant Comments:* Injecting thoughts not in keeping with current topic of discussion.

7) *Self-confessing:* Using the group to share personal problems and gain sympathy.

8) *Fighting and Competing:* Aggression and seeking to "win" your way.

9) *Retaliation:* Seeking to get even with other members.

10) *Special Interest Pleading:* Seeking to achieve a personal goal or the goal of another group, lobbying.

11) *Rush to Decision:* Insisting on a quick decision to get the meeting over with.

12) *Opinion Expressed as Fact:* Expressing an opinion as if it were a fact and disregarding any information provided by others.

E. How each individual contributes to group formation

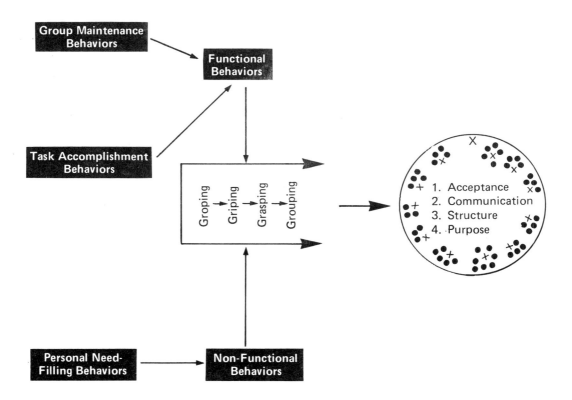

The boss drives men—the leader guides them
The boss depends upon authority—the leader on
  good will
The boss creates fear—the leader develops confidence
The boss assigns tasks—the leader sets the pace
The boss says "I"—the leader, "we"
The boss says "go"—the leader says, "let's go"
                                                    -Anonymous

What I really wanted in the organization was a group of responsible, interdependent workers, similar to a flock of geese. . . . I could see the geese flying in their 'V' formation, the leadership changing frequently, with different geese taking the lead. I saw every goose being responsible for getting itself to wherever the gaggle was going, changing roles whenever necessary, alternating as a leader, a follower or a scout. And when the task changed, the geese would be responsible for changing the structure of the group to accommodate, similar to the geese that fly in a 'V' but land in waves. I could see each goose being a leader.

-Ralph Stayer

You and I—
We meet as strangers, each carrying a mystery with us. I cannot say who you are.
I may never know you completely.
But I trust that you are a person in your own right, possessed of a beauty and value that are the earth's richest treasures.
So I make this promise to you:
I will impose no identities upon you, but will invite you to become yourself without shame or fear.
I will hold open a space for you in the world and allow your right to fill it with an authentic vocation and purpose. For as long as your search takes, you have my loyalty.

-Author Unknown

"Your task—to build a better world, " God said.
I answered, "How?
The world is such a large, vast place,
So complicated now.
And I so small and useless am,
There's nothing I can do."
But God in all His wisdom said,
"Just build a better YOU. "

-Dorothy R. Jones

> *Do not follow where the path may lead. Go instead where there is no path and leave a trail.*
> *-Author Unknown*

> *You can and should shape your own future, because if you don't, someone else surely will.*
> *-Joel Barker*

> *Hope is the beginning of plans. It gives man a destination, a sense of direction for getting there and the energy to get started. It enlarges sensitivities. It gives proper values to feelings as well as to facts.*
> *-Norman Couisins*

> *The farmer came down the lane. "Got a stray," he said. "How do they get lost?" asked the city man. "They just nibble themselves lost," said the farmer; "they keep their heads down, wander from one green tuft to another, come to a hole in the fence—and never can find a hole by which to get back again." The city man answered, "Like people, like every generation of foolish men."*
> *-On the parable of the lost sheep*
> *in the Interpreter's Bible*

2 Purpose
task, influence, decision-making

> *Leadership is the process of persuasion or example*
> *by which an individual (or leadership team) induces*
> *a group to pursue objectives held by the leader or*
> *shared by the leader and his or her followers.*
>
> *-John W. Gardner*

Purpose and Task Effectiveness

A. Groups are organized to accomplish a purpose. A fundamental function of leadership is to help the group attain its goals or purpose.

  1. Effectiveness is measured by the degree goals are being achieved over time.

  2. In terms of accomplishment of purpose, groups tend to first increase and later to decrease in level of effectiveness.

  3.. **P**-eople commit **R**-esources (time, energy, money, skill) to **O**-rganize groups to carry out **A**-ctivities (programs) to accomplish **G**-oals.

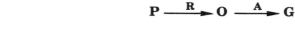

$$P \xrightarrow{R} O \xrightarrow{A} G$$

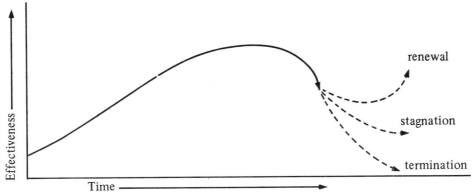

B. *Typical response when effectiveness declines is to turn inward and devote energies to clinging to what is still left, often continuing in a state of stagnation.*

19

C. Improving program effectiveness

Common Causes of Decreased Effectiveness	What is Needed for Renewal and Greater Effectiveness
Vague ends	More specific goals
Unrealistic ends	More realistic goals
Multiple ends	Establishing priority of goals
Group not motivated	Relate short-term to long-term goals, or re-evaluate goals
Goal diversion by unexpected blocks or situational changes	Adapt group goals to new needs or keep goals in view and not be diverted
Goal displacement (when goal becomes maintenance of the organization)	See organization as a tool to goals and not an end in itself
Organizational exploitation by a small sub-group or clique	Focus on needs of all members
Lack of participation due to competition for member's time (family, job or other groups)	Make goals worthwhile for members

Task Leadership: Traits, Functions, Power

A. Much of the study of leadership prior to 1945 concentrated on identifying **"leadership traits,"** the assumption that there exist certain inherent personal traits or qualities that make a "good leader." *Question asked:* What is a leader like?

   1. The trait approach to leadership regards leadership as the property of an individual. It takes the view that "you either have it or you don't."

      ● Focuses on "charisma" and personal qualities of the leader.
      ● Assumes "leaders are born, not made."
      ● Extensive research has been inconclusive in identifying traits. However, lists of "leadership qualities" often appear in leadership books.

   2. **Gary A. Yukl** asserts that the premise that certain leader traits are absolutely necessary for effective leadership "has never been substantiated in several decades of research" although "certain traits increase the likelihood that a leader will be effective, and the relative importance of different traits is dependent upon the nature of the leadership situation."

- Follow are listed some positive traits found most frequently to be characteristic of successful leaders and the negative "fatal flaws" that prevent success:

POSITIVE TRAITS	NEGATIVE TRAITS
Adaptability to situations	Abrasive
Aware of social environment	Aloof
Achievement-oriented	Arrogant
Assertive	Bullying style
Assumes responsibility	Cold
Cooperative	Insensitivity to others
Creative	Intimidating
Decisive	Overdependent on boss or mentor
Desire to influence others	Overly ambitious
Diplomatic	Overmanaging
Energetic	Unable to delegate
Intelligent	Unable to think strategically
Organized	Unable to adapt to boss with
Persistent	different style
Persuasive	Unwilling to change
Self-confident	
Tolerant of stress	

B. The **functional** approach regards leadership as a property of the group itself. *Question asked:* What does a leader do?

1. Leadership is determined by observing how people function in a group. Any person in the group at a particular point in time may be "leading" the group by performing a leadership function. **Robert Bales** identified two clusters of such functions:

   - *Group Maintenance:* Keeping relationships pleasant, encouraging others, maintaining trust, respect, warmth—acts that make people feel comfortable and satisfied with group membership.

   - *Task Accomplishment:* Clarification of issues, initiation of action, development of procedural plan, etc.—acts that enable people to accomplish the goals of the group.

> *The only limit to our realization of tomorrow will be our doubts of today.*
> *-Franklin Delano Roosevelt*

21

2   Assumptions implicit in functional leadership:

- *Any act that helps either group maintenance or task accomplishment is a leadership act.*

- The designated leader has responsibility for being sensitive to functional needs and for seeing that they are taken care of.

- Problems of leadership cannot be separated from problems of group functioning.

- Group members have a shared responsibility to carry out the various tasks of leadership.

- The situation calls for certain actions at certain times.

- Groups differ, requirements for achieving goals differ; therefore leadership required will differ.

- A given function or objective may be served by a variety of behaviors or acts.

- Behavior serving the functions may be performed by a variety of persons in the group.

- A specific behavior may serve *one* function, or both, or one at the expense of the other.

- Required behavior varies—what may serve one function at one time may block the group at another time.

> *If the ladder is not leaning against the right wall, every step we take just gets us to the wrong place faster.*
>
> *-Stephen R. Covey*

C. Another approach to the study of leadership emphasizes **power**. *Question asked:* How much power and authority does the leader have?

1. Leadership is regarded as the exercise of authority.

- Leadership is a matter of political influence and power.
- Leadership depends on the authority the individual has to make things happen. You either have been given that authority or you haven't.

2. Power is one of the means by which a leader influences the behavior of a group, yet the nature of power is often misunderstood. Power may be defined as influence potential, a resource that enables the leader to gain compliance or commitment from others.

   - Power is regarded as finite. If someone else has the power, the leader doesn't. Power may be limited by legislation, negotiation, policy or superordinates.

   - At its worst, the power approach leads to a "king-boss syndrome" of authoritarian behavior.

3. There are two basic kinds of power: *position power* and *personal power.* The best situation is for a leader to have *both* kinds of power.

   - **Position power** tends to flow down in the organization derived from organizational office.

   - **Personal power** (personal influence) is the extent to which followers respect and are willing to follow a leader.

3. Power bases are in the **perceptions** of followers. **French and Raven** and others have identified various bases of power.

   - **Expert power.** The perception that the leader has the necessary education, experience and expertise. The leader deserves to be followed by virtue of know-how.

   - **Information power.** The perception that the leader has access to or is in possession of useful information. The leader deserves to be followed by virtue of control of technical data and information.

   - **Referent power.** The perception of the leader as liked and admired, willing to encourage and help, worthy of confidence and trust. The leader deserves to be followed because of rapport with followers.

   - **Legitimate power.** The perception that the leader has authority to make decisions due to title or position in the organization. The leader deserves to be followed because "that's the boss."

   - **Reward power.** The perception that the leader can provide things followers want. The leader deserves to be followed because the leader is source of rewards.

   - **Connection power.** The perception that the leader has association with influential persons or organizations. The leader deserves to be followed because of connections with others who are important.

   - **Coercive power.** The perception that the leader can impose sanctions. The leader deserves to be followed because of power to punish or hurt.

Leadership Dilemma: Power vs. Empowerment

A. Virtually every designated leader wrestles with this issue: How much power (authority) should the leader exercise in making decisions; how much freedom should the group have in exercising power (empowerment). **Tannenbaum and Schmidt** identify five types of leadership "styles" along a continuum.

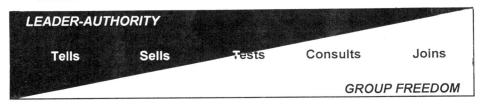

LEADER-AUTHORITY

Tells   Sells   Tests   Consults   Joins

GROUP FREEDOM

1. **Telling**
   The leader identifies a problem, considers alternative solutions, chooses one of them, and then tells followers what they are to do. The leader may or may not consider what group members may think or feel about the decision, but members clearly do not participate directly in the decision-making. Coercion may or may not be used or implied.

2. **Selling**
   The leader, as before, makes the decision without consulting his group. However, instead of simply announcing the decision, the leader tries to persuade group members to accept it. The leader points out how consideration has been given organization goals and the interests of group members and the leader emphasizes how the members will benefit from carrying out the decision.

3. **Testing**
   The leader identifies a problem and proposes a tentative solution. Before finalizing it, however, the leader gets the reaction of those who will implement it. The leader says, in effect, "I'd like your frank reactions to this proposal, and I will take them into account in the final decision."

4. **Consulting**
   The leader here gives the group members a chance to influence the decision from the beginning. The leader presents a problem and relevant background information, then asks the members for their ideas on how to solve it. In effect, the group is invited to increase the number of alternative actions to be considered. The leader then selects the solution/s regarded as most promising, after consulting the group.

5. **Joining**
   The leader here participates in the discussion as "just another member," and agrees in advance to carry out whatever decision the group makes. The only limits placed on the group consensus are those that have been predetermined. (Many teams make decisions this way.)

B. This model has been expanded to include as many as twelve different styles, the additional styles being variations of degrees of "testing."

C. What determines or influences the leader in the choice of leadership style?

1. Forces in the leader as a person:

    ● Value system
    ● Confidence in the group members
    ● Leadership inclinations
    ● Previous leadership experiences
    ● Feelings of security in an uncertain situation

2. Forces in the group members:

    ● Need for independence of or dependence on the leader
    ● Readiness to assume responsibility for decision-making
    ● Tolerance for ambiguity (personality variables)
    ● Interest in the problem
    ● Ability to understand and identify goals
    ● Knowledge and experience of group to deal with problem
    ● Expectation of the group with respect to sharing in decision-making

3. Forces in the situation:

    ● Type of organization
        ▸ values
        ▸ traditions
        ▸ policies
        ▸ expectations for the leader
        ▸ degree of member participation allowed by size of working units, geographical distribution, and degree of inter- and intra-organizational security required to attain goals

    ● Degree of group effectiveness
        ▸ cohesiveness
        ▸ permissiveness
        ▸ mutual acceptance
        ▸ commonality of purpose

    ● The problem itself
        ▸ whether group has the kind of knowledge and experience needed
        ▸ complexity of the problem

    ● Pressure of time
        ▸ the need (real or imagined) for immediate decision

> *The future isn't what it used to be.*
> *-Yogi Berra*

> *I find the great thing in this world is not so much where we stand, as in what direction we are moving: To reach the port of heaven, we must sail sometimes with the wind and sometimes against it—but we must sail, and not drift, nor lie at anchor.*
>
> *-Oliver Wendell Holmes*

Decision Making

A. Misconceptions or faulty assumptions that impede decision making:

1. Assumption that decision making occurs only at the top, or the higher levels of the organization, and therefore can be separated from decision implementing.

    Correction: **There are no one-person decisions** in a group or organization because any decision will eventually involve others who decide to what extent they will carry out the decision. Even those at the lowest echelons and drawing the lowest pay, may have significant influence on what takes place in terms of implementation of a decision. Those dealing most directly with the client have the most substantial influence on the way a decision is in fact carried out.

2. Assumption that decisions are made by positive action on the part of a "decision-maker."

    Correction: Not to decide is to decide (that is, to postpone or to ignore are also decisions). **Decisions (to do, or not to do) are made moment by moment, at every level** of an organization. Likewise, decisions to "slow-down" or not to do one's best.

3. Assumption that good information will insure good decisions.

    Correction: Decisions are made on more than "fact"—**feelings are a substantial part of any decision.** To proceed as if feelings are not involved is to invite problems. But facts are needed. It is usually more dangerous to act without sufficient knowledge than to slow down the processes while information is being obtained.

4. Assumption that a group's decision-making process will improve simply by making the key leader a better decision-maker through study and practice.

    Correction: Problem-solving and decision-making can be improved not so much through the improvement of the individual leader's performance as a decision-maker, as improving his **performance as a *facilitator of decision making***, finding ways and means by which others can be involved in making decisions that affect them.

5. Assumption that there are too many people already involved in the decision-making process, and that the numbers must be reduced.

   Correction: The time and attention given to the involvement of others may be costly, but not so costly in the long run as the failure to carry out properly the decisions of the organization. The fact is, people will support what they help to create. **Those involved in the decision-making process, are likely to feel more responsibility for the decisions that are made.**

B. Improving decision making requires people being "in" on the information and the making of decisions.:

1. Understanding group objectives (shared concerns and aims).

2. Understanding what is going on in the organization (what we don't know we "make up" and spread as rumors).

3. Understanding the role of the individual (who's doing what).

4. Clarifying problem areas and issues (what is it we need to know and understand).

5. Improving problem-solving skills (how to examine assumptions, search for alternatives, evaluate, etc.).

6. Strengthening internal communications (networking across functions and departments).

7. Clarifying the relationships between decision making and action (steps to be taken).

8. Improving the working relationships at all levels.

> *You are the fellow who has to decide*
> *Whether you'll do it or toss it aside.*
> *You are the fellow who makes up your mind*
> *Whether you'll lead or linger behind.*
> *Whether you'll try for a goal that is far*
> *Or be contented to stay where you are.*
> *Take it or leave it, here's something to do*
> *Just think it over, it's all up to you.*
> *-Edgar Guest*

> *Leadership is the exercise of authority and the making of decisions.*
> *-Robert Dubin*

> *In our every deliberation, we must consider the impact of our decisions on the next seven generations.*
> *-From the Great Law of the Iroquois Confederacy*

C. Analyzing the decision-making process

1. Background factors: review existing patterns of relationships and expectations.

2. Review perceptions: of events, persons, the group, the organization.

3. **The analytical process of integrative decision-making:**

```
┌─────────────────────────────────────────┐
│            Problem Recognition            │
│     Goals and Obstacles Identification    │
│          Diagnosis (Why is this?)         │
└─────────────────────────────────────────┘
```

```
┌─────────────────────────────────────────┐
│       Search for Alternative Solutions    │
│           (What might be done?)           │
│            Listing Alternatives           │
│            (Without Evaluation)           │
└─────────────────────────────────────────┘
```

```
┌─────────────────────────────────────────┐
│      Evaluating and Testing Possibilities │
│           (What could be done?)           │
│        Consideration of Consequences      │
│         Selection of Cource of Action     │
│                (Consensus)                │
└─────────────────────────────────────────┘
```

4. Action and Reaction (Implementation and Evaluation)

> *If the horse you're riding dies . . . it's probably a good time to dismount.*
> *-Texas Quote*

Tools for Reaching Consensus

A. Consensus is only possible in a group with those solutions found acceptable or not unacceptable by virtually everyone in the group.

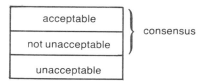

1. **Consensus need not be unanimous**.

   ● Unanimous agreement, if made an absolute condition for consensus, can hold further action hostage to a few, or force "pretend consent" under group pressure.

   ● Groups may wish to establish a ground rule that provides for last resort. For example, a group may agree that a group decision will be declared if at least 85 percent of the group support the solution. Such a ground rule should be clearly a *last resort*, not a shortcut to decision.

   ● Out of respect for the minority, the group may agree to revisit the decision within a specified time period, to listen to dissenting concerns.

2. **Consensus does not mean compromise.**

   ● Compromise starts from positions from which parties give up something they value in return for others giving up something they value. The result is that the compromise settles on what neither *really* wants, and it could very well be that *no one* has any real commitment relative to the action!

3. **Consensus building requires flexibility** in search for a solution that all can support. Consensus requires openness to participation of stakeholders, openness to diversity of points of view, openness to conflict resolution, openness to giving time to the process, openness to risk.

4. **Considerations in consensus building:**

   ● **Building a climate of trust and open communication**. Start with people introducing themselves and describing their connection to the group (if not known to others). Have them comment on how they feel about being at the meeting. Ask them to describe their expectations for the meeting. Honor the right of each to speak without interruption.

- Use both **small-group and large-group activities** to help move people forward in the consideration and resolution of the issues at hand.

- **Deal with real issues (points of tension) and not superficial issues**. Have people talk about feelings relative to the issues. Help people separate issues from personalities involved. Ask, what are the worse-case outcomes of not solving the problem (not doing anything)?

- As people begin to realize they can **speak safely** on a given issue, begin problem-solving in a nonthreatening way.

- **Focus on best-case outcomes** (not worse-case outcomes) relative to ideas being discussed as you press for creative solutions.

- Use a variety of **problem-solving tools** to move the group toward consensus.

E. Techniques for group involvement in decision making

1. **Brainstorming** (about 30 minutes)

   - A process of setting a nonjudgmental climate for maximizing the generation of ideas by a group

     1) Present the problem to group.
     2) Have group members state as many solutions as they can think of (without discussion or evaluation).
     3) Make a list of these solutions.
     4) Then (later) consider the solutions and evaluate them.

2. **Brainwriting** (15-30 minutes)

   - A variant of brainstorming but with ideas generated in writing rather than orally. Individually generated idea lists are passed on to other individuals for further adding of ideas. A total list is then compiled for consideration.

> *Never esteem anything as an advantage to you that will make you break your word or lose your self-respect.*
>
> *-Marcus Aurelius*

3. **Nominal Group Process** (about 1 hour)

    ● A group process where people work in silence (nominally in the presence of each other) while they list possible solutions.

        1) Present the problem to the group.
        2) Members (each individually) list all possible solutions they can think of in a specified time, without talking to each other (10 minutes).
        3) Break groups into sub-groups of about five people, with someone as recorder. Each member reads one solution aloud, the group moving in round-robin fashion from one to another until all solutions from all lists have been stated. Recorder writes each statement on chart in sequence.
        4) Then (later) clarify the list of solutions, before evaluating them. Evaluation may be begun by each member individually listing the top five items he would find most acceptable of all solutions, thus narrowing down the range of solutions. This may be done by each group member assigning a value of "5" to his first selection, a value of "4" to the next and so on, to a value of "1" for his fifth choice. The "votes" can then be tabulated for each item on the whole list.

4. **Fist to Five** (3-5 minutes)

    ● A way to poll the group's feelings at any point in a discussion.

        1) When asked to show a fist to five, group members show:
            ▹ Fist—meaning absolutely not or disagree (idea unacceptable)
            ▹ Three fingers—indicating neutral (not unacceptable)
            ▹ Five fingers—showing agreement (idea acceptable)

5. **Sorting** (about 10 minutes)

    ● A way to narrow brainstormed lists to a workable number of ideas

        1) After obtaining a brainstorming list of specific goals, use three large sheets of flip chart paper and ask group to "sort" the ideas into three categories:
            ▹ "Quick Fixes" (important ideas that can be accomplished quickly or by one person)
            ▹ "Out of Our Hands" (ideas that are not realistic given the present circumstances)
            ▹ "Definite Possibilities" (the rest of the ideas)
        2) Use the "Quick Fix" list as a valuable source for early and easy successes, perhaps assigning volunteers to tackle those issues.
        3) The group is free to concentrate on the more complex issues on the "Definite Possibilities" list.

6. **Affinity Diagram** (about 1 hour)

    ● A way to generate major themes from a large number of ideas, opinions, and issues

    1) Individuals write ideas on cards (or Post-it notes)
    2) Place all cards on table (or Post-its on newsprint wall)
    3) In silence, move the cards or notes into related groups until no one moves any more. Don't discuss.
    4) Next step: Categorize. Create "header cards" for groupings
    5) Draw lines connecting headers, sub-headers, with cards beneath them.

7. **Clustering** (30-40 minutes)

    ● A variant of affinity diagram to merge small-group ideas into a total group product.

    1) Small groups brainstorm the solution to a problem on slips of paper (or large Post-it notes). Each brainstormed idea should be written on a separate slip.
    2) After groups complete brainstorming, one group is asked to post ONE idea from the group and other groups are asked to post any similar ideas directly beneath the first.
    3) A second group posts another idea on the wall and again asks other groups to post similar ideas beneath this one. Continue categorizing the slips in this manner until all ideas are posted.
    4) Groups review columns of ideas and select labels for each of the clusters.
    5) The clusters may then be ranked.

8. **Spend a Buck** (about 15 minutes)

    ● A system for ranking issues or options.

    1) On 3 x 5 cards participants write each predetermined issue or category on a card. Each participant will require as many cards as issues.
    2) Each participant is asked to assume there is a dollar to spend, and to divide the money among the cards in accord with what they see to be the relative importance of ideas. The amount of money each would be willing to spend on that item is written on the card. No one may spend more than a dollar.
    3) Collect cards and tabulate.

> *The man who insists upon seeing with perfect clearness before he decides, never decides.*
>
> *-Henry Frederick Amiel*

9. **The 1-3-6 Technique** (30-40 minutes)

- A system of prioritizing useful when group members are reluctant to speak or when some tend to dominate.

    1) Each participant is given 2-3 minutes to list one or two ideas concerning a topic on a card.
    2) Participants are formed into a group of three. The groups have 7-10 minutes to discuss the ideas of each person in the group and select one or two ideas that the group can support.
    3) Each group of three joins another for a group of six to discuss the choices and choose the best one or two items to represent this group of six.
    4) Ideas from the groups of six are charted for all to see. Every person is given five sticker dots and must choose what he or she believes are the best alternatives. All five dots cannot be put on one alternative; they must be divided in some way among the alternatives.

10. **Fish Bowl** (30-60 minutes)

- A way to discuss ideas generated in several small groups in a large group setting.

    1) Form a circle of chairs in center of room (one chair per group plus one additional chair).
    2) Each small group elects a spokesperson who will express opinions and sentiments for the group. Spokespersons sit in the chairs in the circle.
    3) Spokespersons in the circle of chairs participate in the discussion. Other group members observe and are not allowed to speak. However, if any observer feels that something is being overlooked, he or she may temporarily sit in the empty chair and participate in the discussion. After making their point, they must return to the outside circle to free the empty chair for another observer to participate..

11. **Surveys**

- A systematic gathering of ideas by conducting a survey.

12. **Discussion**

- A systematic discussion by those most involved, focusing on solutions, not assessing blame.

> *Our doubts are traitors, and make us lose the good we oft might win, by fearing to attempt.*
>
> *-Theodore Roosevelt*

33

Ethical Considerations

A. To decide is to choose. To choose is to make value judgments, this course of action over that course of action, this goal over that goal. Decisions inevitably raise moral choices and ethical issues, though these questions may be ignored in terms of "the bottom line", "what our job is here", "getting what we want" , etc.

B. Business issues, political issues, even personal relationship issues, are sometimes dealt with as if ethical concerns are irrelevant.

　1. Elements in ethical judgment:

　　● **Bolman and Deal** identify three principles involved in moral judgment:

　　　1) **Mutuality**—are all parties to a relationship operating under the same understanding about the rules of the game?
　　　2) **Generality**—does a specific action follow a principle of moral conduct that is applicable to all comparable situations?
　　　3) **Caring**—does this action show care for the legitimate interests of others?

　　● **Lax and Sebenius** provide this set of questions to help a leader decide whether an action is ethical:

　　　1) Are you following rules that are understood and accepted?
　　　2) Are you comfortable discussing and defending your action? Would you want your colleagues and friends to be aware of it? Your spouse, children, or parents? Would you be comfortable if it were on the front page of a major newspaper?
　　　3) Would you want someone to do it to you? To a member of your family?
　　　4) What if everyone acted that way? Would the resulting society be desirable? If you were designing an organization, would you want people to act that way? Would you teach your children to do it?
　　　5) Are there alternatives that rest on firmer ethical ground?

People can be divided into three groups: those who make things happen, those who watch things happen, and those who wonder what happened.

-John W Newbern

● Other questions a leader might ask include:

1) Who will be affected by my action/decisions?
2) Does my decision violate any obligations and duties I have to those parties?
3) What are the known negative consequences to these parties?
4) What kinds of costs/benefits will be generated by my decision?
5) What is my intent in making this decision? to do the "right" thing? to better myself? to better my organization?
6) Would I be comfortable to have this action become the basis for organizational policy?

> *Doing more things faster is no substitute for doing the right things.*
>
> *-Stephen R. Covey*

> *When Arun Gandhi last saw his famous grandfather Mohandas Gandhi, the old man gave the boy a piece of paper with a list of what have come to be known as Gandhi's "Seven Blunders of the World" that lead to violence:*
>
> > *Wealth without work*
> > *Pleasure without conscience*
> > *Knowledge without character*
> > *Commerce without morality*
> > *Science without humanity*
> > *Worship without sacrifice*
> > *Politics without principle*
> >
> > *-Mohandas Gandhi*

> *In a real sense, the means represent the ideal in the making—the ends in process. So, in the long run, destructive means cannot bring about constructive ends because the ends are preexistent in the means.*
>
> *-Martin Luther King, Jr.*

Decentralization usually means that instead of one patriarch at the top, we now have seven patriarchs running seven decentralized divisions. All we do is push patriarchy down a level.

-Peter Block

SCIENTIFIC DISCOVERY

The heaviest element known to science was recently discovered by physicists at the Martin Marietta Laboratories here in Denver. The element, tentatively named Administratium, has no protons or electrons and thus has an atomic number of zero. However, it does have one neutron, 125 assistant neutrons, 75 vice neutrons, and 111 assistant vice neutrons. This gives it an atomic mass of 312. These 312 particles are held together in a nucleus by a force that involves the continuous exchange of meson-like particles called morons.

Since it has no electrons, Administratium is inert. However, it can be detected chemically as it impedes every reaction it comes into contact with. According to the discoverers (now employed by Boeing in Seattle), a minute amount of Administratium caused one reaction to take over four days to complete, when it could normally occur in less than one second.

Administratium has a normal half life of approximately three years, at which time it does not actually decay, but instead undergoes a reorganization in which assistant neutrons, vice neutrons, and assistant vice neutrons exchange places. Some studies have shown that the atomic weight actually increases after each reorganization.

Research at other laboratories indicates that Administratium occurs naturally in the atmosphere. It tends to concentrate at certain points such as government agencies, large corporations and universities, and can actually be found in the newest, best maintained buildings.

Scientists point out that Administratium is known to be toxic at any level of concentration and can easily destroy any productive reactions where it is allowed to accumulate. Attempts are being made to determine how Administratium can be controlled to prevent irreversible damage, but results to date are not promising.

-Source Unknown

3 Structure
organization, management, stress

> *I have conceived of many plans, but I was never free to execute one of them. For all that I held the rudder, and with a strong hand, the waves were always a good deal stronger.* —Napoleon

Structure of Organizations

A. Every organization and group, no matter how informal, is structured. Roles are agreed to, responsibilities are accepted, and the group is "organized" to accomplish its purpose.

B. In formal organizations, structure is often indicated on one-dimensional organizational charts that show where each position fits horizontally and vertically.

C. **Mintzberg** and others describe bureaucratic and hierarchical organizational structures as usually including:

1. An **operating core** of people who perform the basic work of the organization producing goods and services in providing for customers or clients.

2. Above the operating core is an **administrative component** of first line supervisors or **middle managers.**

3. Above the middle managers are **top-level managers**. Traditionally they create the mission and provide strategic direction. At the apex is a **chief executive officer** and often a **board of trustees.**

4. Additionally there are two other parts of the administrative structure: a **technostructure of analysts** (who standardize the work and inspect the work of others), and a **support staff** (custodians, nurses, food service, secretaries, etc.) who facilitate the work of the operating core

5. Forms may vary in accordance with size and type of organization but the overall form is traditionally bureaucratic and hierarchical.

D. In the structuring formal organizations, there is a seeking of the "best" structure to serve the unique circumstances of that organization. **Reorganization** and **restructuring** are attempts to improve the structure to conform to a new ideal.

E. **Mintzberg** cites the following management questions that guide leaders in designing formal structures:

1. How many tasks should a given position in the organization contain and how specialized should each task be?

2. To what extent should the work content of each position be standardized?

3. What skills and knowledge should be required for each position?

4. On what basis should positions be grouped into units and units into larger units?

5. How large should each unit be, and how many individuals should report to a given manager?

6. To what extent should the output of each position or unit be standardized?

7. What mechanisms should be established to facilitate mutual adjustment among positions and units?

8. How much decision-making power should be delegated to managers of line units down the chain of authority?

9. How much decision-making authority should pass from the line managers to the staff specialists and operators?

F. Ad hoc structures

1. In contrast to traditional hierarchical organizational structures, some theorists say that in times of change, what is needed is "adhocracy" rather than bureaucracy. Adhocracy refers to a loose, flexible system, a self-renewing organic form tied together mostly by lateral coordination, what **Tom Peters** calls "crazy organizations for crazy times."

2. Adhocracies can exist at either the operating or the administrative level and include ambiguous authority structures, unclear objectives, and contradictory assignments of responsibility! The assumption is that this environment can be more creative, foster exploration, self-evaluation, and learning. Ad hoc structures are most often found in conditions of turbulence and rapid change.

> *We may affirm absolutely that nothing great in the world has ever been accomplished without passion.*
>
> *-Georg Hegel*

3. **Mintzberg** makes these contrasts between bureaucracy and adhocracy.

	BUREAUCRACY	ADHOCRACY
Division of labor	Specialized	Collaborative
Coordination	Standardization	Mutual adjustment
Organization structured to	Provide standardized services/products	Provide innovative services/products
Orientation to change	Resistant	Receptive
Effective operating environment	Stable	Turbulent

G. Turning the pyramid upside down

1. The familiar hierarchical pyramid with its top executive and a few senior vice presidents reporting to him or her, then a row of vice presidents reporting to the senior vice presidents, and eventually down to the workers on the factory floor, with orders coming from the top and filtering down to the bottom, is being challenged on every side.

2. Academic attacks on the pyramid structure of management go back a few decades. Even as early as the 1960's and before, there was much written about "participative management" with ideas going both up and down the pyramid, and with some power shifted to those more intimately familiar with the problems at lower levels.

3. Today, management schools routinely teach students how to delegate authority and empower those further down in the hierarchical structure. Students are told that employees who actually do the job are usually the experts and, thus, are more likely to come up with ways to fix problems than some study team from above. They are instructed on how to form project teams in which everybody is, at least in theory, equal to one another. It may even be that leadership of a team is rotated among its members.

4. The ideas are revolutionary, even subversive, to those in hierarchical positions of power, and to some degree for everyone else who has been reared in and learned in and worked in hierarchies in homes, schools, and workplaces.

5. **Ross and Kay,** among many, insist that the aristocracy of business and government is toppling. Leading companies are shunted briskly aside by others who were unknowns. Companies and governments must reinvent the way they do business or sink.

39

6. There are no "magic bullets" or "quick fixes." Real "turnarounds" take years to implement, reeducation of virtually everyone concerned, and lots of hard work.

7. **Ross and Kay** advocate a "molecular management structure" in which workers, managers, and executives are in direct contact with customers and clients. The boss deals with big strategic issues, leaving employees to put out fires. The flattened molecular structure, they argue, can take advantage of modern technology to customize products or services for each customer, rather than by producing large runs of identical goods. They write that "technological wizardry can be coupled with highly flexible human systems that abandon the stilted lines of management command for versatile work teams that operate with little or no supervision."

> *To succeed, you not only need initiative, you need finishiative as well. When an engine stops knocking, it begins to start pulling.*
> *—Anonymous*

Effective Meetings

A. Types of meetings

1. Business Meetings (carry on official business, hear and act on committee reports)

2. Social Meetings (to increase member interaction, build personal relationships; have fun)

3. Information Sharing Meetings (to keep people informed)

4. Coordination Meetings (to bring together representatives of groups involved in various phases of joint projects)

5. Planning Meetings (to develop plans for programs or activities to be implemented)

6. Fact-finding Meetings (to identify problems, generate information, establish priorities)

7. Brainstorming Meetings or idea-generation meetings (to generate the widest range of alternatives while suspending evaluation)

8. Decision-making Meetings (to consider, evaluate and decide among alternatives)

9. Evaluation Meetings or renewal meetings (to evaluate goals, organizational structure, programs, activities, etc.)

B. A particular meeting may be one of the types above or a combination of two or more types.

C. Differentiation of roles

1. Need for description of responsibilities for officers, standing committees, ad hoc committees, etc.

D. Agenda

1. An agenda provides a purpose, a blueprint for the meeting. Should be in the hands of all, preferably before the meeting.

2. Arrangement of agenda:

   ● schedule critical items early to allow time for discussion and disposition.

   ● also schedule early items to be brought to closure (to provide "successes").

   ● schedule later on agenda items for information or for future consideration.

3. In planning, consider member needs and interests (will they be glad they came?)

4. Is time being well spent? Start on time? End on time? Use of time? Can some things be done without a meeting?

> *Organization is a simple matter, for all of its importance. It is simply a matter of doing things by working together.*
> *-Mary Baker Eddy*

E. Common meeting problems

1. Little planning or preparation for the meeting.

2. Lack of involvement in the planning by those who will be at the meeting.

3. Same meeting repeated, same place, same agenda, same time—time and time again.

4. Holding meetings only because they are scheduled to be held.

5. No agenda or inadequate agenda.

6. Too many items/activities for the time available.

7. Meeting has nothing for early arrivers to do.

8. Long, drawn-out reports.

9. A few people do all the talking.

10. No record of what was said or done.

11. No follow-up (assigned tasks, minutes or summary sent out).

F. Parliamentary procedure

1. Robert's Rules of Order is standard for conducting meetings, but the rules were designed for large meetings—parliaments—and if followed slavishly in small groups can be counterproductive.

2. The rule of making a motion before the subject can be discussed, for example, often leads to amendments and amendments to the amendments during discussion and much confusion. Simply agreeing to discuss the issue *first* before framing a motion can lead to a motion at the end of discussion that reflects a consensus of the group. Robert's formally allows for this procedure as "Committee of the Whole."

> *Do not worry about holding high position; worry rather about playing your proper role.*
> *-Confucius*

> *No one is wise enough by himself.*
> *-Titus Maccius Plautus (about 200 B.C.)*

Managing Time

A. The most frequent "out of control" concerns of leaders involve time.

B. The problems that lead to time wasting tend to be universal in nature though causes and solutions may vary depending on the leader. In any case there are always actions the leader can take to gain control of time.

C. Time wasters and what the leader can do:

1. **Leadership by crisis** (busy putting fires out). May be due to lack of planning, unrealistic time estimates, problem-focused mind-set, reluctance of subordinates to break bad news.

    ●   Leader can allow sufficient time for planning, think ahead, plan ahead, encourage information needed for corrective action.

42

2. **Indecision.** May be due to lack of a rational decision-making process or fear of making mistakes or vain search for total information.

   - Leader can get facts, set goals, investigate alternatives, make decision and implement it, use mistakes as a learning process, make decisions even when some facts are missing.

3. **"Administrivia" and routine.** May be due to lack of priorities, failure to delegate, overmanagement of subordinates, sense of security in dealing with operating details.

   - Leader can concentrate on goals set, delegate to others, look to results rather than details.

4. **Lack of planning.** May be due to not seeing benefit of planning, concern for action now, or perhaps even prior success without planning.

   - Leader can recognize that planning takes time but saves time in the end, that results are more important than activity, that success may be in spite of, not because of lack of planning.

5. **Haste.** May be due to impatience with detail, responding only to the urgent, lack of planning, attempting too much in too little time.

   - Leader can take time to get it right; save the time of doing it over; distinguish between urgent and important; attempt less and/or delegate more; take time to plan.

6. **Lack of priorities.** May be due to lack of goals and objectives.

   - Leader can write down goals and objectives and discuss priorities with subordinates.

7. **Too many meetings.** May be due to poor leadership in meetings, indecision, "jerk inputs," poor planning and organization, badly arranged agendas.

   - Leader can use agendas, stick to the topic, set objectives, distribute information before meeting, distribute minutes, convene only meetings needed.

8. **Visitors and interruptions.** May be due to enjoyment of socializing, inability to say no.

   - Leader can say no, be unavailable, work elsewhere, suggest lunch or breakfast meetings, hold stand-up visit, close the door.

9. **Telephone.** May be due to lack of self-discipline, desire to be informed and involved.

   ● Leader can be brief on calls, screen and "bunch" calls, stay uninvolved except for essentials, use phone answering machine.

10. **Paperwork.** May be due to sheer volume of mail and reading material resulting in a stacked desk of things to read.

    ● Leader can use principle of single handling, read selectively, learn speed reading, delegate screening of material.

11. **Overcommitment.** May be due to broad interests, confusion of priorities or lack of priorities, or too tightly arranged schedule.

    ● Leader can say no, put first things first, relate priorities to schedule of events, allow discretionary time for self-reflection, for the unexpected, and for personal and family time. Keep a "black book" and say no when discretionary time is involved.

D. **Stephen Covey** has developed a time management matrix to illustrate the importance of putting "first things first."

   1. Decisions can be made on the basis of relative urgency and relative importance.

	Urgent	Not Urgent
Important	I Crises Pressing problems Deadline-driven projects Emergencies	II Prevention Production capability activities Relationship building Recognizing new opportunities Planning Recreation
Not Important	III Interruptions Some calls Some mail Some reports Some meetings Proximate, pressing matters Popular activities	IV Trivia Busy work Some mail Some phone calls Time wasters Pleasant activities

   2. Too much time typically is spent in Quadrants I, III, and IV which Covey considers an ongoing invitation for ultimate burnout, continuing stress, forever putting out fires, short term thinking, feeling victimized and out of control, becoming dependent on others or even being fired.

> *Time is an equal opportunity employer. Each human being has exactly the same number of hours and minutes every day. Rich people can't buy more hours. Scientists can't invent new minutes. And you can't save time to spend it on another day. Even so, time is amazingly fair and forgiving. No matter how much time you've wasted in the past, you still have an entire tomorrow. Success depends upon using it wisely by planning and setting priorities. The fact is, time is worth more than money, and by killing time, we are killing our own chances for success.*
>
> *-Denis Waitley*

3. Most people spend too little time in Quadrant II which deals with things that are not urgent, but are important. These items are preventive in character (building relationships, long range planning, reflecting, preparation, learning, etc.) and should result in reducing the number of emergencies that pop up. The more of one's time spent working on things that are not immediate but pay off with large returns in the long run, the more effective is time management.

Dealing With Stress in Organizations

A. Symptoms of organizational stress or burnout

1. Doubts about one's competence and worth, personalizing and internalizing failure, anger is turned inward.

2. Guilt, including continual dissatisfaction with the quality of one's work, feelings of being overwhelmed.

3. Lower productivity, apathy, task avoidance, boredom, carelessness, daydreaming.

4. Psychological rigidity, inflexibility, lack of imagination.

5. Personal withdrawal, especially from people who might make additional demands, general feelings of depression.

6. Indecisiveness—making the simple difficult and fussing over the trivial, preoccupation with details that never seem to get completed.

7. Cynicism and griping, hassled, sour on everybody, feeling others are out to get you, playing the blame game, little irritations bring big reactions.

8. Minor but nagging physical problems, exhaustion and fatigue, susceptibility to illness.

B. Options in responding to organizational stress

1. Taking corrective action to prevent and reverse burnout.

2. Dropping out psychologically. Do only assigned work, adhere rigidly to rules, become compliant, avoid conflict.

3. Attempting to fight back—attack what is regarded as the source of frustration.

4. Attempting to escape through alcohol, drugs, mental illness, "sick days."

5. Resigning, and finding a different situation.

C. Prevention and reversal of burnout

1. Establish emotional contact with others. Share your thoughts and verbalize your feelings and frustrations. Find a good listener, a personal support system.

2. Give up unrealistic expectations and perfectionist demands on yourself. Develop a realistic contract with yourself that includes the amount of work that can reasonably be done.

3. Take professional time for self-improvement and personal revitalization. Build the necessary skills to improve professional competency and efficiency.

4. Schedule diversions that have nothing to do with work. Develop decompression routine. Take regular vacations.

5. Be active physically. Eat sensibly.

6. Deal with conflicts by problem solving.

7. Develop a positive attitude.

Organizational Growth and Restructuring

A. Impact of Age and Size of Organization on Growth and Development

1. A developmental theory developed by **Larry E. Greiner** asserts that growing organizations move through five relatively calm periods of evolution, each of which ends with a period of crisis and revolutionary change.

2. Five Stages of Growth

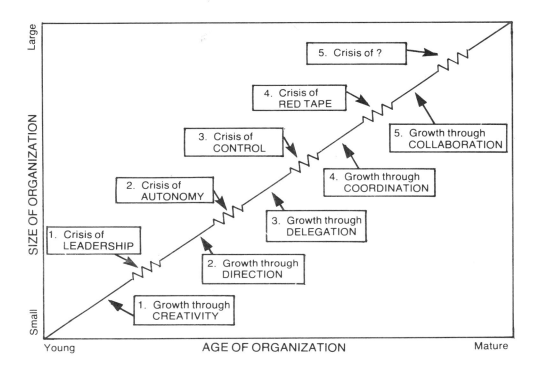

- **First Stage: Growth through Creativity.** Entrepreneurial founders manage "out of hip pocket." *Crisis of leadership* when growth creates need for strong manager to give direction.

- **Second stage: Growth through Direction.** Decisions made centrally by strong management. *Crisis of autonomy* when growth creates need for greater delegation.

- **Third stage: Growth through Delegation.** Decentralized organizational structure motivates, but leads to a crisis of control as management perceives it is losing control. May return to centralization, but more effective to move toward coordination.

- **Fourth stage: Growth through Coordination.** Development of formal systems of coordination which ultimately lead to a *crisis of red tape.* The organization has become too large and too complex. Move to collaborative methodologies.

- **Fifth stage: Growth through Collaboration.** Emphasis on greater spontaneity in management action through teams, ad hoc arrangements, shared involvement in decision-making. Next crisis?

Because power is energy, it needs to flow through organizations; it cannot be confined to functions or levels. We have seen the positive results of this flowing organizational energy in our experiences with participative management and self-managed teams. What gives power its charge, positive or negative, is the quality of relationships. Those who relate through coercion, or from a disregard for the other person, create negative energy. Those who are open to others and who see others in their fullness create positive energy. Love in organizations, then, is the most potent source of power we have available. And all because we inhabit a quantum universe that knows nothing of itself, independent of its relationships.

-Margaret J. Wheatley

I believe that diversity is part of the natural order of things—as natural as the trillion shapes and shades of the flowers of spring or the leaves of autumn. I believe that diversity brings new solutions to an ever-changing environment, and that sameness is not only uninteresting but limiting. To deny diversity is to deny life—with all its richness and manifold opportunities. Thus I affirm my citizenship in a world of diversity, and with it the responsibility to be tolerant. Live and let live. Understand that those who cause no harm should not be feared, ridiculed, or harmed—even if they are different. Look for the best in others. Be just in my dealings with poor and rich, weak and strong, and whenever possible to defend the young, the old, the frail, the defenseless. Be kind, remembering how fragile the human spirit is. Live the examined life, subjecting my motives and actions to the scrutiny of mind and heart so to rise above prejudice and hatred. Care.

-Gene Griessman

Day by day, hour by hour, we misunderstand each other because we cross well-marked boundaries; we blur the sense of you out there and me here; we merge, frequently very sloppily, the subjective with the objective, in various ways. We make of the other person simply an extension of self, either through the attribution of our own thoughts and attitudes to the other person, or by too facile a decision about his nature, after which we go on responding to him as though he were the character we invented. Or we force him/her into the role of surrogate for some member of the original cast.

-Hiram Haydn

48

4 Communication
relating, interacting, helping

> *Positive political skills demand that we find ways to rekindle the entrepreneurial spirit. Ways to treat all members of the organization as entrepreneurs so that employees feel that their units are their own businesses and that they, and they alone, are in the process of creating an organization of their own choosing.*
>
> *-Peter Block*

Communication and Perceptions

A. Communication may be defined as the mutual exchange of information and understanding. Experts tell us that as much as 70 percent of our communication efforts are likely to be misunderstood, misinterpreted, rejected, disliked, or distorted! We communicate at a 30 percent efficiency rate, yet the average person spends 80 percent of his or her waking hours in some form of communication!

B. Communication is based on perceptions and interpretations of truth and reality. Therein lies the richness of communication and collaboration and the problems of human interaction.

  1. Perceptions and interpretations are the product of data taken in through the senses: sight, hearing, smell, taste, and touch. The fact is, we are constantly overloaded with such data. So we develop a selective awareness.

  2. We develop "maps" of our psychological world and we tend to perceive our world with the sensing systems we most prefer. This process has been called "neurolinguistic programming" and associated with **John Grinder, Richard Bandler,** and others.

  3. Persons use their psychological maps to make sense of what they see and hear and feel. For each of us our primary sensory representational system has a lot to do with how we communicate, the language we use, our actions, and how we interact with others.

  4. Four sensory representational systems have been identified: visual, auditory, kinesthetic, and digital.

VISUALS	KINESTHETICS	AUDITORIES	DIGITALS
Map the world in pictures	Map the world from internal and external feelings	Map the world from sounds	Use words, numbers, data to map world
Like space between people	Like to be close to people	Concentrate on hearing, not looking at people	Like it in writing
Words like clear, focus, see, outlook, hazy, show, picture, glimpse, reveal, etc.	Words like touch, handle, block, grasp, sense, feel, impact, hit, etc.	Words like hear, tune, ring, tone, alarm, click, chord, harmonize, etc.	Words like facts, information, rational, analyze, specific, word, etc.
Sit behind the desk, look at diagrams, flow charts, pictures	Sitting at eye level, face to face talk, nonthreatening	Moving around, varied voice speed and delivery, pizazz	Defined terms, data, order and sequence
"I can see that" "Looks good to me"	"How do you feel" "Are you comfortable with this"	"Sounds good to me" "What I hear you saying is"	"That seems reasonable to me" "Have you verified this"

C. **Roger Fisher and Scott Brown** identify six basic elements of a healthy working relationship:

1. **Understanding**—Try to understand how the other sees things. Relationship requires achieving outcomes that satisfy the interests of both, and leaves each feeling fairly treated.

2. **Acceptance**—Deal seriously with those with whom we differ. Relationship requires that we accept each other as someone worth dealing with and learning from. The higher the degree of acceptance, the better the chance of working out differences.

3. **Reliability**—Be wholly trustworthy, but not wholly trusting. Relationship requires trust based on honest and reliable conduct over a period of time.

4. **Rationality**—Balance emotions with reason. Relationship requires reason informed by emotion and emotion guided and tempered by reason.

5. **Persuasion**—Be open to persuasion; try to persuade. The more coercive the means of influence, the less likely it is that the outcome will reflect the concerns of both.

6. **Communication**—Inquire, consult, and listen. Relationship requires that we communicate about our differences. The more effectively and openly we communicate, the better we will understand each other's concerns and the better our chances for reaching a mutually acceptable agreement.

Helping Process

A. General Observations

1. Different names are used to designate the helping process, such as leading, counseling, teaching, guiding, training, educating, listening, etc.

2. They have in common that the helping person is trying to assist another individual in solving a problem.

3. The expectation is that the direction of the help will be constructive and useful to the receiver, (i.e., clarify his/her perceptions of the problem, bolster self-confidence, modify behavior or develop new skills, etc.)

B. Visualizing the Helping Situation.

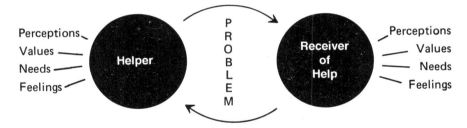

1. The helping situation is dynamic, i.e., characterized by interactions which are both verbal and non-verbal, and relationships.

- The helping person has needs (biological and psychological), feelings, and a set of values.
- The receiver of help has needs (biological and psychological), feelings, and a set of values.
- Both helper and receiver of help are trying to satisfy needs in the situation.
- The helper has perceptions of self, of the receiver of help, of the problem, and of the entire situation (expectancies, roles, standards, etc.).
- The receiver of help has perceptions of self, of the helper, of the problem, and of the entire situation (expectancies, roles, standards, etc.).

2. The interaction takes place in relation to some need or problem which may be external to the two individuals, interwoven with the relationship of the two individuals, or rooted in the relationship between the two individuals. Wherever the beginning point and the focus of emphasis is, the relationship between the two individuals becomes an important element in the helping situation as soon as interaction begins.

3. The receiver's needs, values and feelings, and perception of them as well as perception of the situation (including the problem and the helper) cause the receiver of help to have certain objectives in the interaction which takes place.

4. The helper's needs, values and feelings, and perception of them as well as perception of the situation (including the problem and the receiver of help) cause the helper to have certain objectives in the interaction which takes place.

5. Both helper and receiver of help have power, *i.e.,* influence, in relation to the helping situation. Except for surface conformity or breaking off the interaction, however, it is the receiver of help who controls the question of whether in the final analysis help takes place.

C. It is not easy to give help to another individual in such a way that he/she will be strengthened in doing a better job of handling the situation. Nor is it easy to receive help *from* another, the kind of help which makes us more adequate in dealing with our problems. If we really listen and reflect upon the situations in which we are either in the helper or receiver role, we not only are impressed with the magnitude and range of the problems involved in the helping situation, but also realize that we can keep on learning as a helping person, or a person receiving help, as long as we live.

1. **Some of the difficulties in receiving help from another:** The receiver of help

   - finds needing help hard to admit.
   - perceives problem to be unique.
   - fears losing control; finds it important to be independent.
   - only wants sympathy, not help.
   - distrusts the helper.
   - doubts helper's competency and motivation.
   - fears what will happen.
   - fears what others will think.
   - doesn't see that he/she must change.
   - is defensive; stops listening.
   - has strong need to lean, seeks dependency.

> *Nothing is a greater impediment to being on good terms with others than being ill at ease with yourself*
>
> *-Honors deBalzac*

2. **Some of the helper-behaviors that make it difficult to give help to another:** The helper

- likes to give advice.
- is insensitive to resistance.
- may try to argue or pressure.
- lacks understanding of the helping role.
- lacks awareness of own limitations and resources.
- responds to own needs and overrides needs of others.
- may like to take credit for helping.
- may label or blame.
- lacks awareness of self and own motivations.
- lacks interpersonal skill.
- likes to be a crusader.

3. **To be fruitful, a collaborative helping situation needs these relational characteristics:**

- Climate of **mutual trust and respect**.

- A real **desire to help** on the part of the helper and a real **desire to receive help** on the part of the receiver.

- Recognition that the helping situation is **a joint exploration** of the problem and possible solutions, with the receiver free to make the final decision.

- **Freedom of choice** is essential if the receiver of help is to achieve increased autonomy and independence.

- Listening, with the **helper listening** more than the individual receiving help.

- Behavior by the helper which is calculated to **make it easier for the individual receiving help to talk** and think through the problem and explore solutions.

> There is a destiny that makes us brothers
> None goes his way alone:
> All that we send into the lives of others
> Comes back into our own.
> —Edwin Markham

> There can be no friendship without confidence, and no confidence without integrity.
> —Samuel Johnson

Who Owns the Problem

A. **Thomas Gordon** identifies "ownership of the problem" as the key to appropriate communication responses when problems arise. Leadership effectiveness in dealing with a problem begins with the question: **Who owns the problem?**

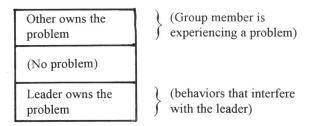

Other owns the problem	} (Group member is experiencing a problem)
(No problem)	
Leader owns the problem	} (behaviors that interfere with the leader)

B. **WHEN THE OTHER PERSON OWNS THE PROBLEM (that is, his/her needs are not being met)**, the other person's behavior in the situation does not impact you personally (that is, you are not a part of the problem).

1. Signs of people with an unmet need or a dissatisfaction (a problem)

   - **Nonverbal Cues**
     Being unusually uncommunicative, sulking, avoiding you, excessive absenteeism, being unusually irritable, not smiling as much as usual, daydreaming, tardiness, looking downcast or depressed, being sarcastic, walking slower (or faster), slouching in their chairs, etc.

   - **Verbal Cues**
     "Should have stayed in bed today." "Oh, forget it." "Get off my back." "If it isn't one thing, it's another." "I feel like quitting." etc.

2. **When the other person owns the problem**, Gordon describes your role as follows:

   - You as helper are a listener, a counselor, a sounding board.
   - You want to help the other, facilitate the other's finding his or her own solution.
   - You can accept the other's solution; you don't need to be satisfied.
   - You're primarily interested in the other's needs.

He has a right to criticize who has the heart to help.

-Abraham Lincoln

54

3. Gordon's **ways of helping when it is the other's problem:**

- **Invitations to talk** (door openers)
  - ▸ expressing your willingness to listen.
    "Would you like to talk about it?" "I've got the time if you want to talk." "I'd sure like to help if I can," etc.

- **Passive listening** (silent listening)
  - ▸ listening without comment.

- **Acknowledgement responses**
  - ▸ nodding.
    "I see." "Oh." "Mm-hmm," etc.

- **Reflective listening**
  - ▸ a longer acknowledgement response.
  - ▸ reflect back the **content**.
    "What I hear you saying is . . ."
    "If I understand you, what you're saying is . . ." etc.

- **Active listening**
  - ▸ decode the **feeling**.
  - ▸ state the feeling.
  - ▸ example:
    Other: "What's the use of trying to change things around here?"
    You decode: *discouraged*
    You: "You're feeling very discouraged." Or, "You sound discouraged."
    Other can now **confirm** it: "That's right," or **correct** it: "I'm more angry than I am discouraged."

C. **WHEN YOU OWN THE PROBLEM (that is, your needs are being interfered with),** you want the other person to change his/her behavior that affects you.

1. Leadership Challenge: How to persuade the other person to change without making him or her lose face or feel resentment toward you.

2. In the terms of **Thomas Gordon**: You own the problem because your needs are not being met. So your response is different from a helper-listener:

- You are a sender, persuader, an advocate.
- You want to help yourself.
- You want to sound off.
- You need to find a solution yourself.
- You must be satisfied with the solution.
- You are primarily interested in your own needs.
- You need to be assertive.

3. You need to confront a group member about his/her behavior. For example:

- One of your workers is much too slow.
- John volunteers to do jobs but often doesn't follow through.
- Mary is curt and impolite in handling phone calls.
- Susan doesn't keep you informed about activities on her committee.
- A supervisor in another department won't cooperate with you.
- Bill is invariably late for meetings.
- Kay interrupts you when you are speaking.

4. **When you own the problem, three courses of action are open to you:**

- You can **attempt to modify the environment**. Changing the situation may be all that is required to change the other's behavior. (For example: separate squabbling co-workers.)

- You can **attempt to modify the other's behavior** by confronting the person with the behavior that is unacceptable to you. Directly assert with "I-messages" (not "you-messages") what behavior it is that is unsatisfactory.

- You can **choose how to deal with a conflict of needs**, if your previous attempts fail in changing the behavior. You have three alternative choices in resolving the conflict:

   - **Method 1: You win; the other loses.** (You use your power or authority)

   - **Method 2: You lose; the other wins**. (You give in or give up)

   - **Method 3: Both win.** (You problem-solve together and find a mutually acceptable solution)

Language of Unacceptance: You-Messages

A. **Thomas Gordon** identifies twelve roadblocks to communication, what he calls "You-messages" or the "language of unacceptance"

1. **Aggressive "you-messages"**

- *Ordering, Directing, Commanding*
   You must do this.
   You cannot do this.
   I expect you to do this.
   Stop it.
   Go apologize to her.

- *Warning, Admonishing, Threatening*
  You had better do this, or else . . .
  If you don't do this, then . . .
  You better not try that.
  I warn you, if you do that . . .

- *Moralizing, Preaching, Imploring*
  You should do this.
  You ought to try it.
  It is your responsibility to do this.
  It is your duty to do this. I urge you to do this.

- *Advising, Giving Suggestions or Solutions*
  What I think you should do is . . .
  Let me suggest . . .
  It would be best for you if . . .
  Why not take a different approach? The best solution is . . .

- *Persuading with Logic, Lecturing, Arguing, Teaching*
  Do you realize that . . .
  The facts are in favor of . . .
  Let me give you the facts.
  Here is the right way.
  Experience tells us that . . .

- *Judging, Criticizing, Disagreeing, Blaming*
  You are acting foolishly.
  You are not thinking straight.
  You are out of line.
  You didn't do it right.
  You are wrong.
  That is a stupid thing to say.

The man's no bigger than the way he treats his fellow man. This standard has his measure been since time itself began.

He's measured not by tithes or creed, high-sounding though they be; nor by the gold that's put aside, nor by his sanctity. He's measured not by social rank, when character's the test, nor by his earthly pomp or show, displaying wealth possessed.

He's measured by his justice, right; his fairness at his play, his squareness in all dealings made, his honest, upright way.

These are his measures, ever near to serve him when they can, for man's no bigger than the way he treats his fellow man.

-Anonymous

- *Name-calling, Ridiculing, Shaming*
  You are a sloppy worker.
  You are a fuzzy thinker.
  You're talking like a "know it all."
  You really goofed on this one!

- *Interpreting, Diagnosing, Psychoanalyzing.*
  You're saying this because you're angry.
  You are jealous.
  What you really need is . . .
  You have problems with authority.
  You want to look good.

2. **"Soothing" you-messages.**

- *Praising, Agreeing, Buttering Up*
  You usually have very good judgment.
  You are an intelligent person,
  You have so much potential.
  You've made quite a bit of progress.
  You have always made it in the past.

- *Reassuring, Sympathizing, Consoling, Supporting*
  You'll feel different tomorrow.
  Things will get better.
  It is always darkest before the dawn
  Behind every cloud there's a silver lining.
  Don't worry so much about it. It's not that bad.

3. **Probing you-messages**

- *Probing, Questioning, Interrogating*
  Why did you do that?
  How long have you felt this way?
  What have you done to try to solve it?
  Have you consulted with anyone?
  When did you become aware of this feeling?
  Who has influenced you?

4. **Indirect you-messages**

- *Distracting, Diverting, Humoring, Sarcasm*
  Think about the positive side.
  Try not to think about it until you're rested.
  Let's have lunch and forget about it.
  That reminds me of the time when . . .
  You think *you've* got problems!

> *No person can heal or reform mankind unless he is*
> *actuated by love and good will towards men.*
>
> *-Mary Baker Eddy*

B. You-messages carry a high risk of damaging relationships.

- They make people feel guilty.
- They may be felt as put-downs, criticism, rejection.
- They may communicate lack of respect for the other.
- They often cause reactive or retaliatory behavior.
- They may be damaging to the recipient's self-esteem.
- They can produce resistance, rather than change.
- They may make a person feel hurt and, later, resentful.
- They are often felt as punitive.

> *One does not improve through argument but through examples. . . . Be what you wish to make others become. Make yourself, not your words, a sermon.*
>
> *-Henri Frederic Amiel*

Language of Acceptance: I-Messages

A. In contrast to "you-messages" which are said to be effective only about 25% of the time, Gordon recommends for the purpose of confronting or attempting to influence the behavior of another, the use of assertive "I-messages" which work 75% of the time (that is, result in a change in behavior).

1. Characteristics of I-messages

- Self-disclosing
- Direct
- Clear
- Authentic/Congruent

2. Benefits of assertiveness

- Your needs get met
- You strengthen your sense of self
- You are better understood by others
- You prevent conflict

> *Sometimes when I consider what tremendous consequences come from little things I am tempted to think there are no little things.*
> *-Bruce Barton*

59

3. Types of I-messages

- **Disclosing I-messages**
  I think
  I feel
  I believe
  I value
  I like/don't like

- **Responsive I-messages**
  No . . .because
  I don't want to . . .because
  I choose to . . .because
  I have decided . . .because

- **Preventive I-messages**
  I need . . .because
  I want . . .because
  I desire . . .because
  I would like to have . . .because

- **Confrontive I-messages**
  I feel . . . . . . (*state feeling*) . . .
       when you . . (*do what behavior*) . . .
            because . . .(*effect of other's behavior on you*) . .

B. A confrontive I-message is a plea for help—an invitation to the other for help—an **invitation** for the other person to change.

- *Example:* "When you come in late, I get upset because I have to bring you up-to-date before we can continue the meeting." (This I-Message to someone who is chronically late)

C. **Shifting Gears**

1. The changee is in the driver's seat. Ultimately that person makes the decision whether to change or not.

2. A common response to an I-message is for the changee to become defensive, apologetic, anxious, upset or resistive. Such responses call for the changer to shift gears, to active listening.

- *Example:*
  Changer: I was really upset when I found several mistakes in your report, because it made me look foolish at the board meeting where I presented the report.
  Changee: Well, you wanted it in such a hurry I didn't have time to double-check all my figures.
  Changer (shifts to active listening): You were under such a time bind, you felt you couldn't take the time to check it out, is that right?

60

One Minute Management

A. **Kenneth Blanchard and Spencer Johnson** have widely shared what they call "One Minute Management"

B. **One minute goal setting**

1. Good performance requires clear goals. People need to be clear on what they are being asked to do (accountability) and what good performance looks like (performance standards).

    ● In one minute goal setting, leader and group member

       1) Agree on the goals.
       2) Know what good behavior looks like.
       3) Write out each goal
       4) Read and re-read each goal.
       5) Observe performance and see if it matches goal.

2. When goals are clear, goals are reachable. You can't hold someone responsible for not accomplishing goals that were not clear in the first place. Goals motivate. The acronym SMART is useful in defining the nature of a goal:

    S - Specific
    M - Measurable
    A - Attainable
    R - Relevant
    T - Trackable

C. **One minute praising**

1. "Catch people doing something right"—and give them a one minute praising which is immediate and specific. Share your feelings so they know how you feel about what they did.

    ● In one minute praising

       1) Catch them doing something right and praise immediately.
       2) Be specific. Tell them what they did right.
       3) Share your feelings. Tell them how good you feel about what they did right and how it helps the organization. (Note disclosing appreciative I-message.)
       4) Pause. Let them feel how good you feel.
       5) Encourage them to do more of the same.
       6) Shake hands or touch in a way that makes clear you support what they're doing.

2. Never follow praising with a reprimand! Keep them separate!

D. **One minute reprimand**

1. Reprimand as soon as possible after the incident. One reprimand at a time. Be specific. Share your feelings (I-message).

   - In a one minute reprimand

     1) Reprimand the person immediately.
     2) Be specific. Tell them what they did wrong.
     3) Share your feelings. Tell them how you feel about what they did wrong—and in no uncertain terms. (Confrontive I-message)
     4) Pause for a few seconds of uncomfortable silence to let them feel how you feel. THEN go on to second half of reprimand.
     5) Shake hands or touch in a way that lets them know you are on their side.
     6) Remind them how much you value them. Reaffirm that you think well of them but not their performance in this situation.
     7) End of reprimand. When it's over, it's over.

2. Reprimand the behavior, not the person. When the reprimand is over, people should think about what they did, not how you treated them!

E. **One minute apology.**

1. Everyone makes mistakes, so it's all right to apologize.

2. Apologize as soon as possible. Be specific. Tell them how you feel about what you did wrong (embarrassed, disappointed, etc.)

   - In a one minute apology

     1) Apologize immediately.
     2) Be specific. Tell them what the apology is for.
     3) Share your feelings. Tell them how you feel. (Disclosing I-message)
     4) Reaffirm yourself. "That isn't my typical behavior, and if I had thought about it more first, I wouldn't have done it."

3. Apology relieves you of expending so much energy trying to prove yourself right.

Dysfunctional Communication

A. **Virginia Satir** calls communication dysfunctional to the degree that it is indirect and vague. It is functional to the degree that it is direct, specific and honest.

1. Satir identifies five freedoms that lead to open communication. She emphasizes that most of us have learned what she calls the "unfreedoms" that distort and frustrate communication.

FIVE UNFREEDOMS THAT DISTORT AND FRUSTRATE COMMUNICATION	FIVE FREEDOMS THAT LEAD TO OPEN COMMUNICATION
"Don't see or hear what you see or hear but what you should see and hear."	The freedom to *see* and *hear* what is here instead of what should be, was, or will be.
"Lie about everything. As long as you can't say what you feel—make it up"	The freedom to *say* what one feels and thinks, instead of what one should.
"Don't feel what you feel, but what you should feel"	The freedom to *feel* what one feels instead of what one ought.
"Don't reach out for what you want, but wait for it to be offered and then pretend you don't want it!"	The freedom to ask for what one wants instead of always waiting for permission.
"Don't take steps on your own behalf, you might rock the boat."	The freedom to take *risks (steps)* on one's own behalf, intead of choosing to be only "secure" and not rocking the boat.

B. Four dysfunctional communication patterns:

1. *Placating* (trying to please so the other person doesn't get upset)

    ●   Says things like: "Whatever you want is OK. I'm just here to make you happy."
    ●   The person begs with his body, "I am helpless" and inside he feels like a nothing, worthless without the person he/she is trying to please.
    ●   The Placater is a "yes-man," apologizing, never disagreeing.
    ●   May suffer pains in the neck (from looking up), strained eyes (from trying to see), headaches (from chronic resentment), whiny, squeaky voice (from begging)!

2. *Blaming* (constant fault-finding, criticizing)

    ●   Says things like, "You never do anything right. What's the matter with you?"
    ●   The person points the accusing finger, "I'm the boss around here," and inside feels lonely, unloved and unsuccessful.
    ●   The Blamer cuts everybody and everything down—(you never. . . you always . . . why don't you ever. . .)
    ●   May suffer from tightness of muscles and organs, increasing blood pressure, difficulty in breathing with voice hard, tight, often shrill, loud!

63

3. ***Super-Reasonable*** (very correct, very reasonable, no feeling--like a computer)

   ● Says things like, "If one were to observe carefully, one would see ... "
   ● The person barely moves, shows "I'm cool, calm and collected" and inside feels vulnerable, feelingless.
   ● The Super-Reasonable does not show feeling, loves to sound intelligent, uses long words, chooses "right" words, and is as motionless as possible.
   ● May suffer from a monotonous dead voice, no feeling from the brain down, and little motion or emotion!

4. ***Distracting*** (irrelevant behavior, words make no sense)

   ● Says things like, "Who cares?"—doesn't come on straight.
   ● Bodily the person shows he/she is off somewhere else and inside says, "Nobody cares, there is no place for me."
   ● The Distracter is like a top, a lot of moving but getting nowhere.
   ● The Distractor is not "together."

> *Our most valuable possessions are those which can be shared without lessening; those which when shared multiply. Our least valuable possessions are those which when divided are diminished.*
> *- William Danforth*

Communication That Builds Self-esteem

A. **Haim Ginnot** identifies three ways to help people build their self-esteem. (Note that in each case the key element is an I-message.)

   1. **When the other person is doing the "wrong" thing:**

      ● Don't talk to the person, talk to the condition.
      ● Describe what you see.
      ● Describe what you feel.
      ● Describe what needs to be done.
      ● Say nothing to the person about herself or himself.

   2. **When the other person is doing the "right" thing:**

      ● Praise descriptively, not judgmentally.
      ● Give recognition to the facts.
      ● Describe the person's efforts.
      ● Don't evaluate the person's personal attributes and character traits.

3. **When the other person demeans himself or herself:**

- Neither agree nor disagree. but acknowledge his or her views and briefly state your own.
- Don't contradict the person's views.
- Don't use logical explanations.
- Don't ridicule the person's views.
- Convey your positive regard.

B. Willingness to accept responsibility and to act responsibly is largely determined by the way we perceive we are being treated. Our perceptions are determined by our communication and interactions with people.

1. **People gain self-esteem and feel responsible**

- when they feel they can make a difference
- when they feel important and needed
- when they feel they can be depended on
- when they feel they have some control of what is happening
- when they feel appreciated
- when they feel respected and trusted
- when they feel in control of themselves
- when they feel they can risk making a mistake
- when they feel they have freedom to make choices

2. **People take responsibility**

- when leaders don't order them around
- when leaders don't threaten them
- when leaders aren't judging them
- when leaders don't put them down
- when leaders don't embarrass them
- when leaders don't talk down to them
- when leaders treat them with respect
- when leaders treat them like a real person
- when leaders let them know when they're doing a good job

Mushroom Farm Lament

We feel we're being kept in the dark.
Every once in a while someone comes around
and spreads manure on us.
When our heads pop up,
they're chopped off.
And then we're canned!

In a way, the only culture that exists for us is in the room in which we are standing at the moment. It is the transformation of the culture of the room we are in that holds the possibility of transforming the culture of the rest of the organization. It is change from the inside out.

-Peter Block

You might say a name, and describe how tall he is, and the color of his eyes and hair. But none of these things is what the person is. A person is invisible activities. WHO, THEN, IS THIS PERSON SITTING NEXT TO YOU?

The person sitting next to you . . . is working away at problems.

He has fears. He wonders how he is doing. Often he doesn't feel too good about how he is doing; and he finds that he can't respect or be a good friend of himself. When he feels that way about himself, he has a hard time loving others; he suffers.

The person sitting next to you has a right to be a person; that is, he has a right to choose and decide, to have a private life of his own. He also has a right to be understood. Unless he can be understood by other people, he is thwarted from being a person.

The person sitting next to you is an inexhaustible sort of existence. Within him are energies that have been only partially awakened. Nine-tenths of his possibility has not yet been touched off. There is all kind of good that is struggling to be born from 'way within that person. There are also worries, fears, hates that are struggling to get themselves expressed Sometimes, if only these could be expressed, he would be free to love other people.

Thus the person sitting next to you is a cluster of memories from the past and expectations of the future. He is really a whole colony of persons forever. So the person sitting next to you is really a city—a community. In that community live the father and mother of this person, the boys and girls with whom he played most, the people with whom he went to school; all the live things of this world that came and interacted with this person. They are still deep within.

The person sitting next to you is the greatest miracle and the greatest mystery that you will ever meet. The person sitting next to you is sacred.

-Ross Snyder

5 Acceptance
culture, community, meaning

> *Ten thousand new teachers each year enter the New York City school system as a result of retirement, death, job turnover, and attrition. These new teachers come from all over the country. They represent all religions, races, political persuasions, and educational institutions. But the amazing thing is that after three weeks in the classroom you can't tell them apart from the teachers they replace.*
>
> *-Albert Shanker,*
> *American Federation of Teachers*

Culture of Organizations

A. Culture refers to the norms, values, and history of the group (or organization) —all the shared understandings held by members of the group. It describes the guiding beliefs and the day-to-day behavior expected of those accepted into the group.

   1. **Organizational culture refers to the unique web of**

      - commonly held perceptions.
      - shared beliefs.
      - images of reality.

   2. Culture provides **meaning** to members of the organization. It provides a way to

      - resolve confusion.
      - increase predictability.
      - provide direction in a situation of ambiguity and uncertainty.

   3. Culture includes largely **unconscious and unexamined assumptions**,

   4. Culture is the **sum total of our meanings and interpretations** of what is happening to us and others in the organization.

   5. Every organization develops distinctive beliefs and patterns over time.

B. Particular cultures may be represented by a metaphor which captures its meaning and the primary view of people in the culture, as well as the way the leaders view themselves.

67

METAPHOR FOR CULTURE	PRIMARY VIEW OF ORGANIZATION	LEADER VIEW OF LEADERSHIP ROLE
FAMILY	Home	Parent
ATHLETIC TEAM	Winning the Game	Coach
WELL-OILED MACHINE	Gears Running Smoothly	Controller
CABARET	Broadway Show	Master of Ceremonies
FACTORY	Input, Output	C.E.O.
CIRCUS	Multiple Activities	Ringmaster
ZOO	Caged Animals	Zookeeper
JUNGLE	Dangerous Savages	Lion Tamer, Policeman
TEMPLE	Sacred Place	Guru
LITTLE SHOP OF HORRORS	Nightmare Walking on Eggs	Self-cleaning Statue (Teflon, nothing sticks)
COMMUNITY	Shared Fellowship	Facilitator

Belonging: Gaining and Maintaining Acceptance

A. **Belonging is gaining acceptance** into an organizational or group culture (the socialization process):

1. Organizations select candidates (new members) whose personal values fit the underlying values of the organization.

2. New people learn the culture through considerable training in the culture often by humility-inducing experiences such as more work than they can reasonably handle, or work for which they are overqualified, or the undesirable tasks no one else wants to do. All this amounts to a kind of initiation rite.

3. People learn to master the performance of tasks and responsibilities, developing their technical knowledge and skills.

4. Cultures reward performance and operational results which are consistent with the underlying values of the culture.

5. People learn to know and accept the organization's values.

6. Cultures provide reinforcing folklore of rites and rituals, stories and myths, and heroes that portray and reinforce the culture.

7. People find and follow role models in the organization, persons who symbolize success in the organization, mentors who provide ongoing models for continuing staff development.

B. An informal network of cultural players (keepers, protectors, system antibodies) watch over the culture to keep people in line and maintain the culture. These cultural players often act as **barriers** to change.

Open and Closed Climates

A. Climate is an aspect of culture but is more specifically a measure of whether people's expectations are being met regarding what they feel it should be like to be a part of the group or institution. It is the fit between the prevailing culture and the individual values of the participants.

1. Climate is a set of perceptions on the part of each participant. A climate may be at any point on a continuum from open to closed. **Andrew Halpin** summarizes the two opposite ends as follows:

CLIMATE FACTOR	OPEN CLIMATE	CLOSED CLIMATE
Disengagement (people don't work together, pull in different directions)	Low	Very High
Hindrance (perception of barriers, burdens, unnecessary busywork)	Low	High
Morale (social needs satisfied, people have sense of accomplishment)	Very High	Low
Intimacy (friendly social relations with each other)	High	Low
Aloofness of Leader (impersonal, goes by the book, social distance)	Low	High
Production/Task Emphasis (highly directive, close supervision)	Low	High
Thrust (moving the organization by example set by the leader)	Very high	Low
Consideration (leaders treat people humanly, do little extras)	High	Low

B. An open system does not rely on static roles, rules, formal goals, rigid structures and fixed patterns, but rather relies on the dynamic qualities of behavioral events, relationships and the web of links and networks in the organization. **An open system enables the creation of a culture for change**. The system is able to react to turbulence by changing its patterns.

69

1. The following table contrasts dynamic open systems with classical closed systems:

DYNAMIC OPEN SYSTEMS	TRADITIONAL CLOSED SYSTEMS
Dynamic relationships. Interlocking cycles of events within and between subsystems. Every individual has something to contribute.	Static relationships. Hierarchical ordering of roles and responsibilities. Hierarchy equals moral superiority.
Power is shared. Differentiation and integration of activities is with subsystems. People doing the job have important information.	Power is centralized. Chief officer has ultimate authority and responsibility and "knows best."
Needs of the environment provide directions for events and activities.	Formal goals provide direction.
Communication consists of system-wide linkages integrating various subsystems.	Communication follows established channels.
Control results from the effectiveness of linkages between internal subsystems and external environment.	Control over production is established by rules.
The function of managerial subsystems is to support the needs of other subsystems.	Superiors manage subordinates.
Conflict is natural and can lead to positive change.	Conflict is dysfunctional and should be eliminated.
Innovation and change is encouraged at all levels.	Change is decided at the top and imposed.
There are many ways to perform a task that are equally satisfactory.	There is one best way to perform a task.

2. According to **Warren Bennis**, an open system creates and includes, at the minimum, acceptance in the culture of such beliefs as

    ● People need to feel significant

    ● Learning and competence matter

    ● People are part of a community

    ● Work is exciting, challenging, fun

> *At the same time that we are almost too willing to yield to institutions that give us meaning and thus a sense of security, we also want self-determination. With equal vehemence, we simultaneously seek self-determination and security. This is certainly irrational. Yet those who don't somehow learn to manage the tension are, in fact, technically insane.*
>
> *-Thomas J. Peters and Robert H. Waterman, Jr.*

Finding Meaning in Organizations

A. Meaning, it has been said, is the most basic human need. Whatever is happening has to somehow make sense, be explainable to ourselves.

1. **Viktor Frankl,** through his hellish experiences in three grim years in Auschwitz and other Nazi prisons, developed his theory of logotherapy which he said, "makes the concept of man into a whole . . . and focuses its attention upon mankind's groping for a higher meaning in life."

2. According to logotherapy, the striving to find a meaning in one's life is the primary motivational force in man. This will to meaning is in contrast to the Freudian view of will to pleasure, or the Adlerian view of will to power.

B. **Lee Bolman and Terrence Deal** identify several ways people provide meaning in the midst of the complexity and ambiguity of organizational phenomena:

1. Myths

    ● provide cohesiveness, clarity and direction to events that otherwise seem confusing and mysterious.

2. Stories and Fairy Tales

    ● provide comfort, reassurance and offer general direction and hope for the future.
    ● provide heroes.

3. Rituals and Ceremonies

    ● provide ways of taking meaningful action in the face of ambiguity, unpredictability, and threat.
    ● provide certainties in the midst of uncertainty.

71

4. Metaphors and Symbols

- provide explanations and interpretations that bring meaning out of chaos.

5. Humor and Play

- allow individuals and organizations to escape from the tyranny of facts and logic.
- view organizations and their own participation as something new and different from the appearance.
- find creative alternatives to existing choices.

6. Theater and Continuing Soaps

- view administrative and technical processes (formal meetings, evaluation systems, accounting systems, management information systems, labor negotiations, etc.) as continuing soap operas not to be taken seriously because scripts rarely change.

> *Anyone who visits more than a few schools notes quickly how schools differ from each other in their "feel." In one school the teachers and the principal are zestful and exude confidence. . . . In a second school the brooding discontent of the teachers is palpable; the principal tries to hide his incompetence and his lack of a sense of direction behind a cloak of authority, and yet he wears this cloak poorly because the attitude he displays to others vacillates randomly between the obsequious and the officious.*
>
> *-Andrew W. Halpin*

Cultural Diversity

A. Recognizing diversity (racial, ethnic, religious, gender, class, etc.) and accommodating diversity is requisite in virtually any organizational context.

B. In diverse workplaces and organizations, there may be some degree of culture clash which highlights the need that all be provided opportunity, equity, and identity.

C. Keys to improving cross-cultural communication

1. Respect for people of all races, religions, ethnicity, culture, whatever.

2. Toleration of ambiguity when reasons for another's behavior are not clear.

3. Relating to people regardless of differences. Seeing differences as strengths that will be beneficial in the organization.

4. Being nonjudgmental (difference is difference, not necessarily a matter of good or bad).

5. Personalizing one's observations of an individual, rather than generalizing to "all people of that kind."

6. Empathy (putting yourself in the other's place, seeing from his or her point of view).

7. Learning more about other peoples, encouraging open dialogue on cultural topics and diversity, discussing the historical, political and economic basis of inequalities encountered by others.

> *Man is a political creature and one whose nature is to live with others.*
>
> *-Aristotle*

> *A reasonably clear conception of organizational health would seem to be an important prerequisite to a wide range of activities involving organizations: research of any meaningful sort; attempts to improve the organization as a place to live, work, and learn; and—not the least—the day-to-day operation of any particular organization.*
>
> *-Matthew Miles*

Building Community

A. Organizations have traditionally operated in a culture defined by legitimacy, hierarchy, and self-interest. However, there has long been recognized an informal organization" operating within the formal structure. The informal organization may be described as "the way things *really* work around here."

B. Traditionally organizations are essentially the arrangement of things (and people) into a coherent whole, controlling, ordering in a linear process, setting up rules and regulations, making corrections as needed, evaluating in terms of stated goals. All this structuring is in attempt to be "rational."

C. Not all groupings of individuals, however, can be characterized as organizations as described above. Families, communities, friendship networks, and social clubs are examples of collections of people that are different from what we think of as organizations. **Thomas Sergiovanni** points out several distinctions between what he calls the traditional metaphor of "organization" and the metaphor of "community."

MATAPHOR OF "ORGANIZATION"	METAPHOR OF "COMMUNITY"
Contractual agreements Bargained rights, discretion, freedom	Social and moral ties, commitments Social structure of concepts, images, values, sentiments, shared beliefs
Personal authority of leader	Authority of shared ideas, common goals, shared ideals, shared purpose
Relationships constructed by others and codified into hierarchy, roles	Relationships close, informal, social ties with others with same intentions, common identity, collegiality
Policies, rules, protocols, regulations, mandates	Norms, mutual obligations toward each other, felt interdependence
Distinction between means and ends	Ends still ends but means are also considered ends
"I" oriented, competitive, acceptance is conditional	"We" oriented, cooperative, sense of belonging and acceptance

D. **Max DePree** describes these two types of relationships as "contractual" and "covenantal." The covenantal relationship is "an expression of the sacred nature of relationships."

1. Covenantal relationships are flexible, and as hospitable to the unusual person as to the usual person.

2. The covenantal relationship, like participative management, champions the right and duty of everyone to influence decisions and understand the implications.

> *The day-by-day behavior of the immediate superior and of other significant people in the managerial organization communicates something about their assumptions concerning management which is of fundamental significance. . . . Many subtle behavioral manifestations of managerial attitudes create what is often referred to as the "psychological climate."*
>
> *-Douglas McGregor*

> *Many an innovation brought in with great fanfare is superficially accepted, and months or years later, things have drifted back to the way they were before. Nobody may have openly resisted the change. Nobody revoked it. It just didn't last.*
>
> *-Goodwin Watson*

Accepting Change

A. **Change is unsettling** because we must give up some behavior we are skilled in, and acquire new behavior in which we lack skill.

   1. **Uncertainty and ambiguity stimulate us to search for meaning** in the new situation, and then to react in terms of the meaning we construct. If, on the basis of the constructed meaning, we believe we will be worse off after the change, we will resist the change.

B. Some Generalizations About Human Behavior

   1. Behavior depends on both the person and the environment.

   2. Each individual behaves in ways which make sense to that person.

   3. An individual's perception of a situation influences behavior in that situation.

   4. An individual's self-concept influences behavior.

   5. An individual's behavior is influenced by personal needs, which vary from person to person and from time to time.

C. Therefore, it is important to:

   1. Build group norms (a culture) that will support change.

   2. Expect hostile, apathetic and dependent reactions. These are symptomatic of the threatening and ambiguous meanings attributed to change.

   3. Expect some failures in the early stages of behavior change. Minimize penalties for failure. Provide rewards for change and opportunities to practice the new forms of behavior.

> *Both tears and sweat are wet and salty, but they render a different result. Tears will get you sympathy, but sweat will get you change.*
>
> *-Jesse Jackson*

D. A conception of forces for and against change

1. The variety of factors involved in change requires that some conceptual scheme be used in analyzing the situation.

2. **Kurt Lewin** saw behavior within a group setting as a dynamic balance of forces working in opposite directions. Some common forces are shown on the following table:

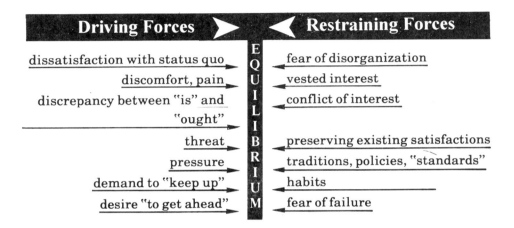

Driving Forces		Restraining Forces
dissatisfaction with status quo	E	fear of disorganization
discomfort, pain	Q	vested interest
discrepancy between "is" and	U	conflict of interest
"ought"	I	
	L	
	I	
threat	B	preserving existing satisfactions
pressure	R	traditions, policies, "standards"
demand to "keep up"	I	habits
	U	
desire "to get ahead"	M	fear of failure

3. Consider, for example, the production level of a work team in a factory. This level fluctuates within narrow limits above and below a certain number of units of production per day. Why does this pattern persist?

    ● Because, Lewin says, the forces that tend to raise the level of production are equal to the forces that tend to depress it.

    ● Among the "driving" forces tending to raise the level of production might be:
    1) the pressures of supervisors on the work team to produce more;
    2) the desire of at least some team members to attract favorable attention from supervisors, in order to get ahead individually;
    3) the desire of team members to earn more under the incentive plan of the plant.

    ● Among the "restraining" forces tending to lower the level of production might be:
    1) a group standard in the production team against "rate busting" or "eager beavering" by individual workers;
    2) resistance of team members to accepting training and supervision from management.
    3) feelings by workers that the product they are producing is not important.

76

- The balance between the two sets of forces, which defines the established level of production, Lewin called a **"quasi-stationary equilibrium."** According to Lewin, this type of thinking about patterns of group behavior applies not only to levels of production in industry, but also to such patterns as levels of discrimination in communities; atmosphere of democracy or autocracy in social agencies; supervisor-teacher-pupil relationships in school systems; and formal or informal working relationships among levels of a professional organization.

4. **Change takes place when imbalance occurs between the sum of the *restraining forces* and the sum of the *driving forces*. This imbalance *unfreezes* the equilibrium.**

5. Imbalances occur if:

   - one or more driving forces are increased
   - one or more restraining forces are decreased
   - a combination of the above
   - a new force is added

6. When an imbalance occurs between the forces and unfreezes the pattern, the level changes until the driving and restraining forces return to equilibrium in a new position.

7. Planned change uses situational forces to accomplish unfreezing, change and stabilization.

8. Exerting strong force (increasing driving forces) through influence or authority in the effort to initiate or maintain a change process may bring about strong reactions against the change. Pressure invites counter-pressure. Tension is likely to mount causing increasing instability and unpredictability.

9. **It is probably more effective to release resisting forces (decrease restraining forces) by opening up communication, by creating a climate in which feelings can be freely expressed, or by helping the opposition actually work through their reasons for resistance.** This emphasizes the need for openness and nonjudgmental approach in the responses of a leader.

> *One of the greatest pains to human nature is the pain of a new idea. It . . . makes you think that after all, your favorite notions may be wrong, your firmest beliefs ill-founded. . . . Naturally, therefore, common men hate a new idea, and are disposed more or less to ill-treat the original man who brings it.*
>
> *-Walter Bagehot, 1873*

E. Creating a culture that **encourages** change

1. **Rosabeth Moss Kanter** suggests these elements as important to a climate that encourages innovation.

- Listen to workers and be receptive to new ideas.

- Provide for faster approvals and less red tape.

- Collaboration between organizational units.

- Provide abundant praise and recognition.

- Provide advance warning of change.

- Make extra resources available.

- Adopt the attitude that we are always learning.

This letter was written to President Andrew Jackson, dated January 31, 1829, by the governor of a leading state, a man who later became president himself:

To: President Jackson

The canal system of this country is being threatened by the spread of a new form of transportation known as "railroads" The federal government must preserve the canals for the following reasons:

One. If canal boats are supplanted by "railroads," serious unemployment will result. Captains, cooks, drivers, hostlers, repairmen and lock tenders will be left without means of livelihood, not to mention the numerous farmers now employed in growing hay for horses.

Two. Boat builders would suffer and towline, whip and harness makers would be left destitute.

Three. Canal boats are absolutely essential to the defense of the United States. In the event of the expected trouble with England, the Erie Canal would be the only means by which we could ever move the supplies so vital to waging modern war.

For the above-mentioned reasons the government should create an Interstate Commerce Commission to protect the American people from the evils of "railroads" and to preserve the canals for posterity.

As you may know, Mr. President, "railroad" carriages are pulled at the enormous speed of 15 miles per hour by "engines" which, in addition to endangering life and limb of passengers, roar and snort their way through the countryside, setting fire to crops, scaring the livestock and frightening women and children. The Almighty certainly never intended that people should travel at such breakneck speed.

Martin Van Buren, Governor of New York

2. In summary, a culture that encourages change must provide

- A collegial environment where people are not isolated from each other.

- Integrated processes that work together and are not fragmented into separated parts.

- Resources earmarked for innovation and experimentation.

- Encouragement for professional risk taking.

- An open climate supportive of problem finding, not problem hiding.

3. The following diagram shows the interrelationship and impact of group maintenance forces, group task needs, and leadership styles on the culture of a group or organization:

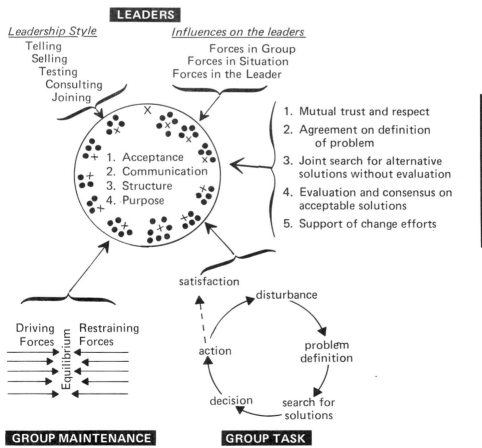

LEADERS

Leadership Style
Telling
Selling
Testing
Consulting
Joining

Influences on the leaders
Forces in Group
Forces in Situation
Forces in the Leader

1. Acceptance
2. Communication
3. Structure
4. Purpose

1. Mutual trust and respect
2. Agreement on definition of problem
3. Joint search for alternative solutions without evaluation
4. Evaluation and consensus on acceptable solutions
5. Support of change efforts

LEADERSHIP

satisfaction

disturbance

action

problem definition

decision

search for solutions

Driving Forces   Restraining Forces

Equilibrium

GROUP MAINTENANCE   **GROUP TASK**

The first order of business is to build a group of people who, under the influence of the institution, grow taller and become healthier, stronger, more autonomous.

-Robert K. Greenleaf

Go placidly amid the noise and haste, and remember what peace there may be in silence. As far as possible without surrender be on good terms with all persons. Speak your truth quietly and clearly; and listen to others, even the dull and ignorant; they too have their story.

Avoid loud and aggressive persons, they are vexations to the spirit. If you compare yourself with others, you may become vain and bitter; for always there will be greater and lesser persons than yourself. Enjoy your achievements as well as your plans.

Keep interested in your own career, however humble; it is a real possession in the changing fortunes of time. Exercise caution in your business affairs; for the world is full of trickery. But let this not blind you to what virtue there is; many persons strive for high ideals; and everywhere life is full of heroism.

Be yourself. Especially, do not feign affection. Neither be cynical about love; for in the face of all aridity and disenchantment it is perennial as the grass.

Take kindly the counsel of the years, gracefully surrendering the things of youth. Nurture strength of spirit to shield you in sudden misfortune. But do not distress yourself with imaginings. Many fears are born of fatigue and loneliness. Beyond a wholesome discipline, be gentle with yourself.

You are a child of the universe, no less than the trees and the stars; you have a right to be here. And whether or not it is clear to you, no doubt the universe is unfolding as it should.

Therefore be at peace with God, whatever you conceive Him to be, and whatever your labors and aspirations, in the noisy confusion of life keep peace with your soul.

With all its sham, drudgery and broken dreams, it is still a beautiful world. Be careful. Strive to be happy.

-Found in Old Saint Paul's Church, Baltimore. Dated 1692.

6 Understanding Behavior
motives and acts

> *Leadership over human beings is exercised when persons with certain motives and purposes mobilize, in competition or conflict with others, institutional, political, psychological, and other resources so as to arouse, engage, and satisfy the motives of followers.*
>
> *-James MacGregor Burns*

Approaches to Motivation and Behavior

A. Three Views of Motivation

1. **Behavior impelled by inner-urges (Freud).**

   - Motivation determined by inner forces and urges.

   - Emphasis on understanding urges and attempting to bring them under control.

2. **Behavior impelled by outer-situational forces (Pavlov-Skinner).**

   - Motivation involves a response to environmental stimuli.

   - Reinforced behavior is repeated.

   - Emphasis on controlling environment to obtain desired response.

3. **Behavior impelled by inherent capacity for growth (Carl Rogers**, and other "third force" psychologists)

   - Motivation is a consequence of man's natural desire to grow and change.

   - Focus is on present behavior—does not ask "Why?" but "What am I doing?"

   - Person must accept responsibility for his/her behavior.

   - No excuses (inner-urges or outer-situation) are accepted.

   - Emphasis is on one's "unleashing" motivation that is already there to accomplish goals that satisfy needs.

Hierarchy of Needs

A. An individual's behavior is influenced by his/her needs, which vary from person to person and from time to time.

B. **Abraham Maslow** shows these needs in a hierarchical arrangement to indicate that a need at one level tends to operate as a primary source of motivation when needs at a lower level are sufficiently satisfied for that person.

*   **Physiological Needs**—most basic needs, important to sustain life itself, such as food, activity, air and sleep.

*   **Security Needs**—a projection of physiological needs into the future including protection from physical harm, assurance of continuing income and employment, etc.

*   **Social Needs**—include a sense of belonging and membership in a group and acceptance by other people.

*   **Self-esteem Needs**—include that which reflects on an individual's self-worth and self-confidence.

*   **Self-actualization**—refers to a sense of accomplishment and the development and utilization of one's potential capacities.

> *He who reigns within himself, and rules passions, desires and fears, is more than a king.*
> *-John Milton*

C. We shall be supported in our efforts to grow and to improve by a psychological force which has only recently come in for much attention. There seems to be in each of us a strong drive toward wholeness. Something in us protests at our own lopsidedness and distortions. **Garner Murphy** writes of realizing human potentialities; **Carl Rogers** finds patients self-correcting; **Abraham Maslow** sees self-actualization as a major motive; **Gordon Allport** uses the term "becoming." If we can become sensitive to our own inner impulses, we shall not need external sticks and carrots to motivate us toward a fuller, richer, better life.

Control Theory

A. **William Glasser** has developed a theory of behavior and motivation which he calls "Control Theory." Behaviors are total, internally motivated, purposeful, flexible and our creative efforts to satisfy five basic needs. In a constant effort to gain more effective control, we, as a control system, choose our behaviors to satisfy our needs. No matter how painful or self-destructive a behavior appears, every behavior is always our attempt to get what we want at the time.

B. All behavior is made up of three components: (1) what we do, (2) what we think, (3) what we feel. According to Glasser, all are choices.

   1. We are motivated completely by forces inside ourselves and not, as most people believe, by response to people and things around us.

   2. We are motivated by our needs.

      ● the need to survive (physiological)

      ● the need for love (to belong, share, cooperate)

      ● the need for power (to control, achieve, be recognized)

      ● the need for freedom (to choose, move around)

      ● the need for fun (to learn, play, enjoy)

   3. All human beings are "control systems" that attempt to control their lives in order to satisfy needs.

   4. Regardless of how we *feel,* we always have some control over what we *do* and what we *think,* and that will change how we feel.

   5. Ask yourself, "Is the criticizing and misery I am now choosing helping me get what I want?" When the answer for the person wanting to regain control of life is *no,* then the way is open to choose a doing behavior that is more satisfying.

83

C. Four components make up a total behavior:

1. Doing (action)

2. Thinking (generating thoughts)

3. Feelings (both pleasurable and painful)

4. Physiology (voluntary and involuntary body mechanisms)

D. Behavior is always a choice. "Do" is shorthand for "think and act." We think. We act. The doing (behavior) is chosen.

E. Feelings and physiology follow the lead of thinking and acting. That is, feelings and physiology are changed by changing the doing and thinking components.

F. We evaluate all we choose to do to determine if it is satisfying our needs.

1. Happy people (with a success identity in terms of meeting needs) are rationally motivated and activated by a sense of strength and empowerment. Their personal world continues to grow larger. They mostly evaluate their own behavior and attempt to improve what they do.

2. Unhappy people (with a failure identity in terms of meeting needs) are more and more emotionally motivated. They feel weak and their personal world is small. They mostly evaluate the behavior of others and spend time criticizing, complaining, judging and attempting to coerce others.

> *Mind is the master-power that molds and makes,*
> *And man is mind, and evermore he takes*
> *The tool of thought, and, shaping what he wills,*
> *Brings forth a thousand joys, a thousand ills:—*
> *He thinks in secret, and it comes to pass:*
> *Environment is but his looking-glass.*
> *-James Allen*

> *Every time you act, you add strength to the motivating idea behind what you've done. Every time you do something, the motivating idea or feeling that prompted you to do it is intensified. The sheer act of acting on any belief or feeling makes you believe or feel it more.*
> *-George Weinberg*

G.. The Brain as a Control System *(William Glasser)*

1. **Old Brain** - governs basic physiological survival and vital functions, what we call "physical" as opposed to "mental."

    - One basic need: Need to survive--to stay alive, reproduce.

2. **New Brain** (cerebral cortex) - governs awareness, voluntary behavior, learning, conscious functioning, what we call "mental" as opposed to "physical."

    - Four basic needs: Needs for love, power, freedom, fun.

3. **Memory**: "The everything-we-know world"

    - Sensory reports of the world (people, situations, things) enter our perceptual system.

    - Reports pass through two filters: (1) a total knowledge filter which regards all information as neutral; and (2) a valuing filter which classifies information as positive, negative or neutral.

    - This value laden world is our perceived world of memory.

4. **"Picture Album"**: Our quality images of "the all-we-want world"

    - Much smaller than our knowledge world is our "quality world" which sorts through the perceptions to determine what (if anything) should be brought into our "album" which contains our best and highest quality pictures of all people, things, and situations that we have learned that make us feel especially good and are most need satisfying.

    - The picture album includes what we value most as everything "worth" knowing. It is our dream world of wants according to our specifications, our cherished beliefs and assumptions.

    - Until (or unless) a perception is admitted to our quality world it has little or no importance to us.

5. **Comparator**: Evaluating information

    - Choosing a perception is a process of weighing the information (perception) on a balance scale against our quality world. Does it add weight (value) in balance with my quality world? Will it satisfy my needs? Will it require organizing or reorganizing (creating) new behaviors? Will it be better for me if I do? What if I don't?

    - Frustration is felt as an urge to behave (do). Destructive negativism (won't, can't) or constructive positive reframing (will, can) affect our choice.

85

6. **Total Behavior**: (Acting, Thinking, Feeling, Physiology)

- Driven by our needs we behave (do).

- Think of yourself as driving (controlling) a car: the 5 cylinder engine represents your basic needs (survival, power, love, fun, freedom). The steering wheel (your wants) is connected to the front wheels (acting, thinking).

- When you are proactive and choose to steer (control) the car, you move the front wheels. The two rear wheels (feeling, physiology) follow. Feelings, body cravings do NOT control. Thinking, action does. We always have some control over what we do and think.

Motivating Factors

A. **David McClelland** has identified three major motivators for positions people prefer for themselves in groups: achievement, affiliation and power (influence).

	High Achievement	High Affiliation	High Power
Goal	Success of well-done task	Mutual friendship	Influence over others

Concerns	Excellence, doing well
	Personal responsibility
	Doing job better
	Unique, important
	  accomplishments
		Being liked, accepted
		Warm, friendly rela-
		  tionships
		Consoling and help-
		  ing others
		Feelings of others
		  and self
			Reputation, position
			Wants ideas to pre-
			  dominate
			Status, prestige
			How to influence
			  others
			Authority

Needs	Personal responsibility
	Calculated risks and
	  chance to innovate
	Recognition of excel-
	  lent performance
		To be with others
		To be friends
		Little structure or
		  constraint
		Freedom to interact
			Structure, rules,
			  policies
			Positions of respon-
			  sibility, authority,
			  prestige
			Authority to act

Strengths	Gets job done
	"Backbone" of group
	Sets attainable goals
	Overcomes obstacles
		Sensitive to others'
		  feelings
		Loyal, enthusiastic
		Tactful
		Interpersonal com-
		  petence
			Confident
			Forceful
			Takes risks
			Articulate

Weaknesses	Rather do task
	  himself
	Does not train
	  others
		Easily hurt
		Passive, avoids con-
		  flict
		Can't say no
		Self-denying
		Doesn't always get
		  task done
			Sometimes domin-
			  eering, arrogant
			Impatient
			May be coercive

B. "Theory X" and "Theory Y." are labels coined by **Douglas McGregor** to describe contrasting sets of assumptions leaders may have about the motivation of people.

Leader's Assumptions of Attitudes of Group Members toward:	THEORY X	THEORY Y
Group Objectives	Indifferent to them	Will work toward them if they perceive rewards associated with doing so
Responsibility	Will avoid it if possible	Will accept responsibility if they are rewarded for acting responsibly
	Prefer to be directed	Capable of self-direction toward objectives that are valuable to them
Work	Dislike all forms of work Will avoid if possible	Consider work as natural as play if they associate rewards with working
Rewards	Want money and security More pay will produce more work	Behave in ways that seek to satisfy a variety of needs
Appropriate means for dealing with group members	Coercion, pressure, threat of punishment Well-specified tasks and close control Pay and monetary incentives	Establish a work environment in which group members can realize recognition, challenge, satisfaction of achievement, etc.

> *I consider ability to arouse enthusiasm among the men the greatest asset I possess and the way to develop the best that is in a man is by appreciation and encouragement. There is nothing else that so kills the ambition of a man as criticisms from his superior. I never criticize anyone. I believe in giving a man incentive to work. So I am anxious to praise and loath to find fault. If I like anything, I am hearty in my approbation and lavish in my praise.*
>
> *–Charles Schwab*

C. **Frederick Herzberg** identified "motivators" (presence of motivating factors) and "de-motivators" (hygiene factors) as they impact on task performance.

1. Hygiene factors refer to "pain-relievers"—conditions required by the group members to maintain good social, mental and physical health but do not provide lasting satisfaction.

2. Motivation factors are the "reward-producers"—conditions leading group members to apply more of their efforts, creative as well as purely physical, to their jobs.

HYGIENE FACTORS (Environmental)	MOTIVATING FACTORS (The Job Itself)
Organizational Policies and Administration	Sense of Achievement
Advancement and Status	Recognition for Accomplishments
Working Conditions	Challenge of the Work and Feeling of Growth and Development
Money	Responsibility

3. Improvement of one or more hygiene factors may result in temporary improvement of job performance, but sustained motivation only comes from the job itself.

Take a piece of wax, a piece of meat, some sand, some clay and some shavings and put them on the fire and see how they react. Each one of the things is being acted upon by the same agent, yet the wax melts, the meat fries, the sand dries up, the clay hardens and the shavings blaze. Just so, under identical influence of circumstances and environment, one man becomes stronger, another weaker, and another withers away. Not so much what is done to us, but what we do, determines our character and destiny.

-Anonymous

God made man to go by motives, and he will not go without them any more than a boat without steam, or a balloon without gas.

-Henry W. Beecher

Transactional Analysis

A. **Eric Berne** and his students (**James**, **Jongeward**, **Harris**) provide in what Berne called "transactional analysis" or TA:

1. A useful conception of human personality and motivation.

2. A view of relationships between two individuals.

3. A way to evaluate the impact of communication.

4. A model for understanding and changing persistent human behavior patterns.

B. Every behavior is acted out of one of the three "ego states." Parent and Child patterns tend to be "fixed" unless consciously changed by the reasoning, choosing Adult state. TA view of the human personality:

"Ego State"	Behavior Mode	Positive Impact	Negative Impact
PARENT (Repetitive, copied, learned behaviors)	Nurturing Parent	Relating Caring Affection	**Overdone:** "smother-love"= dependence **Underdone:** neglect = low esteem
	Critical Parent	Values Norms Opinions	**Overdone:** domination = worthlessness **Underdone:** normlessness, irresponsibility
ADULT (Consciously chosen behaviors)	Rational Problem-solver, the Executive of personality	Rational Thinking Careful Reasoning	Contamination by Parent (prejudices, stereotypes) Contamination by Child (distortions, simplistic answers)
CHILD (Repetition of child behavior when feelings are in control)	Adaptive Child	Socialization	Reaction to Authority: 1) Withdrawal 2) Overcompliance 3) Procrastination
	Little professor	Intuition Creativity	Crazy-making (world view of 4-year old)
	Natural child	Child-likeness Joyousness Curiosity	Childishness Rebelliousness Willfulness

89

> *We cannot become what we need to be by remaining what we are.*
>
> *-Max DePree*

C. The Adult ego state is the "Executive of the Personality" and can control the other states. The Adult ego state thus becomes the key to conscious change.

D. TA view of transactions (communication between two persons). Transactional analysis is the study of the interaction patterns between two individuals. Each communicating party acts out of a Parent, Adult or Child ego state at any given point of time. The resulting transaction may be characterized as *complementary, crossed,* or *ulterior.*

1. **Complementary or Parallel Transactions**—mutual communication.

   - Adult—Adult
   - Parent—Parent
   - Child—Child
   - Parent—Child
   - Child—Parent

   Example of Adult—Adult Transaction

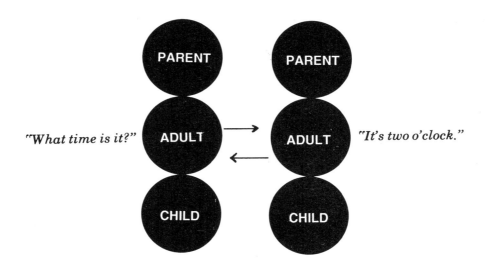

> *All of us are much more like a river than anything frozen in time and space.*
>
> *-Deepak Chopra*

2. **Crossed Transactions**—unexpected response
   (begins as complementary, but is crossed in response)

   Examples of Crossed Transactions

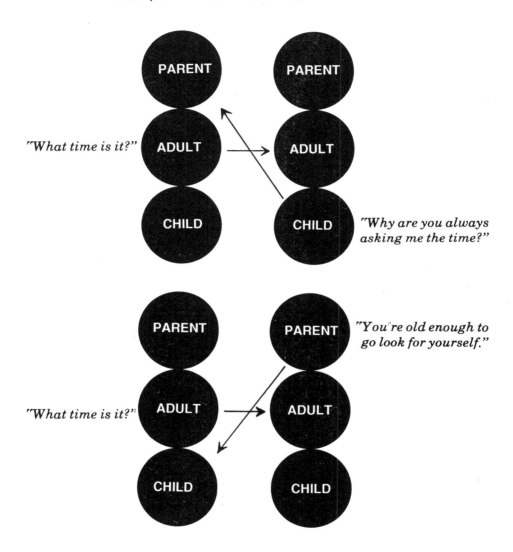

91

3. **Ulterior Transactions**—hidden message
(say one thing and mean another)

Example of Ulterior Transaction

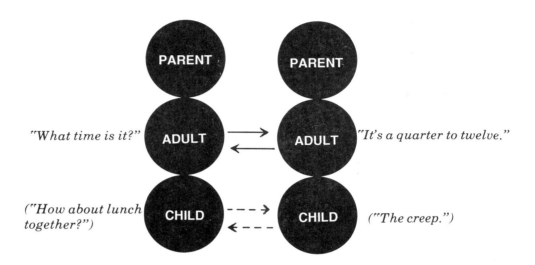

"What time is it?" → ADULT ← *"It's a quarter to twelve."*

("How about lunch together?") ---→ CHILD ←--- *("The creep.")*

4. Either crossed or ulterior transactions cause communication problems.

   ● Crossed transactions mean trouble if the sender is "hooked" by the unexpected message.

   ● Ulterior transactions almost invariably spell trouble because the possibility of misperceiving the hidden message is so great.

E. TA view of behavior

   1. We all have needs for:

      ● **Strokes** (need to be touched, counted, valued). If we don't get positive strokes, we'll seek negative strokes.

      ● **Structure** (we structure time to get, give, or avoid strokes).

         1) Alone (self-stroking)
         2) Rituals (customs, safe acts)
         3) Work or Activities (jobs)
         4) Pastimes (do something in company of another person)
         5) Games (lot of risk and chance; played to get negative strokes)
         6) Intimacy (open, aware, responsible relationship)

- **_Position_** (generalized view of self and other)

    1) You're OK - I'm not OK—want to get away from other
    2) I'm OK - You're not OK—want to get rid of the other
    3) You're not OK - I'm not OK—stalemate of negative strokes
    4) I'm OK - You're OK—giving and receiving positive strokes

> *I am always with myself, and it is I who am my tormentor.*
>
> *-Leo Tolstoy*

2. **Games**

- Games have roles and scripts

    1) **Persecutor Games** (to get even, find fault, start a fight etc.)
        Examples:
        "Now I've got you, you S.O.B."
        Blemish
        "Yes, but. . . "
        Uproar
        Courtroom

    2) **Victim Games** (blame other, enjoy misery, provoke put-downs, etc.)
        Examples:
        "If it weren't for you . . ."
        "See what you made me do . . ."
        "Poor me"
        "Kick me I'm stupid"

    3) **Rescuer Games** (to save others)
        Examples:
        "I'm only trying to help you."
        "What would you do without me?"

- Games are played for negative strokes, to collect bad feelings (trading stamps) and confirm "Not OK" positions. Gray stamps for low esteem; Red stamps for hostility; Blue stamps for depression; White stamps for self-righteousness, etc.

- We may actually manipulate others to play our games so we can collect stamps of our favorite color (called a "racket").

- Redemption time is when we "cash in" our stamps and feel justified in what we are going to do.
    Examples:
    "I've taken this long enough."
    "I'm at the end of my rope."
    "I've had it."

93

Personality Styles

A. One trouble with the emotional side of personality is its tendency to overdo one pattern of satisfaction or another.

B. As an illustration, take three familiar types of leaders (as defined by **Richard Wallen**): the *Tough Battler,* the *Friendly Helper,* and the *Objective Thinker* who tries to avoid both tough and tender emotions.

C. On the chart following are shown characteristic emotions, goals, standards of evaluation, techniques of influence of each type, and value to the group.

TYPE	TOUGH BATTLER	FRIENDLY HELPER	OBJECTIVE THINKER
Emotions	Accepts aggression Rejects affection	Accepts affection Rejects aggression	Rejects both affection and inter-personal aggression
Goal	Dominance	Acceptance	Correctness
Concern	Action	Human Relation-ships	Rationality
Judges others by	Strength, power	Warmth	Cognitive ability
Influences others by	Direction; intimid-ation; control of rewards	Offering under-standing, praise, favors, friendship	Factual data; logical arguments
Value in a group	Initiates, demands, disciplines	Supports, harmon-izes, relieves tension	Defines, clarifies, gets information, criticizes, tests
Communication pattern	Aggressive	Passive	Assertive
Communication hang-up	Blaming, accusing	Placating, plead-ing, agreeing	Super-reasonable, ''computing''
Over-uses	Fight, force	Kindness, com-promise	Analysis
Becomes	Pugnacious	Sloppy senti-mental	Pedantic
Fears	Being ''soft'' or dependent	Desertion, conflict	Emotions, irrational acts
Needs	Warmth, consid-eration, objectivity, humility	Strength; integrity, firm-ness, self-asser-tion	Awareness of feel-ings, ability to love and to fight

94

D. Each personality type can be overdone.

    1. **Tough Battlers** would be better leaders, parents, neighbors and more satisfied persons if they could learn some sensitivity, accept their own inevitable dependence on others, and come to enjoy consideration for others. They would be more successful if they recognized that some facts will not yield to pugnacity.

    2. **Friendly Helpers** would be better leaders, parents, citizens and persons if they could stand up for their own interests and for what is right, even against the pleas of others. They need firmness and strength, and courage not to evade or to smooth over conflicts. They need to be assertive.

    3. **Objective Thinkers** would be better human beings and better leaders if they could become more aware of their own feelings and the feelings of others around them. They need to learn that there are times when it is all right to fight and times when it is desirable to love.

E. The personality typology of Wallen has interesting parallels to the "ego states" of Berne, and both conceptions relate to roles people play in groups as shown in the illustration below:

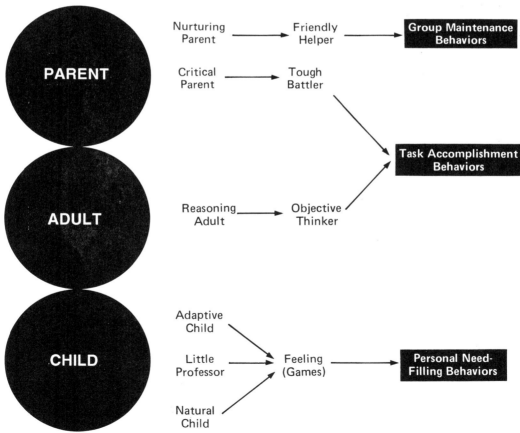

Definitions of Leadership:

The leader is one who succeeds in getting others to follow him.
-W. H. Cowley, 1928

Leadership is the process of influencing group activities toward goal setting and goal achievement.
-R. M. Stogdill, 1948

The leader is the person who creates the most effective change in group performance.
-W. H. Cattell, 1951

Leadership is the initiation of acts that result in a consistent pattern of group interaction directed toward the solution of mutual problems.
-J. K. Hemphill, 1954

Leadership is any attempt to influence the behavior of another individual or group.
-Paul Hersey, 1984

Managers do things right. Leaders do the right thing.
-Warren Bennis and Burt Nanus, 1985

Leadership is the process of moving a group in some direction through mostly noncoercive means. Effective leadership is leadership that produces movement in the long-term best interests of the group.
-John Kotter, 1985

Today we are replacing the manager as order giver with the manager as teacher, facilitator, and coach. The order giver has all the answers and tells everyone what to do; the facilitator knows how to draw the answers out of those who know them best—the people doing the job. The leader as facilitator asks questions, guides a group to consensus, uses information to demonstrate the need for action.
-John Naisbitt and Patricia Aburdene, 1990

We have the right language about change. We know it is a process and not a program. We know it takes time and training and is evolutionary. We know it requires commitment, not coercion. But then we begin to talk about leadership. It is at this point that we revert to our underlying beliefs about control and direction, and our intent for authentic and lasting change gets undermined.
-Peter Block, 1993

7 Leadership
paradigms, perspectives, practice

> *I often feel like the director of a cemetery. I have a*
> *lot of people under me, but nobody listens.*
> -Gen. John Galvin

Paradigm Shifts

A. Conceptions of leadership are undergoing a paradigm shift as older traditional models give way to new models that often dramatically reverse older views and practices of leadership in groups and organizations. The following contrasts some of the differences.

TRADITIONAL MANAGER/LEADERS	NEW PARADIGM OF LEADERSHIP
Leader up front, in charge	Leader supportive, working with
Leader accepts responsibility	Leader shares responsibility
Institution-centered	People-centered
Goal oriented	Process oriented
Straight-lined, linear	Matrixes, multiple fronts
Leader at the helm	Leader "managing by walking around"
Individual assignments and awards	Group assignments and rewards
Leader a loner "lonely at the top"	Leader a connecter, facilitating networks
Emphasis on strategy and tactics, tasks and products	Emphasis on character, principled leadership
Attribute problems to defects in persons	View problems as system issues
Certainty, rationality, control	Creativity, risk-taking, finding meaning
Structural solutions	Array of options
Stability, predictability, wary of change	Open to change, flexible
Authority, firmness	Group participation, self-managed teams
Organizing staff for jobs	Aligning people to shared vision
Controlling and monitoring	Motivating and inspiring
Advocacy	Openness

> *In a day when so much energy seems to be spent on maintenance and manuals, on bureaucracy and meaningless quantification, to be a leader is to enjoy the special privileges of complexity, of ambiguity, of diversity. But to be a leader means, especially, having the opportunity to make a meaningful difference in the lives of those who permit leaders to lead.*
>
> *-Max DePree*

Situational Leadership Theories

A. In an effort to integrate and expand the insights of a number of leadership theories, **Kenneth H. Blanchard and Paul Hersey** developed a conceptual framework designed to help leaders make day-to-day decisions on how various group situations should be handled.

  1. "Situational leadership theory" grew out of earlier leadership models based on two kinds of behavior central to the concept of leadership style: *task behavior* and *relationship behavior.*

  2. Situational leadership theory is based on an interplay among:

   ● the amount of direction *(task behavior)* a leader gives
   ● the amount of socio-emotional support *(relationship behavior)* a leader provides
   ● the **"maturity" level or "readiness"** that followers exhibit on a specific task

  3. Four basic leader behavior styles are identified:

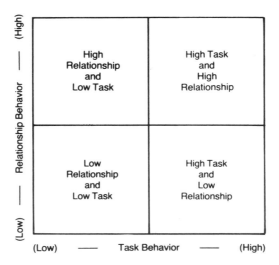

4. **Level of maturity or readiness** is defined as:

    *   the capacity or ability to set high but attainable goals (competence)
    *   willingness and confidence to take responsibility (commitment)
    *   the "maturity" level that followers exhibit on a specific task ("readiness" level of followers)

5. Situational leadership theory contends the following are the best combinations of leadership style and group maturity or readiness

IF GROUP MATURITY IS ---	LEADERSHIP STYLE SHOULD BE:
M 1 Low	S 1 High task/Low relationship
M 2 Low to moderate	S 2 High task/High relationship
M 3 Moderate to high	S 3 High relationship/Low task
M 4 High	S 4 Low relationship/Low task

6. The appropriate leadership style for given levels of follower maturity is portrayed by a curvilinear function in the four leadership quadrants denoting styles of leadership:

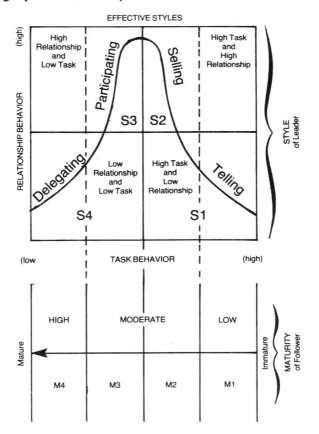

99

LEADERSHIP QUADRANT	LEADERSHIP STYLE
S 1 High task/Low relationship	**Telling**. Directing, Guiding, Structuring. Provide specific instructions and closely supervise performance.
S 2 High task/High relationship	**Selling**. Coaching, Explaining, Persuading. Explain decisions and provide opportunity for clarification.
S 3 High relationship/Low task	**Participating**. Supporting, Facilitating. Share ideas and facilitate in decision making.
S 4 Low relationship/Low task	**Delegating**. Observing, Monitoring. Turn over responsibility for decisions and implementation.

7. These variables are to be considered only in relation to a specific task to be performed. Groups have varying degrees of maturity or readiness, depending on the specific task, function, or objective that is being attempted.

GROUP MATURITY LEVEL	FOLLOWER READINESS
M 1 Low level of task relevant maturity	Low competence/Low commitment Unable, unwilling or insecure
M 2 Low to moderate maturity	Low competence/High commitment Unable but willing or confident
M 3 Moderate to high maturity	High competence/Low commitment Able but unwilling or insecure
M 4 High level of task relevant maturity	High competence/High commitment Able and willing or confident

8. According to situational leadership theory, as the level of maturity of the group increases in terms of accomplishing a specific task, leaders should begin to reduce their directive task behavior and increase their supportive relationship behavior. As the group begins to move into an above average level of maturity or readiness, it becomes appropriate for leaders to decrease not only task behavior but relationship behavior as well. Now people are not only mature in terms of the self-directive performance of the task but also psychologically mature, providing their own socio-emotional support.

100

B. **Fred Fiedler** takes the view that leaders tend to be either task-oriented or relationship-oriented, and it is difficult to change this tendency through leadership training. Therefore, rather than expecting leaders to learn or change to meet different situations, leaders should be selected in light of what different situations call for.

1. Fiedler has concluded that task-oriented leaders perform best in very favorable or very unfavorable situations. Relationship-oriented leaders work best in moderately favorable situations.

2. A group situation is favorable, moderate or unfavorable according to three major factors: (1) *Leader-Member Personal Relations, (2) Task Structure,* and (3) *Position Power of the Leader.*

Situation	Favorable			Moderate		Unfavorable		
Leader-Member Relations	Good	Good	Good	Good	Poor	Poor	Poor	Poor
Task Structure	High	High	Low	Low	High	High	Low	Low
Position-Power	Strong	Weak	Strong	Weak	Strong	Weak	Strong	Weak

Task Leader Performs Best	Relationship Leader Performs Best	Task Leader Performs Best

- *Leader-Member Relations:* Relative degree of respect, trust, admiration and affection between leader and group members.

- *Task Structure:* Degree to which group tasks are specified.
    High task structure allows little choice.
    Low task structure requires group to decide.

- *Position Power:* Authority vested in leader's position.

> *The best leader is·the one who has sense enough to pick good men to do what he wants done, and the self-restraint to keep from meddling with them while they do it.*
> *-Theodore Roosevelt*

101

Managerial Grid

A. **Robert Blake and Jane Mouton** have developed a "Managerial Grid" to help a leader assess and reconcile concern for task accomplishment and concern for people. They emphasize "styles" resulting from the relative strengths of combinations of these concerns.

1. Six styles of leadership have been identified:

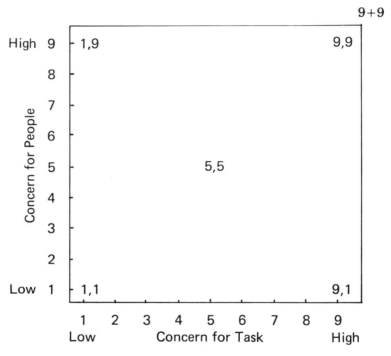

1,1   *Impoverished leader*
This leader has little concern for either task or people, is uncommitted to members. Exerts minimum effort as leader. Stays neutral. Fears being "visible."

1,9   *Country club leader*
This leader adjusts tempo of task in order to minimize pressure on group. Is especially solicitous of member attitudes, morale and well-being, and group atmosphere. Desires approval. Fears rejection.

> *A society of sheep must in time beget a government of wolves.*
>
>   *-Bertrand de Jouvenel*

102

9,1 Task leader

This leader subordinates human concerns entirely to accomplishment of task. Pays attention to group members' performance, but little regard for members' attitudes, morale or satisfaction in task. Maintains control, domination. Fears rejection.

5,5 Middle of the road leader

This leader attempts to balance concern for task and concern for people. Attempts to strike a balance by compromising evenly. Plays safe with policy, tradition, past practice. Fears embarrassment.

9+9 Paternal leader

This leader has a high concern for task and people. Compliance with arbitrary demands is rewarded with approval and benefits. Leader desires control *and* approval.

9,9 Team leader

This leader mobilizes people to accomplish task well, enabling them to feel personally rewarded by achieving the goal. Emphasis on interdependent functioning, group member satisfaction and high performance, relationships of trust and respect.

> *Isn't it strange that princes and kings*
> *And clowns that caper in sawdust rings*
> *And common folks like you and me*
> *Are builders of eternity?*
> *To each is given a bag of tools,—*
> *A shapeless mass and a book of rules;*
> *And each must make, ere life is flown,*
> *A stumbling-block or a stepping-stone.*
> *- R. L. Sharpe*

> *He that knows not, and knows not that he*
> *   knows not, is a fool, shun him;*
> *He that knows not, and knows that he knows*
> *   not, is simple, teach him;*
> *He that knows, and knows not that he knows,*
> *   is asleep, awake him;*
> *He that knows, and knows that he knows, is wise,*
> *   follow him.*
> *-Chinese Proverb*

Organizational Leadership Perspectives

A. **Lee Bolman and Terrence Deal** identify four frames or perspectives of how organizations work. They contend leaders need to "reframe organizations", see their organizations from four perspectives and four different sets of assumptions, **all of which are important and none of which may be ignored**.

1. The assumptions underlying each of these frames are quite different as can be seen from the following summary of the four frames:

GENERAL ASSUMPTIONS	STRUCTURAL FRAME	HUMAN RESOURCE FRAME
Assumptions about Leadership of Organizations	Organizations exist primarily to accomplish goals. Structural form designed to fit particular set of circumstances.	Organizations exist to serve human needs.
Assumptions about the Functions of Organizations	Constrained by norms of rationality in regard to strategies, environment, technology, people.	Organizations and people need each other. Organizations need ideas, energy and talent; people need careers, salaries, and work opportunities.
Assumptions about People in Organizations	Structure focuses on getting the job done. Specialization permits higher levels of individual expertise and performance.	A good fit between individual and organization benefits both: human beings find meaningful and satisfying work, and organizations get the human talent and energy they need.
Assumptions about How Organizations Work	Coordination and control: authority, rules, policies, standard operating procedures, information systems, meetings, lateral relationships, or a variety of more informal techniques. Problems seen as originating in inappropriate structures or systems and can be resolved through restructuring or new systems.	When fit between the individual and the organization is poor, one or both will suffer: individuals will be exploited, or will seek to exploit the organizations, or both.

> *We praise the man who "has the courage of his convictions," but every bigot and fanatic has that; what is much harder, and rarer, is to have the courage to re-examine one's convictions, and to reject them if they don't square with the facts.*
>
> *-Sydney J. Harris*

GENERAL ASSUMPTIONS	POLITICAL FRAME	SYMBOLIC FRAME
Assumptions about Leadership of Organizations	Organizations are coalitions composed of varied individuals and interest groups (hierarchical levels, departments, professional groups, gender and ethnic subgroups).	What is most important about any event is not what happened, but what it means. Events and meanings are loosely coupled: the same events can have very different meanings for different people.
Assumptions about the Functions of Organizations	Most of the important decisions involve the allocation of scarce resources (decisions about who gets what). Because of this, conflict is central to organizational dynamics, and power is the most important resource.	Events and processes in organizations are often ambiguous or uncertain--it is often difficult or impossible to know what happened, why it happened, or what will happen next. The more ambiguous, the harder it is to use rational approaches to analysis, problem solving, decisions.
Assumptions about People in Organizations	There are enduring differences among individuals and groups in their values, preferences, beliefs, information and perceptions of reality. Such differences change slowly if at all.	Faced with uncertainty and ambiguity, human beings create symbols to resolve confusion, increase predictability, and provide direction. Symbols make events seem less meaningless.
Assumptions about How Organizations Work	Goals and decisions emerge from bargaining, negotiation, and jockeying for position among members of different coalitions.	Many organizational events and processes are important more for what they express than for what they produce: they are secular myths, rituals, ceremonies, and sagas that help people find meaning and order in their experience.

105

B. **G. Burrell and G. Morgan** view leadership as a social transaction, but different images of social organization influence its meaning.

1. Four sociological perspectives are identified:

PERSPECTIVE	CHARACTERISTICS OF LEADERSHIP
Structural-Functionalist	Leaders solve problems. Followers trust leaders to solve problems. Experience, rules, regulations, division of labor may substitute for leadership. Emphasize concern for task and concern for people. Emphasize motivating participants.
Political-Conflict	Power relations between dominant and subordinate. Subordinates willingly accept directives from legitimate authority. Conflict common. Change is by radical transformation or the need for change is ignored.
Constructivist	Success or failure attributed to leader. What a leader stands for is more important than what a leader does. Emphasis on maintaining culture. Followers need to understand why things happen; leaders provide explanation.
Critical-Humanist	Leadership serves an important symbolic function of restoring meaning and purpose to daily life. Emphasis on the need to overthrow or transcend or transform the limitations of the existing social order or organization. Traditional sources of authority are subordinated to the individual's responsibility to decide.

Practice of Leadership

A. **John P. Kotter** studied top managers of organizations with several hundreds of employees.

1. He characterized complexity, uncertainty, and dependence as the most striking features of top manager jobs.

2. He found differences, but also similarities particularly in the three basic tasks of the job: setting an agenda, building a network, and using the network to get things done. Their success depended on the cooperation and efforts of hundreds of others.

3. **Kotter** found these challenges as keys to success of top management:

- Set goals and policies under conditions of uncertainty.
- Achieve "delicate balance" in allocating scarce resources across different units or functions.
- Keep on top of a large, complex set of activities.
- Get support from bosses.
- Get support from corporate staff and other constituents.
- Motivate, coordinate, and control large, diverse group of subordinates.

B. **Harlan Cleveland** describes what he calls "The Knowledge Executive" as needing knowledge of leadership as follows:

1. Leadership is based on an understanding of the way an organization could and should work, not only how it does work.

2. Leadership uses deliberation and collective action, not unilateral action.

3. Leadership involves all interested parties: it is concerned about who is in the conversation.

4. Leadership is concerned with vision, not status quo.

5. Leadership concerns problem-solving and problem definition.

6. Leadership is exercised by groups, individuals, and communities.

C. **Thomas Peters and Robert Waterman** studied "high performing" companies. They identified eight leadership actions that characterized "excellence."

1. Bias for action.

- proclivity to act
- reduce paperwork and bureaucratic entanglements

2. Close to the customer.

- close customer contact was an obsession at all levels

3. Autonomy and entrepreneurship.

- encouraged risk and tolerated occasional failures
- structures highly decentralized

4. Productivity through people.

- consistent concern for their people
- training and socialization

107

5. Hands-on, value driven.

- clear on what company stands for
- practices its value system

6. Stick to the knitting.

- avoid becoming conglomerates
- stay with what they know how to do

7. Simple form, lean staff.

- small headquarters staff
- loosely coupled manageable chunks
- fewer layers

8. Simultaneous loose/tight properties.

- combine central control with substantial decentralization, autonomy, and entrepreneurship

D. **Warren Bennis** after years of observation and conversation has defined four competencies for leadership:

1. **Management of attention**—to have a compelling vision that brings others to a place they have not know before.

2. **Management of meaning**—to make dreams apparent to others and to align people with them, that is, to communicate the vision.

3. **Management of trust**—to be reliable.

4. **Management of self**—to know one's skills and deploy them effectively.

E. **James Kouzes and Barry Posner** identified five leadership practices characteristic of successful leaders:

1. Challenging the process

- changing the status quo, experimenting and taking risks.

2. Inspiring a shared vision

- envisioning the future, enlisting others to common purposes.

3. Enabling others to act

- getting people to work together, sharing power and information.

4. Modeling the way

    ● setting the example, leading by doing, building commitment to action, planning small wins.

5. Encouraging the heart

    ● recognizing contributions, celebrating accomplishments.

F. **Stephen R. Covey** has identified "seven habits of highly effective people" which can, when turned around, be stated as the "seven habits of highly ineffective people." The two lists are contrasted below:

SEVEN HABITS OF HIGHLY EFFECTIVE PEOPLE	SEVEN HABITS OF HIGHLY INEFFECTIVE PEOPLE
Be proactive (take action, "response/ability")	Be reactive (doubt yourself and blame others)
Begin with the end in mind (vision)	Work without any clear end in mind (just keep busy)
Put first things first (priorities in use of time)	Do the urgent thing first (the rest you can do if you find time)
Think win/win (seek mutual benefit)	Think win/lose (defeat the other)
Seek first to understand, then to be understood (consideration in communication)	Seek first to be understood (think of self first)
Synergize (creative cooperation)	If you can't win, compromise (get what you can regardless of the cost to other)
Sharpen the saw (continuous improvement and self-renewal)	Fear change (put off improvement)

G. **Stephen R. Covey** identifies the following characteristics of what he calls "principle-centered leaders":

1. They are continually learning.

2. They are service-oriented to a mission.

3. They radiate positive energy, cheerful, optimistic, upbeat.

4. They believe in other people.

5. They lead balanced lives.

6. They see life as an adventure.

7. They are synergistic, seeing the whole as more than the sum of its parts.

8. They exercise physically, mentally, emotionally and spiritually for self-renewal.

H. The National Extension Leadership Development Program under the direction of **Jerold Apps** developed a series of generalizations to describe what he calls "next age leaders." Some of the generalizations follow:

1 **Leadership is a process, not an end point.** Leadership as process means that how we lead is constantly changing, as other elements of society constantly change.

2. **Leadership means experiencing a transformation process.** Leaders see their lives differently, they view their organization differently, and they develop the self-confidence to evoke change in themselves and in their organizations.

3. **Leadership assumes that organizations, like individuals, are constantly learning and changing.** No longer can we assume constancy in organizations with leaders prepared to fit into static situations.

4. **Leaders have a well developed working philosophy of leadership and a variety of leadership skills** that they can apply in a variety of situations.

5. **Leadership is shared and shifting.** Everyone is a leader and everyone is a follower.

6. **Leadership is a way for leaders to assist people in discovering creative potential** in creative problem-solving and creative direction setting.

7. **Leadership contains a strong spiritual dimension.** Next age leaders are guided by a spiritual core of beliefs and values that provides them with a compass for what they do and how they do it but they are open to examining their beliefs and values, and even changing some of them as the result of the examination.

8. **All leadership is guided by an ethical perspective.** Ethics is part of all that we do, what we teach, how we teach, how we interact with people.

9. **Collaboration rather than competition is the cornerstone of leadership activity.** Leaders must lead the way toward collaborating with both sides winning.

10. **Quality must guide at every level in every respect**, in every activity, at every level.

11. Next age leaders must

    - create and communicate a vision, and at the same time understand and meet short term goals.
    - know the difference between management focusing on the present and leadership focusing on the future.
    - build bridges among people and among ideas by bringing together people of diverse backgrounds and experiences.
    - as ideas come into conflict, avoid "win-lose" situations, but rather attempt to transcend conflict and encourage the emergence of new ideas that are often different from and better than the ideas originally presented.
    - constantly challenge ideas, structures, assumptions and beliefs, not willing to accept "givens" without examination and analysis.
    - embrace ambiguity in a world becoming increasingly less predictable and become comfortable with such situations.
    - applaud serendipity and take advantage of unexpected situations.
    - encourage artistry and the creative spirit along with the science and the scientific, and realize that decision making must be a combination of logic and intuition, of objectivity and subjectivity, of science and artistry.
    - at times encourage discomfort, occasionally through creative conflict.
    - appreciate humor.
    - take risks.
    - be teachers.
    - stand back from the hustle and bustle of everyday activity and reflect on what is being done.
    - be whole people, active members of families and communities, balancing an interest in work with interest in physical activity, the arts, and other activities that refresh and give new perspective.

The signs of outstanding leadership appear primarily among the followers. Are the followers reaching their potential? Are they learning? Serving? Do they achieve the required results? Do they change with grace? Manage conflict?
                                        -Max DePree

Every human being has a work to carry on within, duties to perform abroad, influence to exert, which are peculiarly his, and which no conscience but his own can teach.
                                        -William Ellery Channing

111

Another Disorder Classified!

In spite of the many complaints about medical research there are reports of progress. Word is out that a group of researchers have managed after painstaking research to classify yet another human disorder.

This disorder which has plagued humans for many centuries was very difficult to classify because information about it was hard to obtain and objective tests were very difficult to set up because of opposition and even hostility from the subjects.

However, the brave researchers persisted and were able to describe the disorder providing a list of symptoms, incidence, suggested therapies and prognosis. Some of the details are listed below:

Name of disorder: *Intransigent Orthodoxy.*

Type: *Generally attitudinal, psychological.*

Incidence: *Occurs in all walks of life and in all areas of the world. Affects mainly adults. More prevalent in such professions as psychiatry, psychology, university teaching and medicine. Also found in politics and industry, especially among the higher echelons.*

Symptoms: *Hostility and fear of new ideas and concepts. Anger, agitation and even depression when confronted with a new situation or idea. Will spend an inordinate amount of time and energy fighting new ideas and approaches. Mainly characterized by irrational opposition to the introduction of new concepts without regard to their value or proven benefits. There is considerable distress when their opposition is not successful.*

Treatment: *Although there are reports of some moderate recoveries, treatment is very difficult. Evidence and information are generally ineffective.*

Prognosis: *Unfortunately, the disease quickly reaches the chronic stage and it is not subject to treatment. In most cases it has to be considered terminal.*

-Source Unknown

8

Action
shared vision and strategic planning

> *Vision without action is merely a dream.*
> *Action without vision just passes the time.*
> *Vision with action can change the world.*
> *-Joel Arthur Barker*

Vision—Shared Purpose

A. Perhaps nothing is as important for leadership than a vision, a purpose, a clear goal. Effective action requires that a leader have a vision.

   1. But a leader's vision is not enough. Unless it becomes a shared vision, the leader's dream may remain just that—the *leader's* dream..

   2. The leader must be a *communicator* of the vision, but even more, the leader must be a *facilitator*, helping the group or organization arrive at a *shared* vision.

B. When an organization is committed to a shared vision, all energies can be invested in its achievement.

   1. As the world changes, so must the vision. Visionary leadership involves:

- monitoring changes in the realities of the outside world
- making necessary mid-course corrections
- knowing when to initiate a new vision-forming process

   2. The best way to ensure that the vision-forming process is alive and well and continuously practiced in an organization is to multiply the number of visionary leaders at all levels. Vision-forming is everybody's business, thus the importance of participation in the process.

> *It isn't the incompetent who destroy an organization. The incompetent never get in a position to destroy it. It is those who have achieved something and want to rest upon their achievements who are forever clogging things up.*
> *-F. M Young*

> *The few projects in my study that disintegrated did so because the manager failed to build a coalition of supporters and collaborators.*
> *—Rosabeth Moss Kanter*

C. In the visioning process, the role of the leader is what **Burt Nanus** calls the "prudent visionary." Nanus provides this advice:

1. **Don't do it alone.**

   - The leader who decides alone and presents the vision to the organization is asking for skepticism and resistance.

     Remedy: Solicit suggestions and promote wide participation in the search for a vision. This will prepare the organization for changes to come, and may disarm those who would resist these changes.

2. **Don't be overly idealistic**.

   - A vision should represent a worthwhile challenge, but will lose its force if the people see it as too ambitious or unrealistic.

     Remedy: Make sure the vision appears attainable. Select feedback from those most responsible for making it happen. Test the vision with knowledgeable outsiders.

3. **Reduce the possibility of unpleasant surprises.**

   - Many a vision results in surprising consequences:
     What was expected did not occur
     Something unexpected occurred
     Something that was never considered happens

     Remedy: Be thorough in forecasting and anticipating possible future events. Refuse to be lulled by conventional wisdom. Build flexibility into the vision.

4. **Watch out for organizational inertia**.

   - Resistance to change is natural. Existing cultures and organizational constraints often present barriers

     Remedy: Make some alterations in organization. New people favorable to vision or reorganization may break organizational inertia and cause new patterns of relationships

5. **Don't be two preoccupied with the bottom line.**

   ● Bottom-line thinking makes it difficult to think long-term.

     Remedy: Concentrate on doing the right thing to secure the loyalty and support of customers and workers.

6. **Be flexible and patient in implementing the vision.**

   ● Once direction has been determined, and people have bought into the idea, there are many ways of getting "there".

     Remedy: Delegate implementation decisions to those closest to the issues at hand. Allow flexibility in how to implement the vision, to try "small experiments" and learn as they go along.

7. **Never get complacent.**

   ● Keep alert to continuing needs for change. It is hardest to change direction when the situation has been allowed to deteriorate.

     Remedy: Focus on helping the organization to achieve its potential, listen and watch for feedback, empower employees to act, and continue to lead the organization in setting and committing to the vision.

> *You are never given a dream without also being given the power to make it true. . . . You have to work for it, however.*
>
> *-Richard Bach*

Strategic Planning Process

A. **George Steiner** has identified two classic approaches to planning, often viewed as conflicting approaches:

   1. Intuitive, anticipatory planning. Intuitive planners tend to avoid formal, written plans and rely on the informal influence network to bring about change.

   2. Formal, systematic planning. Systematic planners tend to emphasize the development of long-term planning documents and discount intuitive planning.

B. Both types of planning are involved in what is called strategic planning.

115

> *Whatever you can do or dream you can do, begin it.*
> *Boldness has genius, power and magic. Begin it now.*
>
> *-Johann W. von Goethe*

C. Strategic planning is a process by which members of an organization develop a clear vision of its future and the process for achieving that vision.

   1. The vision should be clear, enduring, and forward thinking. It may take several years to achieve.

   2. Planning is concerned with the consequences of decisions, of cause and effect relationships, and alternative courses of action.

   3. Planning is a process which includes developing an organizational philosophy, management systems, major strategies or approaches, and immediate actions toward an agreed upon vision.

   4. The process is concerned with creating consensus on organizational goals and objectives that are established as a means for achieving the over all mission.

   5. Strategic planning focuses on:

       * Inventing the future.
       * Proactive leadership rather than reactive response.
       * Stretching for the ideal conditions rather than the settling for easily obtained everyday goals.
       * Optimism, creativity, group participation.
       * Management: top-down and bottom-up decision making.
       * Relevancy, results-based and measurable plans.
       * A time-line of five years.
       * A plan; a written document, which specifies predetermined courses of action.

D. It is critical that the planning process be tailored to the needs and capabilities of each organization.

   1. The **process is as important as the plan**; for the process itself will largely determine the degree of commitment to the plan.

> *I object to people running down the future. I intend to live the rest of my life there.*
> *-Charles F. Kettering*

E. Below are the major elements which should be considered in strategic planning according to **John Schmidt, George Steiner, Robert Simmerly** and other writers on the subject.

1. **Planning to plan**

   ● Have support for strategic planning at the highest levels of management.

   ● Create organizational readiness for strategic planning.

   ● Create a planning committee to guide the process. During this phase, the organization's leaders must ask and answer such questions as

      1) Who should be involved?
      2) How long it will take?
      3) How will stakeholders be involved?
      4) What information is needed?
      5) Who will develop the data?

   ● Carve out adequate time to make strategic planning a success.

2. **Environmental scanning**

   ● In order to be successful, the plan must consider the organization relative to the environment in which it does and will exist.

   ● **External environmental scanning**:

      1) What are the environmental **opportunities and threats** (external to the organization)?
      2) What are the important trends and issues (demographic, economic, social, political, etc.) that will impact upon your organization?
      3) How probable is it that a particular trend will continue?
      4) How widespread will the trend be?
      5) What data do you have?
      6) How would you assess the impact on your organization of the opportunities or threats facing it?

   ● **Internal environmental scanning**:

      1) What are the organization's **strengths and weaknesses** (internal to the organization, particularly relative· to competing alternatives)?
      2) What are the institutional resources you have available? What is your position in the "market"?
      3) Ask "influentials" and stakeholders their perceptions of your organization's strengths·and weaknesses.
      4) What are the stakeholder's concerns (needs and expectations of key stakeholder groups)?

117

- The scanning process is sometimes called SWOT (for strengths, weaknesses, opportunities, threats) or WOTS UP?

3. **Values clarification**

- The planning team examines their own and the organization's and stakeholders' values, beliefs, traditions, aspirations and culture.

    1) What are the planners' and the organization's goals for development?
    2) What about joint ventures with other organizations?
    3) How can conflicts within and between organizations be managed?
    4) How can diversity issues be dealt with?

4. **Mission formulation**

- The organization's mission is the expression of its vision for the future. This is the beacon which will guide the organization and will establish its image in the community.

- The four primary questions asked in this phase are

    1) *What* function will the organization perform?
    2) *Who* will it serve?
    3) *How* will it perform its function?
    4) *Why* does the organization exist?

5. **Goals and objectives**

- "Goals," it is said, "are dreams that are measurable." Goals break the vision down into component elements. Objectives are a subset of each particular goal.

- Goals provide a statement of direction and offer a frame of reference for planning activities, and a means by which to evaluate these activities.

- Objectives are more specific and less general than goals. An objective can be

    1) measured in time and space
    2) delegated to someone to implement
    3) assigned a deadline for completion

> *Once an organization loses its spirit of pioneering and rests on its early work, its progress stops.*
>
> *-Thomas J. Watson*

118

6. **Strategy development**

   - The planning team conceptualizes specific alternative scenarios and the routes for getting there.

   - Strategies are the major approaches to be employed to accomplish the organization's key goals and objectives.

7. **Performance Audit**

   - The team becomes a part of an everyday audit of the organization's current decisions and performance in order to "prevent the organization from continuing to scan hallucinations" about its capacity to achieve the future being envisioned for it.

8. **Gap analysis**

   - As the ongoing audit reveals gaps between current and envisioned performance, the team must return to strategic planning to rework their scenarios.

9. **Integrating action plans**

   - When the gaps between the organization's current performance and envisioned goals are narrowed, the team integrates the scenarios and actions into a "grand strategy" or "master plan."

10. **Contingency planning**

    - "What if" questions are addressed, such as what if the organization loses an "irreplaceable" staff member or a key facility is destroyed or an outside change occurs. Actions are then proposed to deal with these contingencies.

11. **Action plans**

    - This is where the rubber meets the road. Action plans describe the steps you initiate immediately to begin implementing the strategies.

    - If the rest of the planning work has been done well, the action plans will flow freely, and more importantly the organization will be poised to role up its sleeves and go to work.

He who does not look ahead remains behind.
-Spanish Proverb

---

12. **Implementation**

- Monitor the implementation of the strategic plan. The plan becomes part of every day management decisions as an ongoing process.

- Build in flexibility for change. Continue to scan changes that affect the plan and make adjustments.

- Actively manage the conflict that often occurs when strategic planning is implemented.

> *I do the very best I know how—the very best I can; and I mean to keep doing so until the end. If the end brings me out all right, what is said against me won't amount to anything If the end brings me out wrong, ten angels swearing I was right would make no difference.*
> *-Abraham Lincoln*

> *There is nothing like a dream to create the future.*
> *-Victor Hugo*

Benefits of Strategic Planning

A. Strategic planning always involves hard work, difficult decisions, and a lot of time to digest and rethink ideas. At the same time, it is an exciting adventure which leads to substantial improvements in the effectiveness of the organization.

1. The process results in

- creating an organization's preferred future.
- produces a results-based, action oriented plan for self-improvement.
- helps the organization change in predetermined ways.
- provides "a systems approach to maneuvering an organization over time through the uncertain waters of its changing environment to achieve prescribed aims" (**George Steiner**)
- ensures your organization is running with a common purpose rather than merely running!

120

B. Benefits of a good strategic plan:

1. **Common purpose.**   People tend to achieve peak performance if the goals are clear.

2. **Common sense of direction.** The organization and its stakeholders should be energized by sharing a common vision of the future.

3. **Priorities for change.** Issues which make operational decisions difficult have been resolved through the strategic planning process.

4. **Protection against overextending.** A plan makes it easier to stay focused.

5. **Longer-term effort.** A plan avoids the quick-fix mentality of short-term thinking.

6. **Ensures wiser use of resources.** All resources (time, space, money, people) are systematically focused on the plan.

7. **Allows for flexibility.** Through annual (or more often) updates, the plan provides for responsiveness to changing needs and conditions.

The future belongs to those who believe in the beauty of their dreams.
                                                    -Eleanor Roosevelt

---

I must not interfere with any child, I have been told,
To bend his will to mine,
Or try to shape him through some mold of thought;
Naturally as a flower he must unfold.
Yet, flowers must have discipline of wind and rain,
And though it gives the gardener much pain,
I've seen him use his pruning shears
More strength and beauty to gain for some flower bright;
And he would do whatever he thought was right
To save his flowers from a deadening blight
I do not know—yet it seems to me,
That only weeds unfold just naturally.
                                                    -Anonymous

> *Man is a prisoner of his own way of thinking and of his own stereotypes of himself. His machine for thinking, the brain, has been programmed for a vanished world. This old world was characterized by the need to manage things—stone, wood, iron. The new world is characterized by the need to manage complexity. Complexity is the very stuff of today's world. The tool for handling complexity is organization. But our concepts of organization belong to the much less complex old world, not to the much more complex today's world. Still less are they adequate to deal with the next epoch of complexification, in a world of explosive change.*
>
> *-Stafford Beer*

IS QUALITY IMPORTANT?

Ninty nine per cent good enough means:

2 million documents will be lost by the IRS this year
22,000 checks will be deducted from wrong bank accounts every hour
1,314 phone calls misplaced by telecommunication services per minute
12 babies will be given to the wrong parents each day
268,500 defective tires will be shipped this year
103,260 income tax returns will be processed incorrectly this year
2,488,500 books will be shipped with the wrong cover
5,517,200 cases of flat soft drinks will be produced this year
2 unsafe plane landings at O'Hare International Airport in Chicago daily
18,322 pieces of mishandled mail in the next hour
55 malfunctioning ATM's installed in the next 12 months
1,700,000 pieces of mail would be lost daily
35,000 newborns would be dropped by their doctor or nurse this year
No phone service for 14 minutes each day
Some 200,000 people would receive wrong drug prescription each year
Drinking water would be unsafe to drink 3 1/2 days of the year
Homes would be without electricity seven hours per month

Is 99% good enough?

9

Excellence
quality and continuous improvement

> *We are what we repeatedly do. Excellence, then, is not an act, but a habit.*
>
> *-Aristotle*

Excellence and the Quality Revolution

A. More than any other one individual, **W. Edwards Deming** has given the West a vision of quality—and provided the tools with which to achieve excellence. Born in 1900, Dr. Deming began work with the US Agriculture Department in 1928, and there became interested in quality control. In 1939 he became head mathematician and statistician with the Census Bureau. His lectures on quality control at the time brought little response from American industrialists. In 1947, Dr Deming first visited Japan and taught Japanese managers and engineers the statistical theories and practices necessary to implement quality control. The rest is history. By 1980, American industry began to take notice, and at his passing in 1993, Dr. Deming's ideas of Quality Leadership or Total Quality Management, while not always practiced as he taught, were being introduced into industry, government, education, all types of organizations.

B. Deming's "revolution" was a new view of human enterprise both in content and purpose. He proposed that an enterprise be managed as a system with a common purpose of excellence. There are, he taught, no tradeoffs between quality and productivity with this method of management—everyone gains over the long run.

C. What constitutes excellence? What is quality? Deming's definition: quality is what the customer defines it to be.

   1. **Quality is unyielding and continuing efforts by everyone in the organization to understand, meet, and exceed the needs of its customers.**

      ● In an organization, the customer is the next level below you in the organization, the persons or groups you directly work with or serve. Everyone in the organization is thus a customer and has customers.

   2. The nature of quality

      ● Quality does what it says it does
      ● Quality does it consistently
      ● Quality does it under all conditions
      ● Quality does it cost effectively

> *Routine work drives out nonroutine work and smothers to death all creative planning, all fundamental change in the university—or any institution.*
>
> *-Warren Bennis*

D. Quality can always be improved. The Japanese word **"kaizen"** (pronounced ky'zen) means improvement—continuing improvement in personal life, home life, social life, and working life.

E. The traditional way of obtaining quality and desired excellence has been management by inspection. Deming proposed a very different approach that he called **"continuous quality improvement"** and very different leadership approaches to achieve it.

   1. The table below contrasts the traditional practice and culture of quality by inspection versus quality by continuous quality improvement as taught by Deming:

	QUALITY ASSURANCE BY INSPECTION (Traditional)	CONTINUOUS QUALITY IMPROVEMENT (Deming)
Process for Improving Quality	Inspection-oriented "Bad apple" focused	Culture driven quality improvement Process focused
Management Culture	People as the problem Problems as threats	People as the solution to system and structure problems Problems as opportunities
Process Approach	Everything has a good reason to exist as it is Incremental tinkering	Belief and action: everything can be improved Understanding and shaping processes
Change Strategy	Quick fix "Fire fighting" Incremental improvement Rarely permanent	Root causes and process improvement Systematic tools Quality focus Long-term improvement is possible

2. The next table contrasts the American practice of innovation (the big change) to the Deming practice of continuous improvement (Kaizen) as summarized by **Masaaki Imai.**

	KAIZEN (Japan)	INNOVATION (American)
Effect	Long-term and long-lasting	Short-term but dramatic
Pace	Small steps	Big steps
Time frame	Continuous and incremental	Intermittent and non-incremental
Change	Gradual and constant	Abrupt and volatile
Involvement	Everybody	Select a few "champions"
Approach	Collectivism, group efforts, systems approach	Rugged individualism, individual ideas and efforts
Mode	Maintenance and improvement	Scrap and rebuild
Spark	Conventional know-how and state of the art	Technological break-through, new inventions, new theories
Practical Requirements	Requires little investment but great effort to maintain it	Requires large investment, but little effort to maintain
Effort Orientation	People	Technology
Evaluation Criteria	Process and efforts for better results	Results for profits
Advantage	Works well in slow-growth economy	Better suited to fast-growth economy

> *The world hates change yet it is the only thing that has brought progress.*
> *-Charles Kettering*

> *It is only giving that stimulates. Impart as much as you can of your own spiritual being to those who are on the road with you, and accept as something precious what comes back to you from them.*
>
> *-Albert Schweitzer*

> *The significant problems we face cannot be solved at the same level of thinking we were at when we created them.*
>
> *-Albert Einstein*

The Deming "System of Profound Knowledge"

A. **Deming** developed a "system of profound knowledge" to explain the reasoning behind his leadership approach to quality.

   1. He identified four parts "all related to each other": (1) appreciation for a system; (2) knowledge of the theory of variation; (3) theory of knowledge; and (4) psychology.

   2. The various segments of the system of profound knowledge can not be separated. They interact with each other. Dr. Deming makes these observations:

      ● Knowledge of psychology is incomplete without knowledge of variation. "If psychologists understood variation, they could no longer participate in continual refinements of instruments for rating people."

      ● If statisticians understood a system, and if they understood some theory of knowledge and something about psychology, "they could no longer teach tests of significance, tests of hypothesis, chi-square."

      ● If economists understood cooperation, and the loss and damage from competition, "they would no longer teach and preach salvation through competition. They would, instead, lead us into optimization through cooperation."

      ● The theory of knowledge helps us to understand that management in any form is prediction. The simplest plan requires prediction. Management acts on a causal system, and on changes in the causes. "Grades, ranks, appraisals relate to past performance, but are used without justification for prediction of future performance."

      ● Theory of variation can play a vital part in optimization of a system. "Statistical theory is helpful for understanding differences between people and interactions between people, interactions between people and the system that they work in, or learn in. Theory of variation is helpful for most enumerative studies, and for efficiency in designs of tests and experiments."

- Statistical theory, used cautiously, with the help of the theory of knowledge, can be useful in the interpretation of the results of tests and experiments. "The interpretation of the results of tests and experiments is for future use and is thus prediction."

B. **Deming's conception of "appreciation for a system"**

1. A system Is a series of interdependent functions or activities (sub-processes, stages, components) within an organization that work together for the aim of the organization.

   - There is in almost any system interdependence between the components. The components need not all be clearly defined and documented: people may merely do what needs to be done.

   - All the people that work within a system can contribute to improvement, and thus enhance their joy in work.

   - Management of a system requires knowledge of the inter-relationships between all the components within the system and of the people that work in it.

2. The aim of the system must be stated by the management. Without an aim, there is no system. The components of a system are necessary but not sufficient of themselves to accomplish the aim. They must be managed.

   - The aim proposed for management is for everybody to gain—stockholders, employees, suppliers, customers, community, the environment—over the long term.
   - For example, the aim might be to provide for employees good leadership, opportunities for training, and education for further growth, and other contributors to joy in work.

3. The organization will require someone in the position of aide to the president, to teach and facilitate profound knowledge.

4. The performance of any component is to be evaluated in terms of its contribution to the aim of the system, not for its individual production or profit, nor for any other competitive measure.

   - Optimization of the whole system may require some needed components operate at a loss to themselves.

> *The best preparation for tomorrow is to do today's work superbly well.*
> *-Sir William Osler*

5. If the aim, size, or boundary of the organization changes, then the functions of the components will change for optimization of the new system.

    ● A flow diagram is helpful toward understanding a system. By understanding a system, one may be able to trace the consequences of a proposed change.

    ● Time will bring changes that must be managed to achieve optimization.

6. The greater the interdependence between components, the greater the need for communication and cooperation between them.

7. Management's job is to optimize the system over time. An example of a system, well optimized, is a good orchestra. The players are there to support each other.

    ● All activities should be coordinated to optimize the whole system. Fortunately, precise optimization is not necessary. One need only to come close to optimization.

8. Any system that results in a win-lose structure is sub-optimized. Sub-optimization causes loss to everybody in the system.

    ● Examples of sub-optimization in the management of people: grading in school, gold stars and prizes, merit system, incentive pay, quotas, competition.

9. An additional responsibility of management is to be ready to change the boundary of the system for better service and profit.

C. **Deming's conception of "some knowledge of the theory of variation"**

1. There will always be variation between people, in output, in service, in product. What does the variation tell us about a process, and about the people that work in it?

2. Some understanding of variation, including appreciation of a stable system, and some understanding of special causes and common causes of variation, is essential for management of a system, including leadership of people. Two costly mistakes made in attempts to improve a process:

    ● To treat as a special cause any fault, complaint, mistake, breakdown, accident, shortage, when actually it came from common causes.

    ● To attribute to common causes any fault, complaint, mistake, breakdown, accident, shortage, when actually it came from a special cause.

3. Understand the capability of a process. When do data indicate that a process is stable, that the distribution of the output is predictable? Once a process has been brought into a state of statistical control, it has a definable capability.

4. Knowledge about the different sources of uncertainty in statistical data. How was the data obtained? What are/were the built-in deficiencies? What were the blemishes and blunders in interviewing, or in measurements? What errors in response, non-response, or errors of sampling?

5. Knowledge about interaction of forces, the effect of the system on the performance of people. Knowledge of the dependence and interdependence between people, groups, divisions, companies, countries. Interaction may reinforce efforts, or it may nullify efforts.

6. Understand the distinction between enumerative studies and analytic problems. The results of a test or experiment are enumerative but the interpretation of the results is an analytic problem. It is prediction that a specific change in a process or procedure will improve output in the future, or that no change at all will be a wiser choice. Either way, the choice is prediction.

7. Knowledge about loss functions in relation to optimization of performance of a system.

    ● Which quality-characteristic is causing the most loss to the whole system and is most critical for management to work on?

    ● What knowledge about chaos and loss is the result of random forces or random changes that may individually be unimportant?

8. There is no substitute for knowledge. Enlargement of a committee does not necessarily improve the results of the efforts of the committee unless the additions result in more knowledge.

9. As a rule, profound knowledge must come from the outside and by invitation. Profound knowledge can not be forced on anybody.

> *If we work on marble, it will perish; if on brass, time will efface it; if we rear temples, they will crumble into dust; but if we work upon immortal minds, and imbue them with principles, with the just fear of God and love of our fellowmen, we engrave on those tablets something that will brighten them to all eternity.*
>
> *-Daniel Webster*

> *The human mind once stretched to a new idea never*
> *goes back to its original dimensions.*
> *-Oliver Wendell Holmes*

D. Deming's conception of "theory of knowledge"

1. Any rational plan, however simple, requires prediction concerning conditions, behavior, and comparison of performance of each of two procedures or materials.

2. There is no knowledge, no theory, without prediction and explanation of past events. There is no observation without theory.

   - A statement devoid of prediction or explanation of past events conveys no knowledge.

   - Interpretation of data from a test or experiment is prediction—what will happen on future application of the conclusions or recommendations that are drawn from the test or experiment? The prediction will depend on knowledge or the subject-matter. It is only in the state of statistical control that statistical theory aids prediction.

3. Experience is no help in management unless studied with the aid of theory.

   - An example of itself is no help in management unless studied with the aid of theory. To copy an example of success, without understanding it with the aid of theory, may lead to disaster.

4. No number of examples establishes a theory, yet a single unexplained failure of a theory requires modification or even abandonment of the theory.

5. Communication (as between customer and supplier) requires operational definitions.

6. There is no true value of any characteristic, state, or condition that is defined in terms of measurement or observation. Change of procedure for measurement or observation produces a new number.

7. There is no such thing as a fact concerning an empirical observation. Any two people may have different ideas about what is important to know about any event.

> *Most of us are 100% in favor of improvement as*
> *long as it doesn't require change.*
> *-Anonymous*

E. **Deming's conception of "psychology"**

1. Psychology helps us to understand people, interactions between people and circumstances, interaction between teacher and pupil, interactions between a leader and his people and any system of management.

2. People are different from one another. A leader must be aware of these differences, and use them for optimization of everybody's abilities and inclinations. Management of industry, education, and government operate today under the supposition that all people are alike.

3. People learn in different ways, and at different speeds. Some learn best by reading, some by listening, some by watching pictures, still or moving, some by watching someone do it.

4. A leader, by virtue of his/her authority, has obligation to make changes in the system of management that will bring improvement.

5. There is intrinsic motivation. People are born with a need for relation-ships with other people, and with need to be loved and esteemed by others. There is an innate need for self-esteem and respect.

   ● Circumstances provide some people with dignity and self-esteem. Circumstances deny other people these advantages. Management that denies to employees dignity and self-esteem will smother intrinsic motivation.

   ● No one, child or other, can enjoy learning if constantly concerned about grading and gold stars for performance, or about rating on the job.

6. One is born with a natural inclination to learn and to be innovative. One inherits a right to enjoy work. Psychology helps us to nurture and preserve these positive innate attributes of people.

7. Extrinsic motivation is submission to external forces that neutralize intrinsic motivation.

   ● Pay is not a motivator.

   ● Under extrinsic motivation, learning and joy in learning in school are submerged in order to capture top grades.

   ● On the job, joy in work, and innovation, become secondary to a good rating.

   ● Under extrinsic motivation, one is ruled by external forces. One tries to protect what one has. One tries to avoid punishment. One knows not joy in learning.

   ● Extrinsic motivation is a zero-defect mentality.

131

8. Overjustification comes from faulty systems of reward. Overjustification is resignation to outside forces.

- It could be monetary reward to somebody, or a prize for an act or achievement that was done for sheer pleasure and self-satisfaction. The result of reward under these conditions is to throttle repetition: the person will lose interest in such pursuits. Monetary-reward under such conditions is a way out for managers that do not understand how to manage intrinsic motivation.

E. These propositions of "profound knowledge" run counter to many generally held propositions of traditional leadership and organizational practice. As a practical guide to leaders, Deming translated his conceptions of profound knowledge into "fourteen points," what he called the "obligations of top management." These constitute what is necessary to achieve quality.

> *Really, if you think about it from your point of view as a customer, you want everything: a wide assortment of good quality merchandise; the lowest possible prices; guaranteed satisfaction with what you buy; friendly, knowledgeable service; convenient hours; free parking; a pleasant shopping experience.*
>
> *-Sam Walton*

Deming's Fourteen Obligations for Top Management

A. Total quality management, Deming taught, requires the recognition and application of these points:

1. **Create constancy of purpose for improvement** of product and service, with the aim to stay in business, to provide jobs, to serve customers.

2. **Adopt the new philosophy.** We are in a new economic age. Western management must awaken to the challenge, must learn their responsibilities, and take on leadership for change.

3. **Cease dependence on inspection** (grading and testing) to achieve quality. Eliminate the need for inspection on a mass basis by building quality into the product in the first place.

4. **End the practice of awarding business on the basis of price tag alone**. Instead, minimize total cost.

5. **Improve constantly and forever every process** for planning, production, and service, to improve quality and productivity, and thus constantly decrease cost.

6. **Institute training on the job.**

7. **Adopt and institute leadership.** The aim of leadership should be to help people and machines and gadgets to do a better job. Leadership of management is a need of overhaul, as well as leadership of production workers.

8. **Drive out fear**, so that everyone may work effectively for the organization.

9. **Break down barriers between departments.** People in research, design, sales, and production must work as a team, to foresee problems of production and in use that may be encountered with the product or service.

10. **Eliminate slogans, exhortations, and targets** for the work force asking for zero defects and new levels of productivity. Such exhortations only create adversarial relationships, as the bulk of the causes of low quality and low productivity belong to the system and thus lie beyond the power of the work force.

11. **Eliminate work standards (quotas)** for the work force. Eliminate management by objective, management by numbers, numerical goals. Substitute leadership.

12. **Remove barriers that rob people of pride of workmanship.** The responsibility of supervisors must be changed from sheer numbers to quality. Abolish annual rating or merit rating.

13. **Institute a vigorous program of education and self improvement** for everyone.

14. **Put everybody in the company to work to accomplish the transformation.** The transformation is everybody's job.

Life is making us abandon established stereotypes and outdated views. It is making us discard illusions. The very concept of the nature and criteria of progress is changing. It would be naive to think that problems plaguing mankind today can be solved with means and methods which were applied or seem to work in the past. Today we face a different world for which we must seek a different road to the future. In seeking it, we must, of course, draw upon the accumulated experience and yet be aware of the fundamental differences between the situation yesterday and what we are facing today.

-Mikhail Gorbachev

B. Deming's "seven deadly diseases" that stand in the way of transformation.

1. Lack of constancy of purpose.

2. Emphasis on short-term profits, short-term gains.

3. Annual review of performance, merit rating, annual appraisal.

4. Mobility of management; job hopping.

5. Running an organization on visible figures, with little or no consideration of data that are unknown or unknowable.

6. Excessive medical costs.

7. Excessive costs of warranty and liability.

> *To the extent that leaders enable followers to develop their own initiative, they are creating something that can survive their own departure.*
>
> *-John W. Gardner*

Tools for Continuous Improvement

A. With the emphasis on leadership, collaboration, and some knowledge of variation, it is not surprising that a variety of statistical tools have been used as aids for collective decisions and action.

B. The following table shows several tools and their uses:

QUALITY IMPROVEMENT TOOL	PURPOSE OR USE
Flow Chart	Document actual and ideal path
Cause and Effect Diagram	Explore causes
Check Sheet	Gather data based on observation
Pareto Chart	Display relative importance
Scatter Diagram	Test themes of relationships
Histogram	Display distribution of data
Run Chart	Display simple trends over time
Control Chart	Determine common and special variation in quality

C. A number of "new tools" have been developed by the Japanese and others as aids in working collaboratively and arriving at consensus. The Japanese have combined these tools into a cycle of activity in which the output of one technique becomes an input to the next technique. Each of the tools can be used alone very effectively. However, used together, they enable a group to move from a chaotic situation to an incremental action plan for improvement.

1. **Affinity Diagram**

   - This tool gathers large amounts of language data (ideas, opinions, issues, elements, etc.) and organizes it into groupings based on the natural relationship between each item. It is largely a creative rather than a logical process.

2. **Interrelationship Digraph**

   - This tool takes complex, multi-variable problems or desired outcomes and explores and displays all of the interrelated factors involved. It graphically shows the logical (and often causal) relationships between factors.

3. **Tree Diagram**

   - This tool systematically maps out in increasing detail the full range of paths and tasks that need to be accomplished in order to achieve a primary goal and every related subgoal. Graphically, it resembles an organization chart or family tree.

4. **Prioritization Matrix**

   - This tools takes tasks, issues, or possible actions and prioritizes them based on known, weighted criteria. They utilize a combination of Tree and Matrix Diagram techniques thus narrowing down options to those that are most desirable or effective.

5. **Matrix Diagram**

   - This versatile tool shows the connection (or correlation) between each idea/issue in one group of items and each idea/issue in one or more other groups of items. At each intersecting point between a vertical set of items and horizontal set of items a relationship is indicated as being either present or absent. In its most common use the Matrix Diagram takes the necessary tasks (often from the Tree Diagram) and graphically displays their relationships with people, functions, and other tasks. This is frequently used to determine who has responsibility for different parts of an implementation plan.

6. **Process Decision Program Chart (PDPC]**

- This tool maps out every conceivable event and contingency that can occur when moving from a problem statement to the possible solutions. This is used to plan each possible chain of events that needs to happen when a problem or goal is an unfamiliar one.

7. **Activity Network Diagram**

- This tool is used to plan the most appropriate schedule for any complex task and all of its related subtasks. It projects likely completion time and monitors all subtasks for adherence to the necessary schedule. This is used when the task at hand is a familiar one with subtasks that are of a known duration.

D. Detailed explanations of these tools are obtainable from GOAL/QPC, 13 Branch Street, Methuen, MA, 01844-1953

Managing for Quality

A. In addition to **W. Edwards Deming,** other major theorists on quality management include **J. M. Juran, Armand Feigenbaum,** and **Philip Crosby**. Though they differ somewhat in some emphases, there are common threads running through all of them.

B. The major concepts may be summarized as follows:

1. **Good quality is good productivity.** "Do it right the first time" is seen as a productivity formula as well as a quality formula.

2. **Good quality costs less than poor quality.** Paying to produce bad products, rework or scrap bad products, doing warranty work on bad products are all costs.

3. **Quality can be measured.** Deming cites example after example of measurement of services as diverse as subway systems, filling out forms, to courtesy of the bus driver in answering questions.

4. **Statistical process control.** To understand statistical variation and to make discriminations to adjust the process or leave it alone.

5. **Advocacy of prevention versus detection.** This approach builds credibility, trust and pride in the workforce.

6. **Quality improvement should be a "way of life" for the organization**, rather than a "program" with a beginning and end.

7. **A general philosophy of seeking constant improvement.**

C. **Management's responsibility in managing for quality**

1. Accept the responsibility for transformation and commit to long-term continuous improvement.

2. Define quality of product or service by asking: "What will benefit our customers the most in the future?"

3. Encourage innovation.

4. Stop the blame—fix the system.

5. Solve "stone in the shoe" problems first.

6. Arrange for broad involvement.

7. Create "joy in work" for everybody.

8. Create a "win-win" cooperative culture.

9. Celebrate successes.

10. Lead by example.

D. Barriers to establishing a quality organization:

1. Lack of perceived change in management behavior in the organization.

2. Perception that the process takes too long or that "we are already doing it."

3. Inadequate resources or funds available to implement changes.

4. Inability to get groups together to be trained, or key people not available or "too busy" to be trained.

5. Organizational culture not supportive of change.

6. Lack of consistent priorities during the implementation period.

7. The conviction on the part of the organization that long range management commitment and investment is absent.

> *Life consists not simply in what heredity and environment do to us, but in what we make out of what they do to us.*
>
> *-Harry Emerson Fosdick*

> *The uncompromising attitude is more indicative of an inner uncertainty than of deep conviction. The implacable stand is directed more against the doubt within than the assailant without.*
>
> *-Eric Hoffer*

You and I are in a relationship which I value and want to keep. Yet, each of us is a separate person with his own unique needs and the right to meet those needs.

When you are having problems meeting your needs, I will try to listen with genuine acceptance in order to facilitate your finding your own solutions instead of depending on mine. I will also try to respect your right to choose your own beliefs and develop your own values, different though they may be from mine.

However, when your behavior interferes with what I must do to get my own needs met, I will openly and honestly tell you how your behavior affects me, trusting that you respect my needs and feelings enough to try to change the behavior that is unacceptable to me. Also, whenever some behavior of mine is unacceptable to you, I hope you will openly and honestly tell me your feelings. I will then listen and try to change my behavior.

At those times when we find that either of us cannot change his behavior to meet the other's needs, let us acknowledge that we have a conflict-of-needs that requires resolving. Let us then commit ourselves to resolve each such conflict without either of us resorting to the use of power or authority to try to win at the expense of the other's losing. I respect your needs, but I also must respect my own. So, let us always strike to search for a solution that will be acceptable to both of us. Your needs will be met, but so will mine—neither will lose, both will win.

In this way, you can continue to develop as a person through satisfying your needs, but so can I. Thus, ours can be a healthy relationship in which each of us can strive to become what he is capable of becoming. And, we can continue to relate to each other with mutual respect, love and peace.

-Thomas Gordon

10 Collaboration
conflict and problem solving

> *Man must evolve for all human conflict a method*
> *which rejects revenge, aggression and retaliation.*
> *The foundation of such a method is love.*
> *-Martin Luther King, Jr.*

Collaboration and Conflict

A. Were you to associate freely to the word "conflict" there would likely be three kinds of responses.

   1. One set of terms would have negative connotations: "war," "destruction," "hate," "disorder," "aggression," "violence," "defeat."

   2. A second set of terms would have positive connotations: "collaboration," "opportunity," "excitement," "development," "growth," "adventure."

   3. A third set of terms would be relatively neutral, affectively speaking: "disagreement," "tension," "scarcity," "mediation," "reconciliation," "bargaining."

B. One cannot summarize here all of the propositions about collaboration in conflict resolution that find some support in the literature of various social and behavioral sciences. However, a few propositions may be useful in thinking about valid and invalid strategies for handling human conflict.

   1. Conflict always occurs within a context of interdependence.

      ● Conflict occurs within a relationship between parts of a system of interrelated parts.

      ● If the "parties" in conflict were not interdependent in the sense that the actions of the one "party" have consequences for the opposed "party" and vice versa, conflict could not occur.

      ● This helps in part to explain the fear of conflict—it disrupts the order and the productive output of the system in which it occurs. It may even lead to the dismemberment and destruction of the group.

      ● This proposition also offers hope for constructive resolution through collaboration if perception of the common values of maintaining a system can be kept alive in all parties of the conflict.

2. Two types of conflict:

- Limited good to be distributed. One type of conflict grows out of similarities in the needs and values of parts of a system in the presence of scarce goods to be distributed which are required to satisfy these needs and realize these values.

- Differences related to means and/or ends. Another type of conflict grows out of differences in needs and valuations among parts of a system. The needs and values of one part of a group, for example, may favor one direction of movement for the group; the needs and values of another part of the group may favor another direction of movement. Or the differences may lie not in another direction, but rather in methods and means of moving toward the agreed-upon goal.

3. Collaborative resolution of either of the two types of conflict involves two requirements:

- Each party to the conflict must accept the right of the other party to a claim upon the situation, and must, in effect respect and trust the other.

- All parties must be capable of locating realistically and rationally the sources of the conflict and arriving at mutually acceptable solutions.

Approaches to Conflict

A. Different people prefer different strategies for managing conflicts. These strategies are learned, usually in childhood, and may seem to function automatically. We do not think about how we will act in conflict situations. We just "do what comes naturally," react in the usual way..

1. The fact is, each of us has a preferred personal conflict strategy. Because it was learned, we can always change it if we choose to, by learning different and more effective ways of dealing with conflicts.

2. When you become engaged in a conflict, there are two major concerns you have to take into account::

- **Achieving your personal goals**—you are in conflict because you have a goal that conflicts with another person's goal. Your goal may be highly important to you, or it may be of little importance.

- **Keeping a good relationship with the other person**—you may need to be able to interact effectively with the other person in the future. The relationship may be very important to you, or it may be of little importance.

B. How important your personal goals are to you and how important the relationship is to you affect how you act in a conflict. Given these two concerns, it is possible to identify five styles of managing conflicts:

1. **Collaborating.** Collaborators highly value both their own goals and their relationships. They wisely (like an owl) view conflicts as problems to be solved and seek a solution that achieves both their own goals and the goals of the other person. Collaborators see conflicts as a means of improving relationships by reducing tension between two persons. They try to begin a discussion that identifies the conflict as a problem. By seeking solutions that satisfy both themselves and the other person and maintain the relationship. Collaborators are not satisfied until a solution is found that achieves their own goals and the other person's goals. And they are not satisfied until the tensions and negative feelings have been fully resolved.

   - **When to collaborate:** when both sets of concerns are too important to be compromised; when the objective is to test one's own assumptions or better understand the views of others; when there is a need to merge insights from people with different perspectives on a problem; when commitment can be increased by incorporating others' concerns into a consensus decision; when working through hard feelings that have been interfering with an interpersonal relationship.

   - **Results:** individual abilities and expertise are recognized, each person's (or group's) position is clear, but emphasis is on mutual solution. Results in win-win.

2. **Compromising.** Compromisers are moderately concerned with their own goals as well as their relationships with others. They seek a compromise (like a fox); they give up part of their goals and persuade the other person in a conflict to do the same. They seek a conflict solution in which both sides gain something and lose something—the middle ground between two extreme positions. They are willing to sacrifice part of their goals and relationships in order to find agreement.

   - **When to compromise:** when goals are moderately important but not worth the potential disruption of more assertive modes; when two opponents with equal power are strongly committed to mutually exclusive goals; when temporary settlements are needed on complex issues; when expedient solutions are necessary under time pressure; if a back-up mode is needed when collaboration fails.

   - **Results:** Each party gives up something in order to meet mid-way; results in some loss of each side's position. Results in lose-lose.

> *There is nothing so small that it cannot be blown out of proportion.*
> *-Author Unknown*

141

3. **Accommodating or Smoothing.** Accommodators see the relationship as of great importance while their own goals are of little importance. Accommodators (like teddy bears) want to be accepted and liked by others. They think that conflict should be avoided, smoothed over or ignored in favor of harmony and that people cannot discuss conflicts without damaging relationships. They are afraid that if the conflict continues, someone will get hurt, and that would ruin the relationship. They give up their goals to preserve the relationship. Accommodators say, "I'll give up my goals and let you have what you want, in order for you to like me." They try to smooth over the conflict out of fear of harming the relationship.

- **When to accommodate:** when one realizes one is wrong; when the issue is much more important to the other person; when "credits" need to be accumulated for issues that are more important; when continued competition would only damage the cause; when preserving harmony and avoiding disruption are especially important; when subordinates need to develop and to be allowed to learn from mistakes.

- **Results:** differences are played down, smoothed over or ignored. Results in win-lose.

4. **Competing or Forcing.** Competers try to overpower opponents by forcing them to accept their solution to the conflict. Competer's goals are highly important to them, and relationships are of minor importance. They seek to achieve their goals at all costs. They are not concerned with the needs of others. They do not care if others like or accept them. Competers (like sharks) assume that conflicts are settled by one person winning and one person losing. They want to be the winner. Winning gives them a sense of pride and achievement. Losing gives them a sense of weakness, inadequacy, and failure. They try to win by attacking, overpowering, overwhelming, and intimidating others.

- **When to compete:** when competition is needed against people who take advantage of noncompetitive behavior, when quick, decisive action is needed; on important issues for which unpopular courses of action need implementing.

- **Results:** authority, position, majority rule, or a persuasive minority settles the conflict; may lead to war. Results in win-lose.

> *A rattlesnake, if cornered, will become so angry it will bite itself. That is exactly what the harboring of hate and resentment against others is—a biting of oneself. We think we are harming others in holding these spites and hates, but the deeper harm is to ourselves.*
>
> *-E. Stanley Jones*

5. **Avoiding or Withdrawing or Denying.** Avoiders withdraw into their shells to avoid conflicts. Avoiders (like turtles) give up their personal goals and relationships. They stay away from the issues over which the conflict is taking place and from the persons they are in conflict with. Avoiders believe it is hopeless to try to resolve conflicts. They feel helpless. They believe it is easier to withdraw (physically and psychologically) from a conflict than to face it.

- **When to avoid:** when the issue is trivial; when there is no chance of getting what you want; when the potential damage of confrontation outweighs the benefits of resolution; when one needs to cool down, reduce tensions, and regain perspective and composure; when the need is to gather more information; when others can resolve the conflict more effectively; when the issue seems symptomatic of another fundamental issue.

- **Results:** person decides to solve conflict by denying its existence, or ignoring it, or deciding it's not an issue worth fussing about, or letting fate decide (flip of a coin). Results in win-lose.

C. **Blake, Shepard and Mouton** have developed a model for choosing how to deal with conflict, based upon beliefs held by the parties as to whether conflict is inevitable and whether agreement is considered possible.

1. Three basic attitudes toward conflict and the relative "stakes" involved determine the appropriate passive or active strategies for dealing with conflict

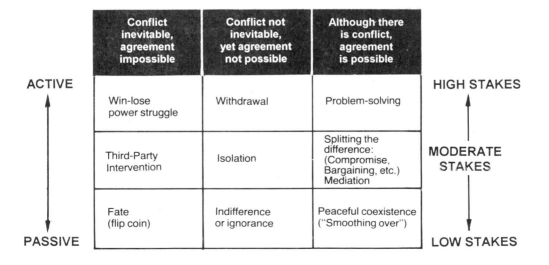

	Conflict inevitable, agreement impossible	Conflict not inevitable, yet agreement not possible	Although there is conflict, agreement is possible	
ACTIVE	Win-lose power struggle	Withdrawal	Problem-solving	HIGH STAKES
	Third-Party Intervention	Isolation	Splitting the difference: (Compromise, Bargaining, etc.) Mediation	MODERATE STAKES
PASSIVE	Fate (flip coin)	Indifference or ignorance	Peaceful coexistence ("Smoothing over")	LOW STAKES

143

Strategies: Win-Win, Lose-Lose, Win-Lose

A. Some strategies for dealing with conflict

	WIN-LOSE		LOSE-LOSE		WIN-WIN
Characterization	Barbaric		Civilized		Collaborative
Strategy	Suppression	All-out War	Limited War	Bargaining	Creative Cooperative Resolution
Description	Overpower the other	Fight in order to win	Arbitration by a third party	Competitive Negotiation (equally depriving one another)	Integrative Decision Making — Problem Recognition; Goals & Obstacles Identification; Diagnosis (Why is this?) → Search for Alternative Solutions (What might be done?); Listing alternatives (without evaluation) → Evaluating & Testing Possibilities (What should be done?); Consideration of Consequences; Selection of Course of Action (Consensus)
Tools for Resolution	Force	War	Imposed Compromise	Mutual compromise	Problem Solving Process
Leadership Approach	Battler		Compromiser		Problem Solver

144

B. **Characteristics of WIN-LOSE and LOSE-LOSE strategies**

1. **Behavior purposeful in pursuing own goals** rather than goals held in common.

2. **Secrecy and lack of openness and trust.** Accurate personal understanding of own needs, but publicly disguising or misrepresenting these needs or desires. (Don't let them know what you really want most, so they won't know how much you are really willing to give up to get it.)

3. **Unpredictable, mixed strategies,** utilizing the element of surprise (to keep the other off-balance). Threats and bluffs used.

4. **Search behavior by parties devoted to finding ways of appearing to become committed to a position** (logical, non-rational and irrational arguments may all be used to serve this purpose).

5. Success is often enhanced where groups, committees, or organizations involved on each side **form negative stereotype of the other (diabolical enemy image)** by ignoring the other's logic, by increasing the level of "we--they" hostility, distortions of judgment and perception, and at the same time strengthening moral self-image and in-group loyalty.

6. **Common win-lose strategies:**

    - authority
    - power, force (mental or physical)
    - failure to respond (ignore)
    - majority rule (over 50%)
    - minority rule (super-majority, two thirds or more)
    - strike
    - fight, war

7. **Common lose-lose strategies**

    - positional bargaining (competitive negotiation)
    - compromise, quid pro quo (each give up something)
    - side payment (bribe)
    - neutral third party (mediate compromise)
    - resorting to rules (regulations)
    - resorting to law (courts)
    - binding arbitration

> *Men do not stumble over mountains,*
> *but over molehills.*
>
> *-Confucius*

145

C. **Characteristics of WIN-WIN strategies**

1. **Behavior is purposeful in pursuing goals held in common**. "I want a solution which achieves your goals and my goals and is acceptable to both of us."

2. **Openness and trust.** "It is our mutual responsibility to be open and honest about facts, opinions, feelings."

3. **Strategy is that of collaborative integrative decision-making** using cooperative, creative methods.

4. **Search behavior is devoted to finding solutions to problems**. Problem-solver controls the process by which agreement is reached, but does not dictate content.

5. **Success requires that stereotypes be dropped**, that ideas be given consideration on their merit, regardless of source, and that hostility not be induced deliberately.

6. **Central to win-win strategies is the application of the problem solving process.** The process goes by many names including:

    - Creative problem-solving
    - Integrative decision-making
    - Cooperative negotiation
    - Collective gaining
    - Integrative bargaining
    - Collegial bargaining
    - Principled negotiation
    - Creative conflict resolution

D. **Results of strategies**

MODE	RESULTS
Battler versus Battler	Stalemate 80% of time
Battler versus Compromiser	Battler wins 90% of time
Battler versus Problem Solver	Battler wins over 50% of time
Compromiser versus Compromiser	Stalemate 80% of time
Compromiser versus Problem Solver	Problem Solver wins
Problem Solver versus Problem Solver	Quick agreement

146

E. **Beliefs necessary for WIN-WIN problem solving (Alan Filley):**

- Belief in the availability of a mutually acceptable solution.
- Belief in the desirability of a mutually acceptable solution.
- Belief in cooperation rather than competition.
- Belief that everyone is of equal value (differences are expected, not judged right or wrong)
- Belief in the expressed views of others as legitimate statements of their position (no second guessing).
- Belief that differences of opinion are helpful.
- Belief in trustworthiness of other members.
- Belief that, though the other party could compete, they and you are choosing to cooperate.

Hard and Soft Bargaining vs. Principled Negotiation

A. **Roger Fisher and William Ury** have developed an alternative to Positional Bargaining which they call Principled Negotiation. It is a system of negotiating on the merits and it utilizes problem solving which, as they show below, contrasts sharply with conventional soft or hard bargaining.

SOFT BARGAINING	HARD BARGAINING	PRINCIPLED NEGOTIATION
Participants are friends.	Participants are adversaries	Participants are problem-solvers
The goal is agreement.	The goal is victory.	The goal is a wise outcome reached efficiently and amicably.
Make concessions to cultivate the relationship	Demand concessions as a condition of the relationship.	Separate the people from the problem.
Be soft on the people and the problem.	Be hard on the problem and the people.	Be soft on the people, hard on the problem.
Trust others.	Distrust others.	Proceed independent of trust.
Change your position easily	Dig in to your position	Focus on interests, not positions.
Make offers.	Make threats.	Explore interests.
Disclose your bottom line	Mislead as to your bottom line.	Avoid having a bottom line
Accept one-sided losses to reach agreement.	Demand one-sided gains as the price of agreement	Invent options for mutual gain.
Search for the single answer: the one THEY will accept.	Search for the single answer: the one YOU will accept.	Develop multiple options to choose from; decide later.
Insist on agreement	Insist on your position	Insist on objective criteria
Try to avoid a contest of will.	Try to win a contest of will.	Try to reach a result based on standards independent of will.
Yield to pressure.	Apply pressure.	Reason and be open to reasons; yield to principle, not pressure.

> *He drew a circle that shut me out—*
> *Heretic, rebel, a thing to flout.*
> *But Love and I had the wit to win:*
> *We drew a circle that took him in!*
> *-Edwin Markham*

Collaborative Problem-Solving

A. Of all the knowledge, sensitivities and skills required by a leader, probably none is more important than facilitation of problem solving.

B. The win-win problem solving process:

1. **Identifying and Defining the Problem**

    - create a mutual problem-solving climate
    - express the problem in a way that does not communicate blame or judgment
    - separate the people from the problem
    - analyze interests of all parties
    - use "I-messages"
    - try to verbalize the Other's side of the conflict
    - use active listening as Other ventilates feelings
    - continue until both accept the definition of problem
    - decide what your goals are
    - don't define problem as a conflict between competing solutions, but in terms of conflicting needs and then generate your solution

2. **Generating Alternate Solutions**

    - create a nonevaluative problem-solving climate
    - be creative in coming up with a variety of solutions
    - ask Other first for possible solutions; avoid being evaluative or critical
    - use active listening; treat ideas with respect
    - offer your solutions; avoid evaluating or discussing any particular one
    - generate as many solutions as possible
    - if things bog down, state the problem again, reassess your goals

3. **Evaluating Alternate Solutions**

    - evaluate the possibilities
    - be honest; are there any flaws in any of the possible solutions? any reason why a solution might not work? will it be too hard to implement and carry out? is it fair to both?
    - during evaluation one of you may come up with a new idea, better than the others, or hit upon a modification that improves an earlier idea

148

4. Decision-making

- a mutual commitment to a solution is essential
- don't try to persuade or push a solution on Other
- unless Other freely chooses a solution acceptable to him or her, chances are it will not be carried out
- when close to a decision, state the solution to make certain you both understand what you are about to decide

5. Implementing the Solution

- agree on action and implementation steps
- immediately after solution has been agreed upon, talk about implementation: who does what by when?
- trust Other; don't talk about failures or penalties
- if Other fails to carry out his or her end of the agreement, confront with I-Messages

6. Follow-up Evaluation of the Solution

- is the solution working? are there weaknesses in the solution?
- decisions are always open for revision, but neither of you can unilaterally modify a decision
- modifications have to be mutually agreed upon, as was the initial decision

C. In recent years there has been a shift from traditional means of conflict control and settlement by means of the exercise of authority roles, judicial processes backed by the legal use of force, arbitration and direct bargaining, and at the international level, the threatened or actual employment of military power.

1. These authoritative or power approaches are still the dominant ones at domestic levels as well as the international level.

2. The traditional approach rests on the view that there will always be a minority whose anti-social behavior has to be controlled in the interests of the social good, and that there will always be conflicts of interest even between those whose behavior is within accepted social norms. The processes of law and order, of adjudication and of power politics, are considered appropriate.

> *The Chinese word for "crisis" is composed of two picture-characters ... the one meaning "danger" and the other meaning "opportunity."*

149

D. A second and more recent approach called "conflict management" is much less confrontational, more perceptive of possibilities and involves collaborative communication often facilitated by a third party.

1. The newer approach is based on view that conflict is natural, and inevitable and even a desirable phenomenon, in social relationships.

2. Third party directed processes are designed to help persons and groups in conflict to be reasonable and cooperative in resolving conflict.

3. Experience suggests this is a reasonable approach to take in dealing with conflicts between persons and groups who share the same goals and values when conflicts are disagreements over means, and to some degree, over priorities.

4. The conflict management approach is not adequate for resolving complex conflicts which involve deeply felt values that cannot be negotiated and may require fundamental changes in relationships and the institutions governing them.

   ● No amount of good will among those negotiating, no amount of training and sophistication in negotiation, can remove the political reality of the existence of fundamental issues over which there can not be compromise.

   ● Conflicts which involve deep issues of ethnic and cultural identity or recognition, and issues of participation usually denied to ethnic minorities, as well as issues of security and basic values, are not negotiable.

E. A third and more recent approach emphasizes the need for a better explanation or theory of conflict, and for processes which are deeply analytical problem solving. **John W. Burton**, Permanent Head of Australia's Foreign Office, and one of the world's leading theorists on international conflict, describes elements in the process:

1. An analysis is required by the parties of all the issues at stake in such a way as to separate interests, which are negotiable, from cultural values on which compromise is difficult, and to separate these from certain needs, such as identity and security, which are not negotiable in any circumstances. Only when such an analysis is complete can there be meaningful discussion of acceptable options.

2. All aspects of relationships, even those of which participants may not initially be fully aware, must be taken into account and become part of the resolution.

> *Things which matter most must never be at the mercy of things which matter least.*
> *-Johann W. von Goethe*

3. Analysis requires a third party who has the necessary knowledge of the nature of conflict and can direct attention to the underlying powerfully motivating concerns, of which the parties themselves may not be fully aware in their struggle to achieve some tactical goals.

- Such a facilitator has a role that goes much further than the role of the process-oriented "conflict management" facilitator. The third party required for analysis is one who has a knowledge base and a theoretical framework that can facilitate the analysis of the problem.

- The separation of interests, values and needs is itself a theory of conflict. It directs attention to aspects that would not otherwise be attended to.

- In addition to helping this analysis, the third party role—too exacting for only one person to perform—is to help reveal insights and suggest options that are deduced directly from such generic theory of conflict.

- The success or failure of the facilitation is dependent upon the adequacy of the theoretical framework and the knowledge and behavior of the third party.

4. Problem solving of this description is not merely a further development in technique, but a generically different approach from either authoritative control or conflict management approaches.

5. A breakthrough from management to problem solving, from settlement to resolution, with implications for all social levels, occurs only as a result of an adequate theory of conflict, and processes deduced from it.

6. Leadership in conflict resolution requires not just training in collaborative techniques, but education in interdisciplinary studies of human behavior.

7. It is not sufficient that authoritative and legal processes simply be supplemented by less confrontational ones. They must be supplemented by analytical processes before there can be predictive and reliable performance in the resolution of conflict.

> *It is better to debate a question without settling it than to settle a question without debating it.*
> *-Joseph Joubert*

> *I can complain because rose bushes have thorns...or rejoice because the thornbush has a rose...It is all up to me.*
> *-Author Unknown*

When one door closes, another opens: but we often look so long and so regretfully upon the closed door that we do not see the one which has opened for us.

-Alexander Graham Bell

Nothing endures but change.
-Heraclitus

There is a story of an experiment with processionary caterpillars carried on by Jean-Henri Fabre, the great French natural scientist. Processionary caterpillars feed upon pine needles. They are so named because they move through the trees in a long procession, one leading and the other following—each with his eyes half closed and his head fitted against the rear extremity of his predecessor!

After patiently working with a group of the caterpillars, Fabre finally succeeded in getting them to the rim of a large flower pot, where he succeeded in getting the first one connected up with the last one, thus forming a complete circle, which started moving around in a procession which had neither beginning nor end.

Fabre expected that after a while the caterpillars would catch on to the joke, get tired of their useless march and start off in some new direction. But not so. Through sheer force of habit, the living, creeping circle kept moving around the rim of the pot—around and around, keeping the same relentless pace for seven days and seven nights. They would doubtless have continued longer had it not been for sheer exhaustion and ultimate starvation. Now, there was an ample supply of food close at hand and plainly visible to the caterpillars, but it was outside the range of the circle, so they continued along the beaten path.

Why? They were following instinct-habit-custom-tradition-precedent-past experience, "standard practice," call it what you will. They were resisting change.

-Anonymous

11 Creativity
intuition, innovation, change

> *Unless individuals, groups and nations can imagine, construct and creatively revise new ways of relating to these complex changes, the lights will go out. Unless man can make new and original adaptations to his environment, our culture will perish. . . . Annihilation will be the price we pay for a lack of creativity.*
>
> *-Carl Rogers*

Intuition and Creativity

A. Research indicates that certain parts of the brain govern specific functions necessary to learning. Most notably, in the human brain, the cerebrum (outer or anterior or upper brain) is divided into two hemispheres.

   1. The interaction between the hemispheres of the brain is very complex. Each hemisphere, while capable of working alone, specializes.

      ● One side, usually the left brain, serves much like a computer, processing information in linear, logical, sequential, piece by piece style.

      ● The other, typically the right brain, governs our ability to envision an object in space, draw images from our life experience and create a "big picture" from the multitudinous pieces of information.

      ● Both sides of the brain are important. For example, we need the left brain to gather all the facts necessary to make a logical decision about the future, but since we can never hope to gather every last one of the facts that might affect us, we must at some point make that decision based on our images of our experience, looking into the future, relying on intuition and imagining the outcome—activities delegated to the right brain.

   2. The most advantageous way of dealing with tomorrow is to have a left and right brain that work together. We must, at the same time, deal with the increasing amount of facts that help us make decisions, and at the same time be future-oriented, intuitive and flexible in responding to change.

3.   Below are contrasted some left brain and right brain characteristics:

PEOPLE RELYING ON THE LEFT BRAIN	PEOPLE RELYING ON THE RIGHT BRAIN
are serious, rational, sequential, controlled	are creative, inventive, intuitive, fun loving
respond to structure in the environment	like random experiments, open endedness
prefer planned activities, keep time	prefer spontaneity, little sense of time
few emotional "highs" and "lows"	free with feelings, higher highs, lower lows
read analytically, seek facts, detail	unify concepts, see "big picture"
make objective judgments	make subjective judgments
solve problems logically, sequentially	solve problems with hunches, insight, leaps
want concrete, certain information	deal with abstract, uncertain information
draw on accumulated organized information	go on "gut" feelings, "discover" solutions
look for differences, categories, distinctions	are analogic, see resemblances, likenesses
rely primarily on language, talking	prefer pictures over words
seek right answer, authority	can see "both sides"

B.   **Roy Rowan** emphasizes the need for "intuitive managers" and focuses on the important role of intuition in leadership.

   1.   **Intuition** has been defined as "quick and ready insight" as "immediate apprehension or cognition, the power or faculty of attaining to direct knowledge without evident rational thought or inference."

   2.   The success of innovative leaders and most innovations depend greatly on the ability of the leaders to utilize their own intuition.

   3.   The blending of practical, scientific knowledge and creative, intuitive thinking makes for effective leadership.

The intuitive mind is a sacred gift, the analytical mind a faithful servant.

                                                         -Albert Einstein

---

C. **Peter Lloyd** says we must "think right or be left behind." Creativity can't be directed, but it can be encouraged. "Creativity only comes when you let go." What distinguishes one person from another are ideas; it is what distinguishes the entrepreneurial spirit. Lloyd provides five tips to stir innovation:

1. **Learn to play**. Before tackling a problem, indulge in a warm-up activity that puts you in a creative frame of mind.

2. **Set deadlines**. Deadlines can spark creative results as long as they don't come too often or too fast.

3. **Promote an environment that nurtures creativity**. Let colleagues know their ideas are valued, and above all, let them take risks and make mistakes.

4. **Practice cross-pollination**. You benefit from the thinking of people with divergent backgrounds. You learn to stretch in a lot of directions.

5. **Don't make excuses**. Everyone has the ability to think "out of the box," to be creative. It is a skill that can be cultivated and developed.

> *The mark of creative managers is not a different way of doing but rather a different way of being. They appreciate that to manage the world around them, they must also manage the world within themselves. They must learn how to manage their inner processes.*
>
> *-Peter Russell and Roger Evans*

D. **Peter Russell and Roger Evans** focus on the "creative manager" and describe the five phases of the creative process:

1. *Preparation*

   ● Preparation involves analyzing the task, gathering data, looking for patterns, trying out ideas, and questioning assumptions.

2. *Frustration*

   ● Frustration occurs when we are unable to resolve the issue; feel bored, irritated, or despondent; and doubt our own ability.

3. *Incubation*

   ● Incubation occurs when we give up trying, put the issue on hold, and hand it over to the unconscious mind.

155

4. *Insight*

- Insight is the inspiration, the "aha," the "Eureka" moment we normally associate with creativity.

5. *Working out*

- Working out involves testing our insights and giving them form.

> *Progress is a nice word. But change is its motivator. And change has its enemies.*
> *-Robert Kennedy*

Responses to Change

A. All people react to change that affects them in very much the same way. **Ken Blanchard** identifies seven predictable responses when people are asked to make a change:

1. People feel awkward, ill-at-ease and self-conscious.

2. People first think about what they have to give up.

3. People will feel alone even though others are going through a similar change.

4. People can handle only so much change.

5. People are at different levels of readiness for change.

6. People will be concerned that they will not have enough resources to carry out the change.

7. If you take the pressure off, people will revert to the old behavior.

B. **Bolman and Deal** suggest that organizational conceptions of change depending on the frames (perspectives) with which the leaders view the organization.

1. From the point of view of the **political frame**:

- Change generates conflict and creates winners and losers. Avoiding or smoothing over those issues drives conflict underground.

- So political change leaders focus on establishing arenas for conflict where issues can be negotiated.

> *We trained hard, but it seemed that every time we were beginning to form up we would be reorganized. I was to learn later in life that we tend to meet any new situation by reorganizing—a wonderful method it can be for creating the illusion of progress while producing confusion, inefficiency and demoralization.*
>
> *-Pertonius Arbiter, Chief Lieutenant of Roman Emperor Nero*

2. From the point of view of the **structural frame**:

   - Change alters the clarity and stability of roles and relationships, creating confusion and unpredictability.

   - So structural change leaders focus on realigning formal roles and relationships and renegotiating formal patterns and policies.

3. From the point of view of the **human resource frame**:

   - Change causes people to feel incompetent, needy, and powerless.

   - So human resource change leaders focus on training for employees, developing new skills, creating opportunities for involvement, and providing psychological support.

4. From the point of view of the **symbolic frame**:

   - Change creates loss of meaning and purpose. People form attachments to symbols and symbolic activity. When the attachments are severed, they experience difficulty in letting go. Existential wounds require symbolic healing.

   - So symbolic change leaders focus on providing transition rituals, mourning the old, saying good-bye, reminiscing, celebrating the new.

Approaches to Change

A. **Kurt Olmosk** has identified eight of what he called "pure strategies of change." All of them have a familiar ring as different approaches traditionally taken by various groups in society.

157

B. The tables below briefly summarize and contrast these approaches:

	FELLOWSHIP	POLITICAL	ECONOMIC	ACADEMIC
Basic assumption	need warm, interpersonal relations	influential people get things done	money can buy the change you want	rational people will change if they have facts
Inclusion	accepts all, everybody equal	based on level and power	people with resources and wealth	people with knowledge and expertise
Good at	mobilizing initial energy	mobilizing power and implementing	implementing decisions	presenting relevant information
Chronic problems	getting financial support, actual implementation	maintaining credibility, fighting backlash	maintaining change and/or satisfaction	implementing findings; getting people to pay attention
Most often used by	volunteer organizations, churches	those already in power	corporations, the very wealthy	people in staff positions, outsiders

	ENGINEERING	CONFRON-TATION	MILITARY	BEHAVIORAL SCIENCE
Basic assumption	if you change surroundings, people change	mobilize anger to force others to notice problems	enough force will cause people to do anything	combine many approaches to complex problems
Inclusion	people with technical skills	people willing to use conflict	people with physical power	people who are affected
Good at	being aware of surroundings, structure	forcing people to look at issues	control, keeping order	using information, involving others
Chronic problems	gaining acceptance of change	finding alternatives, dealing with backlash	rebellion, can never relax	making itself understood
Most often used by	top management	those without power	military, police	organizational development consultants

158

C. Behavioral science approaches to change

1. Rural sociologists, cultural anthropologists, psychiatrists, management and industrial engineers, communications specialists, educators, psychologists, and sociologists as well as others in the social sciences, have contributed to the scientific study of various aspects of the introduction of change.

2. **Everett Rogers** has brought together much of the research on what he broadly calls the "diffusion of innovations." **Ronald Havelock**, another social scientist, summarized a vast amount of research on the "dissemination and utilization of knowledge."

    ●   Drawing on each other's work and collating thousands of studies, they, along with others, have identified some general conceptions of what is today often called "planned change" or "directed change."

3. As one might expect, several factors are involved in determining the extent and speed of adoption of innovations:

    ●   How the innovation is perceived
        ▸   attributes of the innovation as seen by potential user.

    ●   How the innovation decision is made
        ▸   optional decision, a choice by the user
        ▸   authority decision, determined by an authority for the user
        ▸   collective decision, collaboratively determined by user group

    ●   How the innovation is communicated
        ▸   interpersonal communication
        ▸   mass media

    ●   The culture of the social system or organization
        ▸   norms toward innovation
        ▸   openness of communication within systems
        ▸   communication networks

    ●   The activities of the change agent (change leader)
        ▸   how the change leader performs role

4. All these factors are taken into account in considering planned change.

> *Discovery is seeing what everybody else has seen,*
> *and thinking what nobody else has thought.*
> *-Albert Szent-Gyorgi*

> *There is nothing more difficult to plan, more doubtful of success, nor more dangerous to manage than the creation of a new system. For the initiator has the enmity of all who would profit by the preservation of the old system and merely lukewarm defenders in those who would gain by the new one.*
>
> *-Niccolo Machiavelli, 1513*

Planned Change

A. Every organization or group makes some changes whether it wants to or not. Environmental changes, societal changes, technology changes, constantly impact on groups and organizations. And organizations must respond. Such responsive change may be called "reactive change" or "incidental change" or "unintentioned change" or "adaptive change." In any case, the response is more reactive than intentionally planned.

B. **Ronald Havelock** has defined *planned change* as referring to "a change or innovation which comes about through a deliberate process which is intended to make both acceptance by and benefit to the people who are changed more likely."

C. Some related definitions:

1. *Change*: Any significant alteration in the status quo, but usually in a planned change context means an alteration which is intended to benefit the people involved.

2. *Innovation*: Any change which represents something new to the people being changed.

3. *Change process*: How the change or innovation comes about.

4. *Change agent* or *change leader*: A person who facilitates planned change or planned innovation.

5. *Client*: A person, group, organization, or community which the change agent (change leader) works with.

6. *Client system*: Equivalent to "client" but indicating the fact that the "client" is usually a group of people who are interrelated and at least partly interdependent.

7. *Resources*: Persons or things which can be used to improve an innovation or an innovative process. Resources may be available both inside and outside the client system.

8. *Resource Person*: A person who is a resource or who is a provider of resources. The change agent is one type of resource person.

9. *Resource System*: An interrelated **set** of people and organizations capable of providing resources.

10. *User*: Anyone who uses resources in attempting to solve problems; equivalent to "client."

11. *User system*: An interrelated group of users; equivalent to "client system."

12. *Problem-solving*: The process by which clients or users satisfy their needs.

D. The process of planned change

1. **Ronald Havelock** identifies six phases in the process of planned change:

- **Relationship**. The first thing the successful change agent needs to develop is a viable relationship with the client system or a solid base within it. A secure and reasonably well-delineated helping role is an essential place from which to start.

- **Diagnosis**. Once established in the client system, change agents must turn to the problem at hand. The change agent must find out if the clients are aware of their own needs and if the client has been able to articulate those needs as problem statements.

- **Acquiring Relevant Resources**. With a well-defined problem, the client system needs to be able to identify and obtain resources relevant to solutions.

- **Choosing the Solution**. With a defined problem and a lot of relevant information, the client needs to be able to derive implications, generate a range of alternatives, and settle upon a potential solution.

- **Gaining Acceptance**. Even a good solution needs adaptation and needs to be reshaped to fit the special characteristics of the client.

- **Stabilization and Self-Renewal**. Finally, the client needs to develop an internal capability to maintain the innovation and continue appropriate use without outside help. The change agent encourages members of the client system to be their own change agents and to begin to work on other problems in a similar way. As this self-renewal capacity begins to build, it allows the gradual termination of the relationship so that the change agent can move on to other projects, other problems, and other clients.

2. These are **phases**, not chronological steps of a helping process. A phase may come up again and again for reconsideration during the process of consultaticn.

E. Some generalizations about planned change:

1. It is certain that a leader cannot minimize the problems which will result from opposition to a change effort. However, leadership in bringing about change can be more effective if the following points are kept in mind:

- Before a leader initiates change efforts, assumptions should be examined about other persons, the nature of the organization, the value of the goal he is seeking, and the importance of the change itself.

- Change takes place in the day-to-day relationships of people. Whenever we talk about planned change, we are talking about people. To introduce changes as if people were not involved is to threaten the change effort with defeat. No change is ever "little"—it is likely to be a big step for someone.

- People fear change because it undermines their security. In introducing change of any kind, and of whatever magnitude, the leader needs to introduce support and help for the people affected.

- The process of change is helped when the persons who will be affected can participate in the decision-making process and in planning for the change. The greater the participation, the more opportunity people have to identify and deal with personal resistances. The greater the participation, the more assurance people have of being able to influence the direction and the impact of the change, and thus reduce the "restraining forces."

- The attitude of a leader toward other persons is probably more critical than the nature of the change itself.

Innovation-Decision Process

A. **Everett Rogers** defines the "innovation-decision process" as "the process through which an individual passes from first knowledge of an innovation, to forming an attitude toward the innovation, to a decision to adopt or reject, to implementation of the new idea, and to confirmation of this decision."

B. The process consists of a series of actions and choices over time through which an individual (or an organization) evaluates a new idea and decides whether or not to incorporate the new idea into ongoing practice.

C. The distinctive aspect of innovation decision making (as compared to other types of decision making) is the perceived newness of the innovation, and the consequent uncertainty associated with this newness. Uncertainty is an issue because people, even though they may be miserable with the way things are now, will still "prefer the certainty of misery to the misery of uncertainty."

D. **The five stage innovation-decision process**

I. KNOWLEDGE   II. PERSUATION   III. DECISION   IV. IMPLEMENTATION   V. CONFIRMATION

1. **Knowledge.** An individual (or other decision-making unit) is exposed to the innovation's existence and gains some understanding of how it functions.

   ● Prior conditions to the knowledge:
     ▸ previous practice
     ▸ felt needs/problems
     ▸ degree of innovativeness
     ▸ norms of the social systems

   ● Awareness issues
     ▸ what is the innovation (awareness knowledge)
     ▸ how does it work (how-to knowledge)
     ▸ why does it work (principles knowledge)

2. **Persuasion.** An individual forms a favorable or unfavorable attitude toward the innovation.

   ● Individual becomes actively involved in seeking information about the new idea

   ● Key issues in whether a favorable or unfavorable attitude is formed
     ▸ where the individual gets information
     ▸ what messages are received
     ▸ how individual interprets the information received

   ● Individual tries out the idea mentally, by vicariously applying the new idea to present situation or anticipated future situation before deciding whether or not to try it.

   ● To confirm whether evaluative thinking is on the right track, the individual checks with the opinions of peers relative to advantages and disadvantages, compatibility, complexity, whether they think it's a good idea.

163

3. **Decision.** An individual engages in activities that lead to a choice to adopt or reject the innovation.

  ● Seeking to reduce uncertainty by conducting a small scale trial, a pilot or probationary "try it out."

  ● Checking with others who have "tried it out."

  ● Individual may actively reject (even after a trial) and decide not to adopt it or an individual may passively reject, and simply decide not to try it at all.

4. **Implementation.** An individual (or other decision-making unit) makes an overt behavior change by actually putting the innovation into practice.

  ● When putting the idea into use, the individual will need help with operational problems that may arise, and more information and technical know-how.

  ● Unexpected, unanticipated problems often arise that require "support" and "encouragement" during the implementation process.

  ● There may be a lengthy period of time before implementation can be said to be complete.

  ● For some (perhaps most), some degree of re-invention may occur during the implementation stage (that is the innovation is changed or modified by the user).

5. **Confirmation.** An individual seeks reinforcement of an innovation-decision already made, OR the individual may reverse the previous decision (that is, discontinue) if exposed to conflicting messages about the innovation.

  ● Implementation even with re-invention does not complete the process. People have to feel "confirmed," feel they're doing the "right thing," convince themselves this is a good move.

  ● Dissonance occurs as further information or experience may persuade the individual that the innovation should not have been adopted.

  ● If people don't get sufficient reinforcement for the innovation-decision already made, they may reverse the decision, reject the innovation, and discontinue its use.

E. At every point in the innovation-decision process, the individual (or other decision-making unit) may discontinue further consideration of an innovation, may in fact, reject it, though they might later choose to adopt. Similarly, the individual who has chosen to adopt and implement may later discontinue.

Nature of Innovations

A. Though the dimensions of relationships have what some have called the most important bearing on the adoption of an innovation, the nature of the innovation itself is also a factor.

B. There is no end to myths about innovations. Much of what is known, or thought to be known, about change is a mixture of folklore, and common interpretations of experience. It is such notions that the developing scientific literature would contradict. Here are some examples of myths about innovations:

1. **The myth that change comes fast!** Change takes time. Writers have frequently pointed out how long various changes took before general diffusion was achieved. Although diffusion is certainly generally more rapid today than 30 years ago, some lag is usual. Examples:

   ● It took 50 years for the complete diffusion of the innovation known as kindergarten. More than 15 years elapsed before 3% of the nation's schools adopted the change!

   ● Individual farmers took about 15 years to adopt a new hybrid corn.

   ● A study of the adoption of a new drug by physicians indicated that two years were needed for more or less complete diffusion.

   ● More examples of how long it took from the time a new product was conceived until it was generally available on market shelves:

- antibiotics	30 years
- automatic transmission	16 years
- cellophane	12 years
- dry soup mixes	19 years
- fluorescent lights	33 years
- frozen foods	15 years
- instant coffee	22 years
- instant rice	18 years
- nylon	12 years
- photography	56 years
- radio	24 years
- television	63 years
- zippers	30 years
- instant camera	2 years
- long playing records	3 years

2. **The myth that once an innovation is introduced into a system, no further attention is required.** Evidence is to the contrary. Training aids and devices lie unused in storerooms in virtually every organization because teachers, workers, nurses, managers have reverted to their former practices.

- One research report cited an elementary school in which strong commitment to an innovation in teacher behavior was achieved. There was virtually no opposition when the innovation was introduced. But six months later, the researcher found that there was practically no effort being made to implement the innovation. Why? The teacher's felt they lacked the capability to carry it out; they lacked familiarity with the new materials and methods, and the required systemic changes. Teachers found they were unable to change because they lacked the specific skill and training and thus capacity to implement the innovation they had agreed to. So in spite of original good intentions, the innovation failed.

3. **Still another myth suggests that information about the innovation is sufficient for change, that a good idea will succeed on its own merits.** When the facts are known, it is said, they will speak for themselves and convince the client system of the wisdom of adoption of the innovation.

- Hundreds of widely promoted innovations are in fact unaccepted, unused or abandoned as mute testimony to the failure of the belief that information is all that was needed.

C. One way to look at how long the adoption of an innovation will take is in terms of the degree of difference between it and that which it is intended to replace.

D. The impact of the nature of the innovation itself upon its eventual adoption has been extensively studied. Five factors have been identified by **Everett Rogers** and others as important:

1. **Relative advantage**, that is, the degree to which an innovation is perceived as better than that which it supersedes. Relative advantage can be expressed in such terms as economics, prestige, or convenience to the client.

2. **Compatibility**, or the degree to which the innovation is consistent with the existing values and past experiences of the client.

3. **Divisibility or trialability**, the degree to which an innovation may be adopted on a limited basis. Can adoption be stage by stage, a part at a time? An all or none adoption would not have the characteristic of divisibility.

4. **Complexity**, or the degree to which an innovation is relatively difficult to understand and use.

5. **Observability**, or the degree to which practice of the innovation by others can be observed and communicated.

E. **Robert Chin** has identified five levels of change, from easiest to most difficult:

1. **Substitution** of one insulated segment for another is the simplest form of change. (For example, adoption of a new text or workbook is likely to have little or no additional system effects.)

2. **Alteration** may involve a minor change but one that can have unforeseen systemic affects. (For example: the workbook requires additional laboratory space and equipment with which the teacher is unfamiliar.)

3. **System disturbance or perturbation** resulting from temporary variations in the equilibrium of the system. (For example: moving to another classroom, changing offices, a strike.)

4. **System restructuring** of which Chin states, "Change of this order is basic social change." Reorganization, a major reshuffling, a new technology (An example might be the adoption of a new curriculum.)

5. **Value orientation change,** most complex of all and disorienting to the system, requiring a change in some of the deeply held assumptions and beliefs about the way things are. (Examples: eliminate grades, adopt cooperative learning)

Research and Development Perspective

A. The research and development model of the creation of innovations and their diffusion has stood the test of time.

1. It is the model that has made the scientific method famous, from the agriculture technology revolution to putting a man on the moon!

B. The model is rooted in rationality, prescribed research methodology, the division of labor (universities, research institutions, government, industry, etc.), and the notion that (most of the time) high investments will pay off ultimately in quality, quantity, and long term gain, as practices and benefits are extended to the mass audience.

1. It is the basic model of industrial R & D, and governmental R & D support as with the agricultural research and extension system.

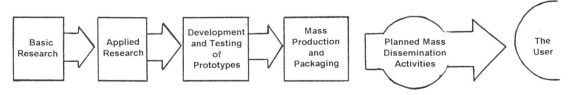

Basic Research → Applied Research → Development and Testing of Prototypes → Mass Production and Packaging → Planned Mass Dissemination Activities → The User

2. Among those identified with the model are **Henry M. Brickell, David Clark**, and **Egon Guba.**

3. There is an assumption of an orderly developmental process from research to development to use. The researcher discovers, defines and verifies, the assumption goes; then the technologist develops the idea; finally, the practitioner puts it to use, in this sequence:.

- Basic research
- Applied research
- Development and testing of prototypes
- Mass production and packaging (commercialization)
- Planned mass dissemination activities (marketing)
- The User (adoption)

C. R & D seldom seems to work in so linear fashion. There is in fact a great deal of crossing back and forth between research, development and use.

Social Interaction Diffusion Perspective

A. The social interaction diffusion model emphasizes personal relationships in the diffusion of innovations.

1. The model focuses on networks and group memberships and identifications.

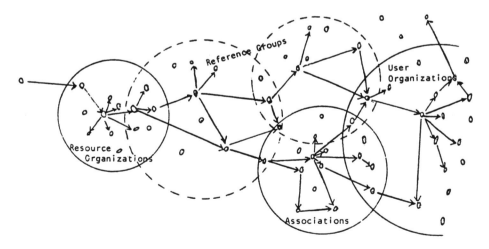

2. The model deals with social structure, and power and influence structures, and the impact of "opinion leaders."

3. The importance of such factors as proximity (nearness to each other) and cosmopoliteness (cosmopolitan world view as opposed to localite) as factors in adoption.

4. Among those identified with the model are **Everett Rogers, James Coleman, Elihu Katz, Herbert Menzel, Richard Carlson,** and **Paul Mort.**

5. The model has been used to study the diffusion of farm practices, the spread of new drugs among physicians, etc.

B. The much researched model identifies five categories of persons with regard to their likelihood to adopt an innovation and identifies typical characteristics of persons in each category as revealed in research findings.

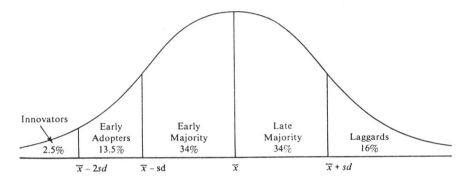

1. **Innovators** - 2.5% (the venturesome first 2.5% to adopt an innovation).

   ● Characteristics:
     ▸ willing to accept risks
     ▸ highest in socio-economic status
     ▸ used scientific, impersonal sources of information
     ▸ cosmopolite in orientation
     ▸ tend to be younger rather than older
     ▸ tend to be relatively wealthy (can afford to risk)
     ▸ tend to have the most education

2. **Early Adopters** - 13.5% (those who valued the respect others had for them, who brought innovation adoption to 16%)

   ● Characteristics:
     ▸ regarded by others as role models
     ▸ high in socio-economic status
     ▸ made contact with local change agents for information
     ▸ localite in orientation
     ▸ greatest degree of opinion leadership in this group

> *If you are open to new possibilities in your life, then that alone will give you access to those possibilities—readiness is all.*
>
> *-Deepak Chopra*

169

3. **Early Majority** - 34% (those who were deliberate before they acted and brought adoption up to 50%)

   ● Characteristics:
     ▸ as peers approve, they consider adopting themselves
     ▸ above average socio-economic status
     ▸ contacted their opinion leaders and change agents
     ▸ exhibited some opinion leadership toward others

4. **Late Majority** - 34% (the skeptical "show me" types whose action ultimately brings adoption up to 84%)

   ● Characteristics:
     ▸ respond to pressure from peers
     ▸ below average socio-economic status
     ▸ contacts with peers for information
     ▸ little opinion leadership

5. **Laggards** - 16% (the traditionalists who may not ever adopt)

   ● Characteristics:
     ▸ oriented to the past
     ▸ lower socio-economic status
     ▸ contacts with neighbors, friends, relatives for information
     ▸ tend to be semi-isolates
     ▸ tend to be older
     ▸ tend to be lower income
     ▸ tend to have least education

C. Sociologists and others who have studied the phenomena of institutional and societal change have conceptualized the formation of several groups in response to a projected change:

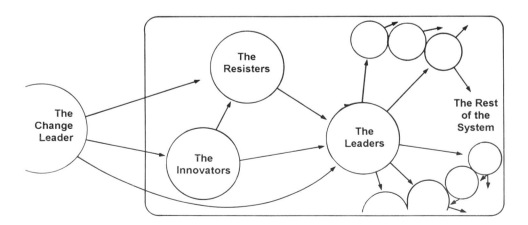

1.   *Innovators*—who will be supportive and enthusiastic about the change.

2.   *Resisters*—who will oppose the change and "defend the system" against the invading idea. Opposers act as "social antibodies" of the system.

3.   *System Leaders*—informal "opinion leaders" to whom the rest of the system looks for "cues" as to response.

4.   *The Rest*—usually a large majority who look to their "opinion leaders" and accept the change as legitimate as their informal leaders do.

D.   The way It works

1.   *System Leaders* (opinion leaders) keep an "eye on" the innovators and an "ear open" to the resisters, usually giving the "go ahead" only after having made some modifications in the change.

2.   *Innovators'* success does not insure adoption, as they are regarded as "odd-balls" or eccentrics by the rest of the system.

3.   *Resisters* will usually continue to oppose until the "bitter end."

4.   The "keys" to diffusion of the change into the system are the system leaders (opinion leaders), as their approval and acceptance trigger further acceptance by their followers.

E.   Opinion leadership

1.   **Everett Rogers** defines opinion leadership as the degree to which an individual is able to influence informally other individuals' attitudes or overt behavior in a desired way with relative frequency. Opinion leaders thus play an important role in the diffusion of innovatlons.

2.   **Opinion leaders** tend to have higher social-economic status, more education, more mass media exposure, more cosmopoliteness, greater social participation, more contact with change leaders, and are generally somewhat more innovative than their followers, particularly when the system norms favor change. But when system norms are traditional, opinion leaders will not be particularly innovative.

3.   Opinion leaders who tend to be opinion leaders on a variety of topics are called **polymorphic** opinion leaders. Those who tend to provide opinion leadership on only one topic are called **monomorphic**. Generally the more complex a system, the more likely opinion leadership is limited to the area of the opinion leader's particular expertise.

F. Communication factors

1. In human communication most often the transfer of ideas occurs between a source and a receiver who are alike, similar, that is, they are homophilous. Most of us enjoy the comfort of interacting with others who share common meanings, attitudes and beliefs, and a mutual language. The problem is, we are not as likely to be exposed to new ideas this way! **Homophily** tends to be a barrier to diffusion.

2. On the other hand, **heterophily** (interaction with others of diverse views, attitudes, beliefs, experience) tends to open thought to other possibilities, challenge our assumptions and interpretations, and as a result, we are more likely to contact innovative opinion leadership.

3. For some time it was thought that mass media had a direct, immediate and powerful "hypodermic effect" on a mass audience. More recently this has been seen as too simple and mechanistic a view, that there is at minimum, a "two-step flow" that involves interpersonal influence. Messages from the mass media tend to flow first to opinion leaders who in turn pass the messages on to their followers.

Problem Solver Perspective

A. The problem solver model perspective emphasizes the user's need as the paramount consideration.

1. Diagnosis is part of the process as is the utilization of the internal resources of the user/group in solving the problem.

2. The change agent is an "outsider" whose role is to help the user/group find the solution and see it as theirs.

3. Self-motivated change has the firmest motivational basis and best prospects for long-term maintenance.

4. Among those identified with the model are **Goodwin Watson, Ronald Lippitt, Herbert Thelen, Matthew Miles,** and **Charles Jung**.

5. The model is widely used by consultants in many contexts and in organizational development.

B. Regardless of formal job title and position, there are four primary ways in which a person can act as a change leader in solving problems.

> *You cannot teach a man anything; you can only help him find it in himself.*
>
> *-Galileo*

1. According to **Ronald Havelock** the change leader may act as:

    - A solution giver (leader provides answer)
    - A catalyst (leader focuses on creating a disturbance)
    - A resource linker (leader brings in consultant/s to solve problem)
    - A process helper (leader facilitates a collaborative approach to problem solving)

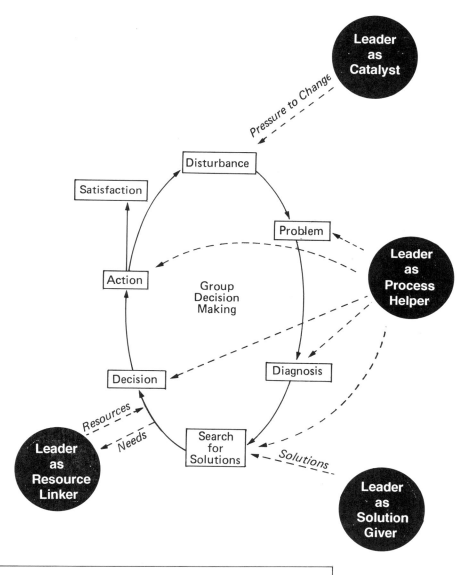

> *What lies behind us and what lies before us are tiny matters, compared to what lies within us.*
> *—Oliver Wendell Holmes*

C. The problem solving model is basically a rational model.

1. The problem starts with a "disturbance" and a felt need to deal with it.

2. A decision to "do something" about the problem.

3. An active attempt to define and diagnose what the problem is.

4. A search for possible solutions.

5. Selection of a solution and decision to apply it.

6. Application of the solution to see if it will satisfy the need. If not, the disturbance continues and problem solving begins again.

D. Traditional problem solving approaches such as "solution giver" is regarded as "old fashioned," reactive and authoritarian and creates resistance to imposed solutions. The "catalyst", though sometimes necessary, is seen as little more than a troublemaker. On the other hand, the "resource linker" or "process helper" approaches are valued as more enlightened for problem solving.

Linkage Perspective

A. **Ronald Havelock** sees leadership for change as a communication process, as a two-way linkage process that occurs only in a relationship between a change leader and another.

1. The two way helping relationship involves

- The sender's (change leader, helper) perception of the receiver (learner, client system).
- The learner's perception of the sender.
- Each person's perceptions of the message (words and meaning of the innovation or change).
- The receiver's response to the medium of delivery (how the message was transmitted).
- The sender's response to the feedback received.

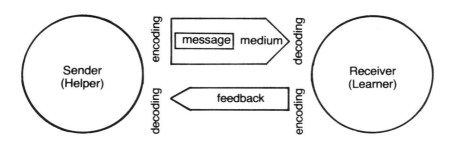

B. The linkage perspective incorporates the other perspectives

1. The user (receiver) must be able to understand (and simulate) the research, development, and evaluation processes employed by the resource system (helper) in the fabrication of solutions (Research and Development Perspective).

2. Successful linkage experiences build channels for efficient communication and dissemination (Social Interaction Diffusion Perspective).

3. Resource system (change leader, helper) must recapitulate or adequately simulate the user's (receiver, learner) problem-solving process (Problem Solver Perspective).

4. Resource and user must provide reciprocal feedback (Linkage Perspective).

C. **Ronald Havelock** studied a vast amount of research on change relative to the four aspects of the communication process: (1) **sender system**, (2) **receiver system**, (3) **message**, and (4) **medium**. He summarized the research findings under seven broad generalizations of key elements involved in change.

1. *Linkage.* Linkage, in barest essentials, means connections between people. Innovativeness is directly proportional to the strength and variety of linkages within the receiver system and between the system and the diverse relevant sender systems.

2. *Structure.* Effective change usually takes place within a coherent framework, a structure which designates a rational sequence of goal setting, planning, and execution, and a definition, and coordination of sub-tasks. Successful innovators do not all follow the *same* structure, but they all follow *some* structure. Coherent structure is also an important element of the innovation itself.

3. *Openness.* Openness to new ideas is virtually synonymous with "innovativeness." Successful change requires some degree of openness by both receiver and sender, *e.g.:* (a) openness to receiving new ideas; (b) active eagerness to seek out new ideas; (c) active desire for self-renewal; (d) openness to *give* new ideas to others; (e) openness to listening to the problems of others; and (f) openness to giving authentic non-evaluative feedback.

4. *Capacity.* This is a summary concept which ties together the highly inter-correlated variables of wealth, power, status, education, intelligence, size and sophistication of the system. High capacity systems are more likely to be innovative because, in a figurative and literal sense, they have more "risk capital" at their disposal.

5. *Reward.* It is a fundamental psychological fact that rewarded behavior tends to be repeated. The sender won't send if he doesn't get rewarded for sending and the receiver won't receive if he doesn't get rewarded for receiving. Processes which lead to successful change must include a sequence of intermediate steps which have pay-off value to all the parties involved.

6. *Proximity.* A good deal of research evidence points to the fact that proximity to the sources of innovation is a good predictor of innovative behavior. The greater the opportunity for meaningful contact and mutual stimulation between innovation originators and other members of the social system, the greater will be the likelihood of diffusion to those others. When resources are close at hand, they are used more often.

7. *Synergy.* A final point to keep in mind is the need for considerable redundancy in change processes. A single exposure to a new idea is rarely, if ever, sufficient stimulus. A diversity of approaches, messages, media need to be put together and "orchestrated" before most people will be influenced to change.

Consequences of Innovations

A. Every innovation has consequences, some anticipated and some that are unanticipated. Likewise, nonadoption of an innovation also has consequences.

B. Much innovation literature has a "pro-innovation bias." The assumption of beneficial results for adopters often blinds change leaders to potential negative side-effects for adopters.

1. Change leaders need to consider all possibilities in identifying potential positive and/or negative consequences that might result from adoption of the innovation.

   ● Possible desirable or undesirable consequences
     ‣ functional vs. dysfunctional effects to an individual or system
     ‣ who are the "winners" and "losers"
     ‣ various effects of the innovation on adopters
     ‣ consequences to other than adopters

   ● Possible direct or indirect consequences
     ‣ direct changes that occur in immediate response to an innovation
     ‣ indirect changes that occur as later consequences

   ● Possible anticipated or unanticipated consequences
     ‣ windfall profit to early adopters
     ‣ response to form, function and meaning of innovation
     ‣ effect of change on organizational equilibrium
     ‣ gap widening consequences (between haves and have nots)
     ‣ impact on ethos and quality in the social system

176

C. Undesirable, indirect, and unanticipated consequences of innovations usually go together, as do the desirable, direct, and anticipated consequences.

    1.   How can a change leader consider all (or at least most) the possible consequences?

- Listen to the opposers, the resisters of the innovation. What are their concerns? What are their arguments against the innovation? How do they say the innovation will affect the system? Why do they say the innovation will not work? Etc.

- Think through their concerns. The most important role of the opposition is what they can tell you about what would otherwise be unanticipated, undesirable, or indirect consequences.

- Make modifications, adjustments, changes in plans to deal with concerns being raised. This will not mean that the opposition will then become supporters. They are likely to continue to oppose. But you will have dealt with at least some of the consequences you would not have taken into account if you had not listened to them.

- Think of opposers as the "antibodies" of the system whose role is to keep the system from changing. Their concerns about what will happen to the system will provide the change leader important information to be considered.

Change Leader Roles

A. **Everett Rogers** identifies a sequence of seven change agent (change leader) roles:

    1.   **Develop a need for change.** Often a change agent must initially help his clients to become aware of the need to alter their behavior. This may involve assessing needs, pointing out new alternatives, dramatizing the importance of problems, convincing people they are capable of confronting these problems.

    2.   **Establish an information-exchange relationship.** Develop rapport with clients, establish credibility relative to the agent's competence, trustworthiness, and empathy.

    3.   **Diagnose problems.** Analyze problems as to why existing alternatives or practice is not meeting needs. View the situation empathetically from the standpoint of the client. Change agents must "zip themselves into their clients' skins, and see their situation through their eyes."

    4.   **Create an intent to change in the client.** The change agent must be client-centered, rather than innovation-oriented, focusing on the client's problems. Seek to motivate the client's interest in the innovation to achieve their goals.

> *The executive leadership of an organization has two responsibilities: one is maintenance of the system the way it is, and the other is changing the system so that it performs better. In other words, the leader is both a change agent and a resister of change.*
>
> *-Ronald Havelock*

5. **Translate intent into action.** Work with opinion leaders, activate peer networks. Recognize the key element is the interpersonal network influences from near-peers at the persuasion and decision stages in the innovation-decision process.

6. **Stabilize adoption and prevent discontinuances.** Direct reinforcing messages to clients who have adopted. Clients may need assistance and support at the implementation and/or confirmation stage in the innovation-decision process.

7. **Achieve a terminal relationship.** The end goal for the change agent is to develop self-renewing behavior on the part of the client system. The change agent's role is to be no longer needed.

B. The table below summarizes some of the roles of the change leader and the corresponding roles of the change client (learner):

ROLE OF CHANGE LEADER (AGENT, SENDER, HELPER)	ROLE OF CHANGE CLIENT (USER, RECEIVER, LEARNER)
Promote, advocate	Become aware of need or problem
Provide information, tell	Become interested, seek information
Demonstrate, show	Evaluate, mentally try out innovation
Train, teach	Trial, test innovation
Help	Install innovation
Service, support	Adopt innovation
Nurture, follow-up	Institutionalize innovation

> *There is no such thing as the perfect solution. Every solution, no matter how good, creates problems.*
>
> *-Author Unknown*

C. Some generalizations about strategies for effecting system change

1. The effectiveness of a planned change is often directly related to the degree to which members at all levels of an institutional hierarchy take part in the fact-finding and the diagnosing of needed changes and in the formulating and reality-testing of goals and programs of change.

2. Diffusion of the change is enhanced by the active participation of formal and informal leadership (opinion leaders) in decisions related to the change, including modifications (by serving on study committees, planning committees, implementation committees, etc.).

3. Change leaders should not identify too closely with the first to adopt (innovators) or devote extensive time trying to gain support of opposers (laggards), but rather work closely with opinion leaders (prospective early adopters and early majority).

4. The place to begin change is at those points in the system where some stress and strain exist. Stress may give rise to dissatisfaction with the status quo and thus become a motivating factor for change in the system.

5. To change a subsystem or any part of a subsystem, relevant aspects of the environment must also be changed. Anticipate consequences.

6. To change behavior on any one level of a hierarchical organization, it is necessary to achieve complementary and reinforcing changes in organization levels above and below that level. Obtain needed support.

7. If thoroughgoing changes in a hierarchical structure are desirable or necessary, change should ordinarily start with the policy-making body.

> *Change is not linear or able to be mapped out in advance. No matter how well we plan it . . . it will not unfold in a linear way; there'll be surprises, there'll be detours, there'll be unpredictable things that happen for better and for worse. Successful change agents are those poised to learn as the surprises occur.*
>
> *-Michael Fullan*

> *Questioning is like standing at a gate and reaching to raise the latch. It is a sign that one has reached a state of development where an awareness of truth prompts the interrogation. Nothing can or ever will be forced through to one who has not lifted the latch of receptivity. Live each day alerted to the realization that voices speak to ears that listen.*
>
> *-Josephine H. Brooks*

179

> *If we can trust the workings of chaos, we will see that the dominant shape of our organizations can be maintained if we retain clarity about the purpose and direction of the organization. If we succeed in maintaining focus, rather than hands-on control, we also create the flexibility and responsiveness that every organization craves. What leaders are called upon to do in a chaotic world is to shape their organizations through concepts, not through elaborate rules or structures.*
>
> *-Margaret J. Wheatley*

> *But I'm coming to believe that all of us are ghosts. . . . It's not just what we inherit from our mothers and fathers. It's also the shadows of dead ideas and opinions and convictions. They're no longer alive, but they grip us all the same, and hold on to us against our will. All I have to do is open a newspaper to see ghosts hovering between the lines. They are haunting the whole country, those stubborn phantoms—so many of them, so thick, they're like an impenetrable dark mist. And here we are, all of us, so abjectly terrified of the light.*
>
> *-Henrik Ibsen*

> *Systems thinking, the integrating concept of the learning organization, is the discipline of seeing the structures that underlie complex situations and for discerning high from low leverage change. The essence of the discipline lies in a shift of mind from seeing linear cause-effect chains to seeing interrelationships and from viewing the world in snapshots to seeing processes of change.*
>
> *-Peter M. Senge*

12 Learning Organizations
reflective action

> *Real learning gets to the heart of what it means to be human. Through learning we re-create ourselves. Through learning we become able to do something we never were able to do. Through learning we reperceive the world and our relationship to it. Through learning we extend our capacity to create, to be part of the generative process of life. There is within each of us a deep hunger for this type of learning.*
>
> *-Peter M. Senge*

Systems Theory

A. All living systems—be they organic like a cell, or the human body, or supra-organic like a society or an ecosystem—have a dual nature: they are both wholes in themselves, and simultaneously, integral parts of larger wholes. These wholes that are integral parts of larger wholes have been called "holons."

    1. In the organization of living systems, emergence is a universal and striking feature. At each holonic level new properties and new possibilities emerge, which could not have been predicted.

    2. Mind or consciousness arises by virtue of "feedback loops" that permit living systems to self-correct, adapt and evolve.

B. **Margaret J. Wheatley** writes in her book, *Leadership and the New Science,* "We are beginning to recognize organizations as systems, construing them as 'learning organizations' and crediting them with some type of self-renewing capacity. . . . Organizations are seen as conscious entities, possessing many of the properties of living systems."

    1. Traditional theoretical constructs of the nature of systems have been strongly influenced by Newtonian images of the universe. Systems are managed by separating things into parts, force is exerted from one person to another, planning assumes the world is predictable, we assume we can see the world objectively.

    2. The lessons of the new science (**Einstein, Bohr, Heisenberg**, and modern physics, biology, chemistry and theories of evolution and chaos) offer a dramatically different way to view the world and systems and organizations.

- Materialistic and machine images that focus on things rather than relationships, are beginning to give way to a new perspective, to a quantum mechanical view of reality where particles come into being and are observed only in relation to something else, where relations are primary, where order exists within disorder and disorder within order, where change and stability are complementary aspects of growth, where space is filled with fields, and unseen forces of interpenetrating influences and invisible structures connect.

C. Systems theory draws on the work of **Wiener** in cybernetics, and **Von Bertalanffy** in general theory of systems, **Miller** in theory of living systems and **Boulding** in "general theory of practically everything."

   1. **Bolman and Deal** summarize systems theory and cybernetics in the following propositions:

      - A system is a set of interacting and interrelated parts. [Holistic.]

      - Human organizations are appropriately viewed as open systems with permeable boundaries, continually engaged in importing, transforming, and exporting matter, energy, information, people. [Open.]

      - Human organizations are capable of surviving and growing, rather than inevitably decaying and dying, if they are able to work out a mutually beneficial relationship with their environment. [Renewing.]

      - Every system is a supersystem for systems contained within it and a subsystem for systems containing it. [Interrelationships.]

      - A system is more than the sum of its pats. A system's properties emerge from the relationship among its parts and from the system's relationship to its environment. [Patterns forming and reforming.]

      - Organizations tend to maintain steady states, a dynamic equilibrium in which diverse forces are approximately balanced. The more that a system is threatened with disequilibrium, the more resources it will marshall to maintain or restore its balance. [Balanced steady state.]

      - To maintain a steady state, open systems need adaptive processes, including feedback loops, that enable the systems to sense relevant changes in the internal or external environment and to adjust their properties accordingly. [Capacity for self-correction, self-adjusting reinforcing and balancing feedback loops and delays.]

> *An organization that creates information is nothing but an organization that allows a maximum of self-organizing order or information out of chaos.*
>
> *-Ikujira Nonaka*

> *What is needed is an act of understanding in which*
> *we see the totality as an actual process that, when*
> *carried out properly, tends to bring about a harmo-*
> *nious and orderly overall action . . . . in which*
> *analysis into parts has no meaning.*
>
> *-David Bohm*

Creating a Learning Organization

A. Disciplines of a learning organization

1. Leadership in a learning organization starts with the principle of creative tension. Creative tension comes from seeing clearly where we want to be, our "vision," and recognizing where we are, our "current reality." The gap between the two generates a natural tension. The creative tension can be resolved in two ways: by raising our current reality toward the vision, or by lowering our vision toward the current reality.

2. **Peter Senge** insists that all organizations must become learning organizations. Senge asserts, "the team that became great didn't start off great—it *learned* how to produce extraordinary results."

3. A "great team" applies "five disciplines" of a learning organization: personal mastery, mental models, building shared vision, team learning, and systems thinking. Systems thinking (the "Fifth Discipline") fuses the other four disciplines into a coherent whole.

    ● **Personal Mastery** (capacity to bring about desired results)
        ‣ Clarifying and internalizing your personal vision.
        ‣ Focusing energies on components of the vision.
        ‣ Seeing reality objectively relative to your vision.
        ‣ Dealing with creative tension (positive energy created by gap between reality and vision) and dealing with emotional tension (negative energy created by your limiting beliefs).

    ● **Mental Models** (capacity to reflect on notions and assumptions behind perceptions and behavior)
        ‣ Scrutinizing generalizations and deeply ingrained assumptions that may hamper sound decision making.
        ‣ Assessing the mental pictures or "images that influence how we understand the world and how we take action."
        ‣ Examining mental models that move us forward or hold us back.
        ‣ Balancing inquiry and advocacy.
        ‣ Distinguishing espoused theory from theory in use.

183

- **Shared Vision** (capacity to build shared commitment in a group, shared goals, values, missions, and pictures of the future)
  - ‣ Seeking genuine shared vision that breeds excellence and learning because people want to pursue these goals.
  - ‣ Encouraging caring commitment rather than mere compliance.
  - ‣ Communicating and asking for support.
  - ‣ Recognizing and defusing defensive routines by encouraging self-disclosure and openness.
  - ‣ Seeing shared visioning as an ongoing process.

- **Team Learning** (capacity to develop shared meaning to create results team members desire)
  - ‣ Learning by practice the art of aligning and creating shared meaning.
  - ‣ Discovering what undermines team success, and learning together how do deal with team problems.
  - ‣ Learning to suspend assumptions and creatively explore complex and subtle issues.
  - ‣ Learning to dialogue and listen to each other as colleagues.

- **Systems Thinking** (the capacity to integrate the four disciplines into a coherent whole system way of thinking)
  - ‣ Seeing patterns and interrelationships between parts.
  - ‣ Focusing on the whole system rather than isolated parts.
  - ‣ Seeing interrelationships, not things, and processes.
  - ‣ Avoiding solutions that deal only with symptoms.
  - ‣ Moving beyond blame (poorly designed systems more than incompetent individuals cause problems).

B. Senge's **"Laws of the Fifth Discipline."**

1. **Today's problems come from yesterday's solutions**.

2. **The harder you push, the harder the system pushes back**. The more you try to improve things, the more effort is required.

3. **Behavior grows better before it grows worse.** Short-term success may result in long-term decline.

4. **The easy way out usually leads back in.** Relying on familiar solutions will guarantee that problems persist. "If you do what you've always done, you'll get what you've always got."

5. **The cure can be worse than the disease**. The familiar solution is sometimes not just ineffective, but can be dangerous in the long run.

6. **Faster is slower**. The system will compensate for fast growth by slowing down, even if it means death.

7. **Cause and effect are not closely related in time and space**. Most of the time, cause and effect do not occur close together, so dispense with simple cause-and-effect thinking and learn to see what is at the root of problems.

8. **Small changes can produce big results, but the areas of highest leverage are often the least obvious**. Small, well focused actions can produce significant improvements. It's often hard for people to see where the high leverage points lie.

9. **You can have your cake and eat it too, but not at once**. When one changes from "snapshot" to a "process" mode of thinking, dilemmas (like high quality, low cost) appear differently (both are possible but not immediately).

10. **Dividing an elephant in half does not produce two small elephants.** Systems are "alive" and their character depends on the whole.

C. Dialogue and discussion

1. **David Bohm** makes a distinction between dialogue and discussion.

- In **dialogue** team members listen to each other with deep regard and suspend their own views to better hear those of others.

- In **discussion**, on the other hand, views are presented and defended as the team searches for the "best" view. There may be a sense of wanting to "win" and see one's view prevail.

2. According to Bohm, three conditions are necessary for real dialogue to occur.

- All participants must suspend their assumptions. They must see assumptions as assumptions and not fact and "hold" them in front of the group as if suspended for all to see.

- All participants must find a balance between giving and receiving, between advocacy (presenting own views) and inquiry (exploring other's views) as colleagues.

- A facilitator, who "holds" the context of the dialogue, must be present.

3. After the dialogue, decisions must be made and then the need is for discussion, to determine action to be taken.

> *Things do not change; we change.*
> *-Henry David Thoreau*

D. Circles of causality

1. **Peter Senge** points out that "though we may see straight lines, reality is made up of circles."

- Linear thinkers are always looking for a thing or person who is responsible. Systems thinkers take on greater responsibility for events, because their perspective suggests that everyone shares responsibility for problems generated by the system.

2. Learning systems (that is, systems that are changing) involve reinforcing and balancing feedback loops and delays.

- **Reinforcing feedback** in systems is an engine for either growth or decline. The "change" causes a "snowball effect" accelerating growth or decline.

- **Balancing feedback** is the system's response to check the "vicious cycle" of reinforcing feedback. Balancing feedback provides balancing limits and stability. It provides self-correction to the system so it can maintain itself and get some work done.

- **Delays** are the interruptions between actions and their consequences. Delays account for the time required for learning, development, progress, and adjustment to the change and its consequences.

E. Senge's **"Organizational Learning Disabilities"**

1. **"I am my position."** People understand their daily tasks, but see themselves in a system in which they have little power and no need to take responsibility for poor results.

2. **"The enemy is out there."** People focus on their positions and don't see how their actions have an effect beyond their boundaries so they find an external agent to blame for problems that arise. The problem is that usually the"out there" and the "in here" are part of the same system.

3. **The illusion of taking charge**. Mistaking proactiveness as an antidote for reactiveness, people tackle problems fast by taking action against the enemy "outside." Truly proactive means seeing how we contribute to our own problems and solving them first.

4. **The fixation on events.** People see life as a series of events, each of with an "obvious" cause. Current day events distract us from seeing long-term patterns of change and threats that lie behind the events.

5. **Maladaptation to gradually building threats to survival**. Illustrated by the parable of the boiled frog. (If you put a frog in boiling water it will attempt to escape. But if you put the frog in room temperature water, it will stay put, and though you gradually turn up the temperature, the frog will not try to escape; it will get groggier, and sit there and boil!)

6. **The delusion of learning from experience**. People learn from experience, but often, in fact, the consequences of many of their most important decisions are in the distant future and not experienced directly.

7. **The myth of the management team**. Teams may not, in fact, function as teams because they fight for turf and avoid anything that will make them look bad. To keep up the appearance of a cohesive team, they hide disagreement and come up with watered-down decisions that everyone can live with.

Action Science

A. **Chris Argyris** defines an "action scientist" as one who engages in "self-reflection" and seeks both to promote learning in the client system and to contribute to general knowledge by creating conditions for inquiry in the practical context of client systems.

1. "Theories-in-use" is a way of describing everyday behavior for individuals and organizations. Theories-in-use includes knowledge about behavior of organizations, and every domain of human activity including strategies for resolving conflicts, making a living, closing a deal, etc. These "theories-in-use" provide a means for maintaining some degree of constancy in our "world picture."

2. Theories-in-use may (or may not) be compatible with one's "espoused theories" (what one says one believes).

3. There are two general models of "theories-in-use."

   • The traditional Model I Theory-in-use is is essentially the opposite of Model II Theory-in-use.

B. **Model I Theory-in-use** (traditional paradigm)

1. **Effect**: Reduces the probability of generating valid knowledge and detecting and destroying errors

2. **Governing variables include**

   • controlling the purpose of the meeting or encounter
   • maximizing winning, minimizing losing
   • minimizing generating or expressing negative feelings
   • maximizing rationality

3. **Strategies include**

   • advocating in order to be in control and win
   • unilaterally saving face

4. **Consequences in the organization**

- miscommunication
- mistrust
- lack of risk taking
- rivalry, competition
- protectiveness
- self-fulfilling prophecies
- self-sealing processes
- escalating error
- little freedom of choice
- **single-loop learning** (a single learning cycle):
  - ▸ discover inconsistencies within espoused theories or theories-in-use or incongruent behavior.
  - ▸ invent new meanings or new behavior to reduce inconsistency and incongruity.
  - ▸ produce the meanings invented by trying new behaviors.
  - ▸ generalize the new learning beyond the specific case.

> *The* learners *inherit the future.* *The* learned *find themselves living in a world that no longer exists.*
>
> *-Eric Hoffer*

C. **Model II Theory-in-use** (new paradigm)

1. **Effect**: Increases the probability of generating valid knowledge

2. **Governing variables include**

- valid, confirmable information
- free and informed choice
- internal commitment to the choice

3. **Strategies include**

- advocating combined with inquiry and public testing
- facilitative collaboration
- interpersonal relations and group dynamics
- minimizing unilateral face saving
- reflective experimentation

4. **Consequences in the organization**

- reduction of self-sealing and error-escalating processes
- surfacing of threatening issues to be dealt with
- disconfirmable statements become apparent
- reflect on errors and redesign actions to be taken
- public testing of theories of action
- effective problem solving

- **double-loop learning** (learning cycles within learning cycles):
  - ▸ discover inconsistencies and incongruities and discover difficulties in discovery, so invent how to discover, produce the behavior needed for discovery, and generalize the discovery process.
  - ▸ invent new meanings and discover difficulties in inventing, so invent how to invent, produce the invention, and generalize about the invention process.
  - ▸ produce the new meanings and discover difficulties in producing, so invent how to produce, produce the production, and generalize about the production process.
  - ▸ generalize the new meanings to similar and to different settings and discover difficulties in generalizing, so invent how to generalize, produce the generalizations, and generalize about effective generalization process.

The Reflective Practitioner

A. Adult learning and critical thinking

  1. All adults learn. Learning is as natural as breathing and living.

   - All learning involves unlearning. All adults are to a greater or lesser extent "trapped" by mental models that cause them to reject new insights that conflict with deeply held internal images of how the world works, images that limit them to familiar ways of thinking and acting.

   - All adults are motivated to learn when they see a purpose (benefit) in learning, that is, when they believe that learning will enable them to cope better or resolve problems.

   - All adults can learn what they believe they can learn. How they see themselves as learners, and their attitudes toward learning or "school" are important parts of the self-concept.

   - All adults learn when their adulthood is not threatened. More than anything adults do not want to be treated (or be taught) like children. They want their experience and abilities to be valued.

   - Age of itself is the least reliable predictor of adult ability to learn. The best predictor of learning ability is current participation in continuing learning!

   - Learning is an active process involving readiness and commitment. Learning is most effective when there is learning by doing, just-in-time learning, learning-on-the-job, learning that involves immediate application to life situations, learning that provides evidence of progress or "pay-off."

2. Learning requires critical reflection, questioning, exploring, examining, discovering, reframing, inventing, and thus to some degree, transforming some of our assumptions underlying our beliefs, values, accepted truths, perceptions, behaviors, and social structures.

- Assumptions are taken-for-granted beliefs we have about reality.
- Assumptions are the rules of thumb that guide our actions.
- Assumptions are the common sense beliefs and conventional wisdom, the "everybody knows that..."
- Assumptions are rarely wholly right or wholly wrong. Most assumptions have more validity in some situations than others.

3. A crucial component of reflective practice is recognizing the conditions and contexts that render assumptions invalid or less valid.

4. **Stephen Brookfield** calls this process **"critical thinking."** Critical thinking is the productive and positive activity people engage in when creating and re-creating aspects of their personal, workplace, and social lives.

- The implicit assumption is that adults through critical reflection will choose superior perspectives as they better understand the meaning of their experience.

- New learning by its nature transforms existing knowledge into a new perspective and in so doing empowers the learner.

5. Critical thinking values reflection in day to day activities with respect to belief systems, habitual behaviors, and social structures, maintaining a willingness and readiness to learn, especially when routine behavior is not "working."

B. A process for implementing reflective practice for continuous learning (**Karen Watkins, Victoria Marsick**)

1. Clarify the thinking and reasoning we bring to the situation and make that thinking explicit.

2. Open yourself to questions about what and how you are learning, thinking, doing.

3. Notice feelings, facts, and intuition about the context of the situation.

4. Test out hunches, guesses, intuitive feelings, before acting.

5. Investigate many points of view.

6. Name (frame) the problem, and then continue to re-name (reframe) it.

7. Uncover values, beliefs, assumptions, and norms that guide your thinking and actions.

8. Experiment, and in so doing, seek reality-based feedback.

C. **Donald Schon** describes the activity of the "reflective practitioner" as follows:

1. A situation in action brings spontaneous, **routinized responses**—a knowing-in-action of strategies, understandings and ways of framing the task or problem without conscious deliberation.

2. A **"surprise" occurs** when routine responses lead to an unexpected outcome.

3. Surprise leads to **reflection within an action-present**. Reflection consciously considers both the unexpected event and the knowing-in-action that led up to it.

4. Reflection-in-action has a critical function, **questioning the assumptional structure of knowing-in-action**, thinking critically of the thinking that led up to this and possibly restructuring strategies of action, understandings of phenomena, and reframing problems.

5. Reflection gives rise to **on-the-spot experiment**, trying out new actions, testing tentative new understandings, making moves to change. On-the-spot experiment may work, or it may produce surprises that call for further reflection and experiment.

D. **Reflective action at the workplace** as described by **Watkins** and **Marsick:**

1. People have experiences that pose a challenge which they convert to a learning opportunity by framing or reframing the problem as they assess what they see, filter it through mental models from past experiences, and use their judgment to name what they see.

2. They then think about what to do and learn as they examine and explore the experience. They assess their assumptions about the context itself, the people involved, expected ways of acting, anticipated resources, or anticipated impact. This helps them decide how they want to act.

3. They take action to respond to the challenge, learning as they reflect in-and-on the action before, during, and after they experiment and examine results.

4. They assess their actions and draw conclusions and plan for future learning based on assessment of both the intended and unintended consequences.

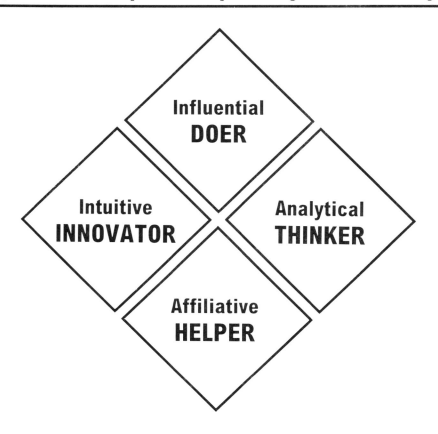

> *Be ye therefore perfect, even as your Father which is in heaven is perfect.*
>
> —*Christ Jesus*

> *I, I, I, I itself, I,*
> *The inside and outside, the what and the why,*
> *The when and the where, the low and the high,*
> *All I, I, I, I itself, I.*
>
> —*Anonymous*

> *I will gain a baiance on the side of good,*
> *my true being.*
>
> —*Mary Baker Eddy*

13 Transformative Leadership
dynamic synergy

> So long as a man imagines that he cannot do this or
> that, so long is he determined not to do it; and
> consequently, so long it is impossible to him that he
> should do it.
>
> —Benedict Spinoza

Four Modes of Perceiving Our World

A. Theoretical conceptions from the literature on leadership, change,
    motivation, learning, and personality frequently identify four "styles."

1. **Carl Jung** observed that man normally experiences the world through
    four modes: sensing, thinking, feeling and intuiting.

    ● **Sensing** is the reality function—our senses (sight, hearing, touch,
      taste, smell) tell us that something exists.

    ● **Thinking** is the logical function—our thoughts interpret that
      something, analyze and make sense out of it.

    ● **Feeling** is a value function—we make a value judgment about the
      object (whether we like it, how we feel about it).

    ● **Intuiting** is a possibility function— through hunches and guesses we
      see possibilities inherent in the object.

2. Persons who are strong in one mode tend to be weaker in another, but
    everyone has potential for all four styles. Our modes or styles represent
    learned behaviors.

B. Many models of leadership tend to focus on only two or three of these
    dimensions: sensing and feeling, or sensing and feeling plus thinking.
    Intuiting, a fourth dimension, has often been ignored as being irrational and
    irrelevant until more recently.

1. Several models based on two dimensions of human behavior contrast concern with task accomplishment to concern with relationships. Some of these are shown below and usually posit the desirability of some middle position between the two extremes:

	SENSING	FEELING
Traditional Dichotomy	Dominant (leaders)	Submissive (followers)
Gender	Masculine (macho)	Feminine (helper/nurturer)
Gray	"Men are from Mars"	"Women are from Venus"
Cartwright/Zander	Goal Attainment	Group Maintenance
Blake/Mouton	Concern for Task	Concern for People
Stogdill/Coons	Initiating Structure	Consideration
Friedman	Type A Personality	Type B Personality
Levy	Left Brain	Right Brain

2. Other models add a third "thinking" (choosing, structuring, analyzing, reasoning) dimension to sensing and feeling, again often emphasizing the desirability of some balance between the three:

	SENSING	THINKING	FEELING
McClelland	Power	Achievement	Affiliation
Wallen	Tough Battler	Objective Thinker	Friendly Helper
National Training Laboratory	Desire to Lead	Task Abilities	Group Maintenance Abilities
Hersey/Blanchard	Leader Task Behavior	Leader Effectiveness (choosing behaviors)	Leadership Relationship Behavior
Fiedler	Position-Power	Task-Structure	Leader/Member-Relations

C. More recently, most models include a fourth dimension of "intuiting" variously emphasizing finding meaning, seeing the big picture, being creative, inventive, or fun loving! The next table contrasts several four dimensional models which bear similarity to Jung's four modes of sensing, thinking, feeling, and intuiting:

Carl Jung	SENSING	THINKING	FEELING	INTUITING
Lee Bolman Terrence Deal	Political Frame	Structural Frame	Human Resource Frame	Symbolic Frame
G. Burrell G. Morgan	Political-Conflict (power relations)	Structural-Function-alist (solve problems)	Constructivist (follower concerns)	Critical-Humanist (symbolic meaning)
Peter Senge	Personal Mastery (desired results)	Mental Models (reflect on images)	Shared Vision (commitment)	Team Learning (shared meaning)
Rosabeth Moss Kanter	Power skills (influence)	Segmentation (organization)	Empowerment (human relations)	Culture (meaning)
Stephen Covey	Scientific Manage-ment (control)	Human Resource (efficiency)	Human Relations (kindness)	Principle-centered (meaning)
David Kolb	Converger (practical)	Assimilator (theoretical)	Diverger (wholistic)	Accommodator (adaptive)
Anthony Gregorc	Concrete Sequential (hands on, ordered)	Abstract Sequential (words, images)	Abstract Random (nuance, mood)	Concrete Random (creative, intuitive)
Ned Herrmann	Limbic Left Brain (organized, order)	Cerebral Left Brain (logical, rational)	Limbic Right Brain (interpersonal)	Cerebral Right Brain (synthesize)
Dudley Lynch	Posterior Left Brain (doer, competitor)	Anterior Left Brain (analyzer)	Anterior Right Brain (belonger)	Posterior Right Brain (creator)
Grinder/Bandler	Visuals	Digitals	Kinesthetics	Auditories
Virginia Satir	Blamer	Super-reasonable	Placator	Distracting
Eric Berne	Critical Parent	Adult	Nurturing Parent	Intuitive Child
William Glasser	Power (gain importance)	Freedom (choosing)	Belonging (love/cooperate)	Fun (learn/play)
Michael Mercer	Results-focused	Detail-focused	Friendly-focused	Partying-focused
Gary Smalley	Lion (in charge)	Beaver (careful with details)	Golden Retriever (loyal, caring)	Otter (fun-loving, playful)
Don Lowry	Gold (Organizer)	Green (Architect)	Blue (Communicator)	Orange (Challenger)
T. Allessandra M. O'Connor	Director (control)	Thinker (precision)	Relater (appreciation)	Socializer (prestige)
Margaret Wheatley	Organizing Force of Order out of Chaos	Organizing Force of Information	Organizing Force of Relationships	Organizing Force of Field of Meaning
Gospel Accounts of Christ Jesus	Jesus as the active doer (Mark)	Jesus as the knowledgeable teacher (Matthew)	Jesus as the compassionate friend (Luke)	Jesus' spirituality (John)
Russell Robinson	**Influential Doer** (action)	**Analytical Thinker** (excellence)	**Affiliative Helper** (collaboration)	**Intuitive Innovator** (creativity)

195

Influential Doers

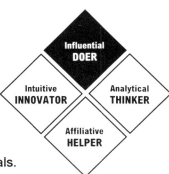

A. Motto of Influential Doers:

"Results are the important thing in this dog-eat-dog world."

B. Influential Doers as Team Members

1. Influential Doers keep team focused on mission and goals.

2. Doers make it their business to encourage that things get done in line with the mission.

3. They are concerned about strategy, and who does what and when. They realize the importance of cooperation by all team members and that each does his/her part.

4. At times, Doers may resist revisiting the mission or redefining roles after a project has begun.

5. They may express little interest in learning basic team skills or considering individual needs of other team members.

C. CHARACTERISTICS OF INFLUENTIAL DOERS

1. *Goal of Influential Doers: Action.*

   - Get the job done, get others to work, get results.
   - Accomplish mission and goals.

2. *Motivator: Need to lead.*

   - Exercise power, control, be in charge.
   - Need to complete task.

3. *Personal Concerns: Personal influence.*

   - Immediate actions to be taken.
   - Make things happen.
   - Recognition for being in charge.
   - Status, prestige, reputation, position.
   - Wants ideas to predominate.

4. *Organizational Culture Desired: Structured.*

   - Defined responsibilities.
   - Rules, policies, directives, clear lines of authority.
   - Predictable environments.
   - Established procedures, schedules.
   - Traditional structures.

5. *Decision Making Style: Authoritative.*

- Quick, based on personal observations.
- "Judgment call" based on need for action.
- Authority, rulings, regulations, past practice.
- Enforced by pressure, threats, intimidation.

6. *Learning Style: Hands-on.*

- Organized, methodical, to the point.
- Concrete-sequential.
- Learn by doing, activity on task.
- Seek correct answers.
- Value completion and accuracy.

7. *Conflict Management Style: Battling.*

- Fight, force, coercion, suppression of other.
- Hard bargaining. Shifting strategies.
- Sharp criticism.
- Disagreements tend to become win-lose encounters where winning becomes everything.

8. *Sensory Representation: Visual.*

- Map the world in "pictures" ("I can see that.")

9. *Communication Patterns: Telling.*

- Get to the point.
- Demanding, ordering.
- Blaming, accusing.

10. *Characteristic Strengths: Proactive.*

- Decisive. Give direction. Take initiative.
- Exercise authority.
- Take responsibility. Delegate responsibility.
- Organize, structure, discipline.
- Practical, realistic, hard working, efficient, thorough, reliable.
- Willing to set goals, risk action, accept challenges.
- Articulate, confident, forceful.
- Predictable.

11. *Characteristic Weaknesses: Domineering.*

- Arrogant. Manipulative. Impatient. Pugnacious.
- Fears being "soft" or dependent.
- Low tolerance for ambiguity. Has "the answer."
- May not see long range impact.
- Push themselves or others to the limit.

197

12. *Under Pressure or Stress: Impulsive.*

- Act hastily.
- Harden position.
- Blame others.
- Complain.

13. *Time Orientation: Present.*

- Immediate concerns.
- No delay.
- Deadlines. On time or just before.

14. *Life Style: Practical.*

- Organized, active, business-like. Have list of things to be done.
- Competitive.
- Work comes before play.

D. **PREFERRED LEADERSHIP SKILLS OF INFLUENTIAL DOERS**

1. **Results-oriented Action Skills**

- Initiating action
- Organizing
- Supervising
- Controlling
- Overseeing
- Goal setting
- Managing
- Prioritizing
- Directing

- Task structuring
- Assigning tasks
- Moving forward
- Risking action
- Advocating
- Persuading
- Planning
- Coordinating
- Delegating

E. *May be viewed by others as*

1. Bossy, shortsighted, status-seeking, thinking only of self, acting hastily, not trusting others, dominating, pushy, uncaring, harsh, tough.

> *A mature person is one who does not think only in absolutes, who is able to be objective even when deeply stirred emotionally, who has learned that there is both good and bad in all people and in all things, and who walks humbly and deals charitably with the circumstances of life, knowing that in this world no one is all-knowing and therefore all of us need both love and charity.*
>
> *-Eleanor Roosevelt*

Analytical Thinkers

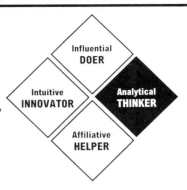

A. **Motto of Analytical Thinkers:**

"Thinking it through is better than going off half-cocked."

B. **Analytical Thinkers as Team Members**

1. Analytical Thinkers keep the focus on task.

2. They provide the team with technical information, solid data, and expertise.

3. They do their homework, and push the team to high performance and quality standards.

4. They are dependable, committed and hard working but may lose patience with long discussions.

5. Others may see them as getting bogged down in the details or not concerned enough about team climate and team process.

C. **CHARACTERISTICS OF ANALYTICAL THINKERS**

1. ***Goal of Analytical Thinkers: Excellence.***

   - Be rational, think it through.
   - Do it right the first time.

2. ***Motivator: Need to achieve.***

   - Need to do quality work.
   - Need for detail, data, facts.

3. ***Personal Concerns: Quality.***

   - Demonstrating their cognitive ability.
   - Satisfaction in a job well done.
   - Orderly and systematic flow of tasks.
   - Continuous improvement.
   - Recognition for excellent performance.

4. ***Organizational Culture Desired: Intellectual.***

   - Atmosphere where logic, accuracy, excellence prevail.
   - Climate that values intellectual ability and careful thought.
   - Quality-oriented environment with independent thinkers bent on solving complex problems.

199

5. *Decision Making Style: Rational.*

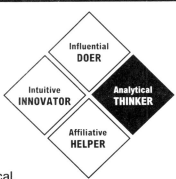

- Seek information.
- Analyze data.
- Apply theory.
- Weigh alternatives.

6. *Learning Style: Conceptual.*

- Organized study, logical, theoretical, analytical.
- Abstract-sequential.
- Learn by reading, lectures.
- Value reasons and understanding why.

7. *Conflict Management Style: Problem-solving.*

- May delay to further analyze problem.

8. *Sensory Representation: Digital.*

- Map world through words, symbols, sequenced information ("that seems to be a reasonable approach").

9. *Communication Patterns: Explaining.*

- Put in writing.
- Assert facts.
- Super-reasonable, "computing."

10. *Characteristic Strengths: Evaluative.*

- Logical thinking.
- Set attainable goals, calculate risks. Overcome obstacles.
- Take personal responsibility for doing work well.
- Develop prototypes, pilots, models.
- Industrious, persistent, serious, exacting.
- Carefully plan in step by step, orderly, logical fashion.
- Follow-through on every detail.

11. *Characteristic Weaknesses: Over-cautious.*

- Indecisive while seeking more information to analyze and study further.
- Rather do the task alone to be sure it's done right.
- Do not like to train others.
- Contemptuous and critical of ideas not thought through.
- Fear emotions and irrational acts.
- May be rigid and dogmatic in defending views and move to a stubborn "no budge" position.

12. **Under Pressure or Stress: Super-logical.**

- Nitpick with facts and details.
- Organize thoughts.
- Become extremely firm and overly cautious.
- May lose patience with the need to get others involved.

13. **Time Orientation: Linear.**

- Relate past to present and present to future.
- Early for meetings.

14. **Lifestyle: Competent.**

- Intellectual.
- Achieving.
- Orderly clutter.
- Takes pride in accomplishments.

D. **PREFERRED LEADERSHIP SKILLS OF ANALYTICAL THINKERS**

1. **Excellence-oriented Detail Skills**

- Analyzing
- Data collecting
- Information seeking
- Assessing resources
- Testing feasibility
- Critiquing
- Rational planning
- Evaluating
- Clarifying issues

- Defining problems
- Diagnosing
- Fact finding
- Stating objectives
- Charting
- Using statistical tools
- Summarizing
- Elaborating
- Logical thinking

E. **May be viewed by others as**

1. Perfectionist, rigid, over-analyzing, unemotional, too controlled, non-dynamic, over-serious, too critical, picky, indecisive.

> *Whoever would be a teacher of men let him begin by teaching himself before teaching others; and let him teach by example before teaching by word. For he who teaches himself and rectifies his own ways is more deserving of respect and reverence than he who would teach others and rectify their ways.*
> *-Kahlil Gibran*

Affiliative Helpers

A. Motto of Affiliative Helpers:

"Relationships are what really matter, to get along."

B. Affiliative Helpers as Team Members

1. Affiliative Helpers are group process and team oriented.

2. They are concerned with listening to each other, getting everyone involved, consensus building, feedback, and positive team climate.

3. Sometimes it may seem they are interested in process as an end in itself.

4. They may be viewed as not giving enough attention to completing task assignments or making progress toward team goals.

C. CHARACTERISTICS OF AFFILIATIVE HELPERS

1. *Goal of Affiliative Helpers: Collaboration.*

   - Cooperation, working together.
   - To be liked, to be friends.

2. *Motivator: Need for affiliation.*

   - Need for acceptance, belonging.
   - Interaction with others.

3. *Personal Concerns: Personal relationships.*

   - Group process.
   - Feelings, mood, nuances.
   - How others will be affected.
   - How to be helpful.
   - Receiving sincere appreciation.

4. *Organizational Culture Desired: Nurturing.*

   - Atmosphere that is supportive.
   - Freedom to interact within broad guidelines with little structure or constraint.
   - Environment where people understand and help each other, where there is peace and harmony.
   - Status quo with no surprises.
   - Climate of trust and loyalty.

5. *Decision Making Style: Participative.*

- Concern for others.
- Seek consensus. Involve everyone.
- Soft bargaining.
- Postpone action until agreement.

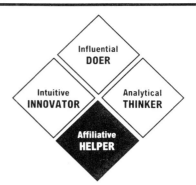

6. *Learning Style: Interactive.*

- Holistic, subjective.
- Sociable, informal, adaptable.
- Abstract-random.
- Learn by discussion, group activities.
- Value cooperative learning, working with others.

7. *Conflict Management Style: Compromising.*

- Seek middle ground for agreement.
- Do not like conflict.
- Seek reconciliation, smooth over, harmonize.
- May try to break tension with a supportive or humorous remark.
- May leave to avoid the conflict.

8. *Sensory Representation: Kinesthetic.*

- Map world from internal and external feelings ("How do I feel and how do you feel about that").

9. *Communication Patterns: Agreeing.*

- Like face to face contact.
- Passive, placating, soothing.
- Small talk.

10. *Characteristic Strengths: Supportive.*
- Caring, helpful.
- Concerned with other's feelings.
- Introspective, loyal, tactful.
- High interpersonal competence.
- Considerate, friendly, encouraging, respectful, willing, agreeable, diplomatic.
- Spontaneous, express feelings.
- Appreciate each person's contributions.

11. *Characteristic Weaknesses: Sentimental.*

- Easily hurt by criticism or impersonal treatment.
- Fear desertion or conflict.
- Hard time saying "no"; may be overextended and not get task done.
- Self-denying; pliable.
- Unsure, self-blaming.
- Hooked into rumor mill.

203

12. **Under Pressure or Stress: Emotional.**

- Passive-aggressive; appear to agree but resist.
- Crying, pouting.

13. **Time Orientation: Past.**

- Refer to past,
- Personal ties, memories.
- Not punctual.
- Procrastinates.

14. **Life Style: Amiable.**

- Going and doing with people.
- Sociable.
- Stick with familiar.
- Value friends, pictures, mementos.

D. **PREFERRED LEADERSHIP SKILLS OF AFFILIATIVE HELPERS**

1. **Relationship-oriented collaborative skills.**

- Harmonizing
- Encouraging
- Compromising
- Consensus taking
- Supporting
- Communicating
- Gate keeping
- Tension relieving
- Cooperating
- Reconciling
- Teamworking
- Linking
- Norm setting
- Protecting traditions
- Mediating
- Enabling
- Expressing group feelings
- Following

E. *May be viewed by others as*

1. Oversensitive, overpersonalizing, overemotional, conforming, too concerned about others, postponing, not serious about getting the job done.

> *How closely men resemble books!*
> *For instance, when one merely looks*
> *At covers dull, or bright with sheen,*
> *He ne'er can tell what is between*
> *Until he reads. A gaudy dress*
> *May be the cloak of emptiness*
> *While bindings plain and poor and thin*
> *May hold a wealth of thought between.*
> *-Courtney Challis*

Intuitive Innovators

A. Motto of Intuitive Innovators:

"Try it. There's more than one way to skin a cat."

B. Intuitive Thinkers as Team Members

1. Intuitive Innovators provide a challenging function; they frequently question team goals, methods, decisions.

2. They bring freshness and critical thinking.

3. They suggest alternatives, other possibilities, and question the team's work.

4. They create an openness that widens discussion.

5. Sometimes they may try to push the team too far and may not know when to back off from their ideas.

C. CHARACTERISTICS OF INTUITIVE INNOVATORS

1. *Goal of Intuitive Innovators: Creativity.*

   - Discover another way, get out of a rut.
   - Improve, make it different.
   - Creatively adapt.
   - Find a solution.

2. *Motivator: Need to innovate.*

   - Need to creatively come up with ideas, to be original.
   - To try a new way.

3. *Personal Concerns: Personal Change.*

   - Self-discovery, reflection.
   - Self-reliance.
   - Desire to be unique.
   - Recognition for ideas.
   - Have fun.
   - Create something different.

4. *Organizational Culture Desired: Innovative.*

   - Environment that is creative, open to future possibilities, changing, unconstrained, non-competitive, lively, with people strongly focused on ideals.

205

5. *Decision Making Style: Explore options.*

    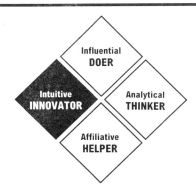

    - Seek creative solutions.
    - Consider intuitive alternatives.
    - Examine assumptions.

6. *Learning Style: Experimenting.*

    - Inventive, creative, innovative.
    - Investigative, curious, inquisitive.
    - Concrete-random.
    - Learn by trial and error, intuitive hunches, guesses.
    - Open-ended problem solving. Ask what if? why?
    - Mental leaps rather than systematic logic.

7. *Conflict Management Style: Reframing.*

    - Innovative problem solving.
    - Redefining issues and problems.
    - Press for discussion of differences, other courses of action.

8. *Sensory Representation: Auditory.*

    - Maps world from sounds.
    - Provides pizazz to interpretations.
    - Hears a different drummer ("I heard something in me say...").

9. *Communication Patterns:* **Interpreting.**

    - Varied interpretations.
    - Think "ahead." Think globally.
    - Say what "pops in."
    - Inject new ideas.
    - Tell stories, analogies.

10. *Characteristic Strengths: Intuitive.*

    - Critical thinking.
    - Reject preconceptions.
    - Seek alternate assumptions, other explanations, additional possibilities.
    - Relish change. Flexible.
    - Sense of humor.
    - Insightful, imaginative, creative.
    - Energetic, stimulating, enthusiastic.
    - Visionary, idealistic.
    - Tackle new problems with zest.

11. *Characteristic Weaknesses: "Far Out."*

- More concerned with "might be" than practicality.
- Appears to "jump to conclusions."
- Many unfinished tasks. Lack of follow-through.
- Condescending and critical of "stick-in-the-muds."
- Easily bored. Inattentive to detail.
- May play devil's advocate too long.

12. *Under Pressure or Stress: Withdraw.*

- Pull away into self and become cautious and disinterested.
- Become uptight and scrappy, tantrum and take it personally.

13. *Time Orientation: Future.*

- Beyond now.
- May lose track of time, forget appointments, commitments.

14. *Life Style: Adventurous.*

- Variety, newness.
- Fun, excitement.
- Risk taking.
- Value new and different.

D. **PREFERRED LEADERSHIP SKILLS OF INTUITIVE INNOVATORS**

1. **Change-oriented Creativity Skills.**

- Reframing
- Brainstorming
- Visualizing
- Creating ideas
- Reinventing
- Generating alternatives
- Trouble-shooting
- Creative problem solving
- Critical thinking
- Imagining solutions
- Rethinking
- Reflection
- Examining assumptions
- Creative adaptation
- Dialogue
- Inquiry
- Designing
- Systems thinking

E. *May be viewed by others as*

1. Unrealistic, impractical, fantasy-bound, scattered, flaky, out-of-touch, fanatic, disorganized, excitable, pie in the sky.

> *To raise new questions, new possibilities, to regard old problems from a new angle, requires creative imagination and marks real advance in science.*
>
> *-Albert Einstein*

207

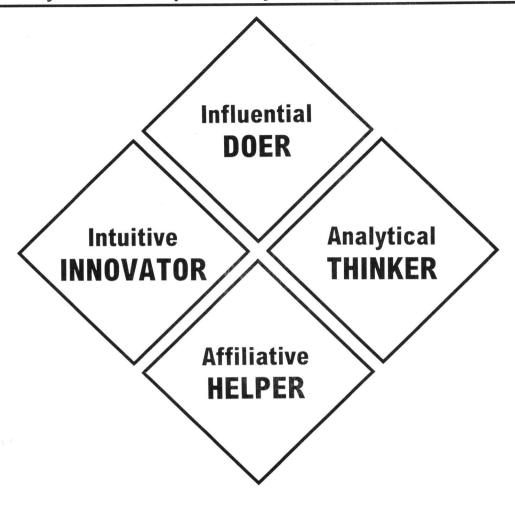

Group Participation Styles

A.. Our ways of perceiving and analyzing the world impact on our behavior in all kinds of groups—work groups, teams, social groups, professional groups, ad hoc groups, committees, boards, task forces, family groups.

B. To some extent the four group participation styles are contextual (how we behave depends on how we perceive the situation), but generally our habitual ways of perceiving and analyzing the world persist regardless of the situation.

   1. Participation styles help explain why we may have such difficulty working with some persons, particularly when we are high in one participation style and another is high in another style.

   2. The following summary shows how a person who favors a particular style is likely to view another who is partial to a different style.

	Influential Doers see .... as	Analytical Thinkers see .... as	Affiliative Helpers see .... as	Intuitive Innovators see ....as
Influential Doers	Compatible if agree on goals and means	Simplistic Acting hastily Bossy Short-sighted Status-seeking	Ruthless Wheeler-dealer Self-centered Uncaring Harsh Not trusting	Dictatorial Dominating Pushy Conniving Willing to do anything to get their own way
Analytical Thinkers	Slow-moving Overcautious Picky Indecisive Non-dynamic	Compatible if agree on data and details	Rigid Impersonal Over-analyzing Boring Uptight Unemotional Perfectionist	Lacking in imagination Narrow Bean-counter Too critical Over-serious
Affiliative Helpers	Talkers Time wasters Bleeding hearts Not serious about getting job done	Disorganized Over-emotional Immature Touchy-feely Oversensitive Conforming	Compatible if like each other and enjoy being together	Erratic Overreactive Too concerned about others Over-personal-izing
Intuitive Innovators	Dreamers Out-of-touch "Nuts" Unrealistic Impractical Fantasy-bound	Overly philo-sophical Undisciplined Free-form Pie in the sky Scattered	Fanatical Fascinating Flaky Excitable	Compatible if agree on new ideas

> *It used to be Peter and Andrew, James and John. Now it is Peter and John. Calvary had brought these men into closer fellowship with each other. By nature and temperament they were very different. Peter was a doer, John was a dreamer; Peter was a motivator, John was a mystic; Peter had his feet on the rock, John had his head in the clouds. . . . Peter and John were opposites. By nature they would get on each other's nerves, but now they walked together.*
>
> *-John Phillips in Exploring Acts*

209

C. The following table summarizes and contrasts the four group participation styles.

   1. The contrasts strongly point to the importance of a **balance among the four styles to achieve ideal group participation.**

	INFLUENTIAL DOER	ANALYTICAL THINKER	AFFILIATIVE HELPER	INTUITIVE INNOVATOR
Goal	Action	Excellence	Collaboration	Creativity
Motivation	Need to lead	Need to achieve	Need for affiliation	Need to innovate
Personal Concerns	Influence	Quality	Relationships	Change
Organizational Culture	Structured	Intellectual	Nurturing	Innovative
Decision Making	Authoritative	Rational	Participative	Explore options
Learning Style	Hands-on	Conceptual	Interactive	Experimenting
Conflict Management	Battling	Problem-solving	Compromising	Reframing
Strength	Proactive	Evaluative	Supportive	Intuitive
Weakness	Domineering	Over-cautious	Sentimental	"Far-out"
Under Stress	Impulsive	Super-logical	Emotional	Withdraw
Planning	Realign power, air conflicts	Consider objectives, resources	Promote participation	Produce symbols, find meanings
Reorganizing	Distribute power, form coalitions	Realign roles and responsibilities	Balance human needs and roles	Seek new order
Meetings	Competitive occasions	Formal event for decisions	Shared feelings Involvement	Celebrate and transform culture
Evaluation	Opportunity to use power	Way to improve performance	For helping individuals grow	Shared ritual
Time Orientation	Present	Linear	Past	Future
Communication	Telling, bossing, influencing	Explaining, transmitting facts	Agreeing, share needs, feelings	Interpreting, offer other ideas
Effective Leadership	Advocacy, coalition building	Analysis, design, social architecture	Support, empowerment	Inspiration, framing experience
Ineffective Leadership	Management by fiat, manipulation	Management by detail and rules	Management by abdication	Management by smoke and mirrors

2. Ideally, **we should strive for human balance**. We can try out and learn some behavior patterns we have usually neglected. We can experiment with behaviors opposite of those on which we have too often relied. We can, with effort and persistence, learn to develop those parts of ourselves that have fallen into disuse. **The result is to achieve a range of style adaptability and fourfold competence, a dynamic synergy of styles and skills.**

> *We are all capable of more than we do.*
> *-Mary Baker Eddy*

Leadership Style Profile Types

A. Determination by an individual of the relative strength of each of the four basic group participation styles (denominated Influential Doer, Analytical Thinker, Affiliative Helper, and Intuitive Innovator) enables the individual to create a personal "Group Participation Styles Profile." This individual profile enables one to identify, out of fifteen possibilities, a personal "Leadership Style Profile Type", each type representing a preferred approach to group leadership. See instruments later in this chapter, pages 223-229.

B. Each of the four group participation styles can be viewed as a continuum of relative strength ranging from low to high. None of us is totally one style, but most of us have style preferences, preferring one or two styles over the others, that is, we are "high" in one or more styles and relatively lower in others.

- Being relatively lower in a style represents a potential for development and learning. The habits of decades don't change in days, but we can always start here and now to make changes in our ways of behaving.

C. The HIGH/LOW Profiles reveal SEVEN PROFILES of "Lead Leader Types" and EIGHT PROFILES of "Specialist Leader Types."

1. **Lead Leaders of all types have in common the desire to lead**. They are relatively high in the Influential Doer style and at least one other style. They like being in charge, taking responsibility, influencing others, getting results.

2. **Specialist Leaders prefer not to be in charge**; they are relatively lower in the Influential Doer style, so tend to work in various supportive, staff or consultative roles under the leadership of one of the Lead Leader types. They perform specialized leadership roles.

211

LEADERSHIP STYLE PROFILE TYPE	INFLUENTIAL DOER	ANALYTICAL THINKER	AFFILIATIVE HELPER	INTUITIVE INNOVATOR
Transformative Leader	High	High	High	High
Management Team Leader	High	High	High	Low
Analytical Change Leader	High	High	Low	High
Relational Change Leader	High	Low	High	High
Task Leader	High	High	Low	Low
Relational Leader	High	Low	High	Low
Initiating Change Leader	High	Low	Low	High
Change Specialist	Low	High	High	High
Staff Specialist	Low	High	High	Low
Problem Solving Specialist	Low	High	Low	High
Human Relations Specialist	Low	Low	High	High
Task Specialist	Low	High	Low	Low
People Specialist	Low	Low	High	Low
Action Specialist	High	Low	Low	Low
Idea Specialist	Low	Low	Low	High

> *Knowing others is wisdom.*
> *Knowing the self is enlightenment.*
> *-Lao-Tzu*

No single style could suffice under the day-to-day, even minute-by-minute, varying conditions of different personalities and moods among their employees, routine process vs. changing or sudden deadlines, new and ever-changing government regulations and paperwork, ambiguous roles of workers, wide ranges in job complexity from simple to innovation-demanding, changes in organizational structure and markets and task technologies and so on. Contingency theory has come to mean, therefore, that the effective manager has, and knows how to use, many leadership styles as each is appropriate to a particular situation.

-James Owens

D. **Thumbnail Sketches of Fifteen Leadership Style Profile Types:**

1. **TRANSFORMATIVE LEADER**

    - (HIGH Influential Doer, HIGH Analytical Thinker, HIGH Affiliative Helper, HIGH Intuitive Innovator)

    - The transformative leader performs effectively in virtually any situation, having a balance of the qualities and skills of the influential doer, analytical thinker, affiliative helper and intuitive innovator. The transformative leader represents a leadership paradigm that values a range of characteristic attributes of each of the styles, and possession of a variety of skills at getting tasks done, achieving excellence and quality, working cooperatively with others, and bringing about change. Characteristics of each of the four group participation styles are moderated or balanced by elements of the other styles. Transformative leaders (also called transformational leaders) are proactive, rational, collaborative and creative innovators who continually improve their reflective practice and organizational skills, team learning and shared vision skills, task mastery and achievement skills, and reframing and systems thinking skills.

Time past and time future
   What might have been and what has been
      Point to one end, which is always present . . .
The detail of the pattern is movement.

-T. S. Elliot

> *If you want one year of prosperity, grow grain.*
> *If you want ten years of prosperity, grow trees.*
> *If you want one hundred years of prosperity,*
> *grow people.*
>
> *-Chinese proverb*

2. MANAGEMENT TEAM LEADER

- (HIGH Influential Doer, HIGH Analytical Thinker, HIGH Affiliative Helper, LOW Intuitive innovator)

- The management team leader is much in demand. This leader combines the skills of the doer, the thinker and the helper. However, major change may present a problem for these leaders as they prefer to modify the present system with few and small changes. This leader believes in the potential of team members, involves them effectively in decision making and collaboration, facilitates action and mutual responsibility, promotes joint organizational efforts, and the achievement of quality and excellence.

3. ANALYTICAL CHANGE LEADER

- (HIGH Influential Doer, HIGH Analytical Thinker, LOW Affiliative Helper, HIGH Intuitive Innovator)

- The analytical change leader combines the skills of the doer, thinker, and innovator. Here is a leader for change who gets things done and thinks change through. But there may be a tendency to be less willing to include others in change planning and evaluation. These leaders tend to rely on their own competence and expertise and expect others to recognize this and go along.

4. RELATIONAL CHANGE LEADER

- (HIGH Influential Doer, LOW Analytical Thinker, HIGH Affiliative Helper, HIGH Intuitive Innovator)

- The relational change leader combines the skills of the doer, helper and innovator. This leader's approach to change is to involve people and enlist them in the project. A project may be postponed or abandoned unless virtually everyone agrees to the change. Sometimes in the desire to get everyone to agree, projects may be too compromised to work well. Study and analysis may be insufficient, especially if people share the leader's enthusiasm and want to move quickly.

5. **TASK LEADER**

- (HIGH Influential Doer, HIGH Analytical Thinker, LOW Affiliative Helper, LOW Intuitive Innovator)

- Task leaders once reigned supreme, and still represent a very common pattern of leadership. Authoritative task leaders combine the skills of the doer and thinker earning a reputation for getting things done and doing them well. Their people skills tend to be lower and group members often complain about such leaders for their lack of human relations skills. These leaders tend to resist change (unless they initiate it) because it disorganizes their work patterns. Such leaders need to develop linkages with those having the skills of people specialists and change specialists, and work to develop these skills in themselves.

6. **RELATIONAL LEADER**

- (HIGH Influential Doer, LOW Analytical Thinker, HIGH Affiliative Helper, LOW Intuitive Innovator)

- The relational leader puts people first and combines the styles of doer and helper. This leader wants to lead but may not have developed the requisite organizational and thinking skills. It is not unusual for the task to be sacrificed if the leader feels the people cost is too high. Maintaining good human relationships is the most important thing to the relational leader. Initially they are loved by all for their human qualities, but ultimately are criticized for their lack of careful planning and ineffective organization, unless they have task specialists on their staffs.

7. **INITIATING CHANGE LEADER**

- (HIGH Influential Doer, LOW Analytical Thinker, LOW Affiliative Helper, HIGH Intuitive Innovator)

- Initiating change leaders, combining the skills of doer and innovator, relish change. When there is a change to be made they'll take the lead and do what it takes to make it happen. They may be surprised by the consequences and the resistance their approach creates. They need to develop collaborative skills in involving others and to develop analytical skills in creating more effective strategies.

> *The test of a first-rate intelligence is the ability to hold two opposed ideas in mind at the same time and still retain the ability to function*
> *-F. Scott Fitzgerald*

8. **CHANGE SPECIALIST**

- (LOW Influential Doer, HIGH Analytical Thinker, HIGH Affiliative Helper, HIGH Intuitive Innovator)

- You want change? The change specialist can help. This specialist brings change skills to the task, plus collaboration skills, and analytical skills. They are ideal team members. As change specialists they will be willing to help leaders put together a change program that will work, and to help them effectively involve those who will be expected to carry out the change.

9. **STAFF SPECIALIST**

- (LOW Influential Doer, HIGH Analytical Thinker, HIGH Affiliative Helper, LOW Intuitive Innovator)

- The staff specialist is someone who is competent and responsible in carrying out tasks assigned and skilled in human relations, good at getting work done and at working with others, and willing to let the formal leader do the leading (and take the credit).

10. **PROBLEM SOLVING SPECIALIST**

- (LOW Influential Doer, HIGH Analytical Thinker, LOW Affiliative Helper, HIGH Intuitive Innovator)

- A problem solving specialist is high in analytical thinking skills and high in innovative and experimental change skills. This specialist is ideal for trouble shooting and problem solving, just the person to help bring creative resolutions to task and system problems.

11. **HUMAN RELATIONS SPECIALIST**

- (LOW Influential Doer, LOW Analytical Thinker, HIGH Affiliative Helper, HIGH Intuitive Innovator)

- The human relations specialist is valued in maintaining staff morale and as someone concerned with improving the atmosphere and climate of the system. High in helping skills and change skills these specialists seek innovative ways to create and build a collaborative climate.

> *There is little point in general models if they do not give rise to specific conceptual derivations and empirical applications which illuminate, in however modest degree, significant day-to-day practice.*
>
> *-Jacob W. Getzels*

12. TASK SPECIALIST

- (LOW Influential Doer, HIGH Analytical Thinker, LOW Affiliative Helper, LOW Intuitive Innovator)

- Task specialists can be counted on to do quality work. Excellence is the goal. They often prefer to work alone to assure that tasks get done right the first time. Their highest recognition is a job well done. They serve leaders well with specific task assignments.

13. PEOPLE SPECIALIST

- (LOW Influential Doer, LOW Analytical Thinker, HIGH Affiliative Helper, LOW Intuitive Innovator)

- People specialists feel an ongoing responsibility for group morale and the social emotional climate of the system but may have little or no interest in the task. They are sensitive to the nuances of what is going on with people's feelings and can provide valuable information to leaders willing to listen. Of all types, they are likely to be the most willing to do routine tasks provided their social needs are being met.

14. ACTION SPECIALIST

- (HIGH Influential Doer, LOW Analytical Thinker, LOW Affiliative Helper, LOW Intuitive innovator)

- Action specialists come ready for action. They may try to take charge and are ready "to make things run and get things done." They need to temper their initiating and directing skills by valuing and developing more thinker, helper and innovator skills. Action specialists need to listen to others to avoid rejection by those who see them as "just wanting to boss other people around."

15. IDEA SPECIALIST

- (LOW Influential Doer, LOW Analytical Thinker, LOW Affiliative Helper, HIGH Intuitive Innovator)

- Idea specialists come "loaded with ideas." Their readiness and willingness to "jump into change" and "change things around" need the tempering of doing, thinking and helping skills. The development of such skills added to their intuitive idea generation will moderate what others may see as a person out-of-touch, disorganized, and fantasy bound.

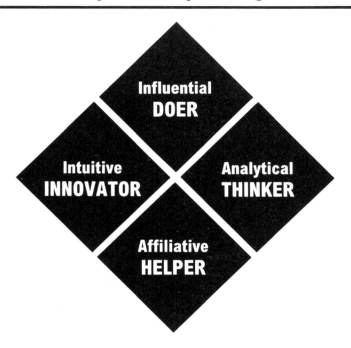

Dynamic Synergy of Styles and Skills

A. The point of recognizing our own "four group participation styles," is to emphasize **the importance of developing a "balance" among the four modes.** We are all a mix of the four styles, though one or more style may be relatively stronger in us. The issue is not to deny or throttle our strengths, but to nurture and develop our areas of lesser strength. We need to become more whole, more complete, more rounded, and learn to function creatively and flexibly and thoughtfully in the face of changing situations of ambiguity and uncertainty.

B. **The transformative leader is an ideal toward which we all can strive.** The transformative leader brings to each group or organization of which he/she is a part, requisite skills for action, collaboration, excellence, and creativity. He/she has collaborative skills to complement action skills, excellence skills to complement creativity skills, action skills to complement excellence skills, creativity skills to complement collaborative skills, excellence skills to complement collaborative skills, creativity skills to complement action skills, and so on in dynamic synergy.

C. The greater **the variety of leadership skills** a leader develops and appropriately utilizes, the more effective the leader is likely to be in various group situations. Every individual has the capacity to learn and develop any leadership skill with practice. The problem is that all of us tend to continue to develop those skills we have already mastered and feel comfortable doing and we tend to neglect development of those skills we have not mastered and do not feel comfortable doing. Transformative leadership requires the broadest range of leadership skills and a commitment to continuing learning.

218

1. **Seventy-two Leadership Skills for Transformative Leaders:**

INFLUENTIAL DOER
Action Skills

Advocating
Assigning Tasks
Controlling
Coordinating
Delegating
Directing
Goal Setting
Initiating Action
Managing
Moving Forward
Organizing
Overseeing
Persuading
Planning
Priortizing
Taking Action
Supervising
Task Structuring

ANALYTICAL THINKER
Excellence Skills

Analyzing
Assessing Resources
Charting
Clarifying Issues
Critiquing
Data Collection
Defining Problems
Diagnosing
Elaborating
Evaluating
Fact Finding
Information Seeking
Logical Thinking
Rational Planning
Stating Objectives
Summarizing
Testing Feasibility
Using Statistical Tools

AFFILIATIVE HELPER
Collaboration Skills

Communicating
Compromising
Consensus Taking
Cooperating
Enabling
Encouraging
Expressing Group Feeling
Following
Gate Keeping
Harmonizing
Linking
Mediating
Norm Setting
Protecting Traditions
Reconciling
Supporting
Team Working
Tension Relieving

INTUITIVE INNOVATOR
Creativity Skills

Brainstorming
Creating Ideas
Creative Adaptation
Creative Problem Solving
Critical Thinking
Designing
Dialogue
Examining Assumptions
Generating Alternatives
Imagining Solutions
Inquiry
Reflection
Reframing
Reinventing
Rethinking
Systems Thinking
Trouble-shooting
Visualizing

D. Fortunately, a **transformative team** can be achieved without even one member of the team being a transformative leader!

E. Just as individual transformative leadership is defined as having a balance of group participation styles, so transformative teams can be defined in terms of a balanced mix of leadership style profile types, each team member bringing a particular mix of proactive, rational, collaborative and creative strengths to develop a synergism within the whole team which, as a team, continues to learn and improve its proactive leadership skills, collaborative teamwork skills, excellence and quality improvement skills, and creative innovational and change skills.

1. Those high in **Influential Doer** skills ask such questions as:

   ● What has to be done to accomplish the goal?
   ● What exactly is the situation?
   ● What has been done?
   ● How do we get started?

2. Those high in **Analytical Thinker** skills ask such questions as:

   ● What are the pros and cons?
   ● What are the logical consequences?
   ● Is there data to support expected outcomes?
   ● What are the costs/benefits?

3. Those high in **Affiliative Helper** skills ask such questions as:

   ● How will the people concerned react to the outcome?
   ● Who is committed to carry out the solution?
   ● How much do I care about what may happen?
   ● Will the outcome contribute to group harmony?

4. Those high in **Intuitive Innovator** skills ask such questions as:

   ● What are other ways for solving this problem?
   ● What are the implications beyond the facts?
   ● What are the possibilities open for us?
   ● What is this problem analogous to?

> *Inventions of alternates is just what scientists seldom undertake except during the pre-paradigm stage of their science's development and at very special occasions during the subsequent evolution. So long as the tools a paradigm supplies continue to prove capable of solving the problems it defines, science moves fastest and penetrates most deeply through confident employment of those tools.*
>
> *-Thomas S. Kuhn*

F. A team can achieve maximal functioning with a mix of leadership style profile types. The key is that each member of the team values the differences and appreciates the unique contributions every other member brings to the team:

    ● Three dimensional Management Team Leaders, Analytical Change Leaders, Relational Change Leaders, and Change Specialists

    ● Two dimensional Task Leaders, Relational Leaders, Initiating Change Leaders, Staff Specialists, Problem-Solving Specialists, and Human Relation Specialists

    ● One dimensional Task Specialists, People Specialists, Action Specialists, and Idea Specialists

G. **In the mathematics of teams, various combinations of threes and twos and ones make FOUR and the equivalent of Transformative Leadership is achieved in teamworking!**

H. This is not to imply that each individual should not strive toward Transformative Leadership as an individual goal of self-development. It is the privilege of each and all to become all each individual can become. **The portrait of this ideal of Transformative Leader might look something like this:**

    1. The Transformative Leader knows how to facilitate the creation and communication of a shared vision.

    2. The Transformative Leader knows how to practice collaborative decision-making.

    3. The Transformative Leader knows how to foster and implement team building and team learning.

    4. The Transformative Leader knows how to develop individual commitment to quality, mastery and continuous improvement.

    5. The Transformative Leader knows how to transform disagreement and conflict into problem-solving and innovation.

    6. The Transformative Leader knows the importance of encouraging people to challenge existing structures, assumptions, and mental models.

    7. The Transformative Leader knows how to facilitate the practice of systems thinking, seeing the interrelatedness of all systems.

    8. The Transformative Leader knows how to involve others in continuing dialogue, inquiry, and reflection-in-action.

221

9. The Transformative Leader identifies with the role of change agent as a designer and facilitator of creative innovational thinking and implementation of change.

10. The Transformative Leader believes in people and treats others with trust and respect.

11. The Transformative Leader possesses a clear and positive sense of purpose and a standard of ethical values.

12. The Transformative Leader can live comfortably with complexity, ambiguity and uncertainty.

13. The Transformative Leader knows how to facilitate his/her own and other's continuing learning.

14. The Transformative Leader knows how to balance competing work and personal demands.

> *I am one, but I am one.*
> *I cannot do everything but I can do something*
> *What I can do, with God's help I will do.*
> *I am one, but I am one.*
> *-Anonymous*

> *The knowledge of human potential is the highest form of knowledge. Learn to use this knowledge to increase your physical, mental and spiritual well-being. For that is the key to peace and harmony within the self, and the world.*
> *-Deepak Chopra*

> *Change—real change—comes from the inside out. It doesn't come from hacking at the leaves of attitude and behavior with quick fix personality ethic techniques. It comes from striking at the root—the fabric of our thought, the fundamental, essential paradigms, which give definition to our character and create the lens through which we see the world.*
> *-Stephen R. Covey*

TRANSFORMATIVE LEADERSHIP

DYNAMIC SYNERGY

ACTION! EXCELLENCE! COLLABORATION! CREATIVITY!

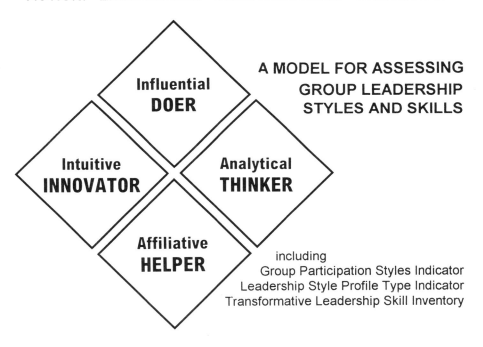

Influential **DOER**

Intuitive **INNOVATOR**

Analytical **THINKER**

Affiliative **HELPER**

A MODEL FOR ASSESSING GROUP LEADERSHIP STYLES AND SKILLS

including
Group Participation Styles Indicator
Leadership Style Profile Type Indicator
Transformative Leadership Skill Inventory

> *One need ask only one question: "What for?" What am I to unify my being for? The reply is: Not for my own sake.*
> *-Martin Buber*

> *If there is no transformation inside each of us, all the structural change in the world will have no impact on our institutions.*
> *-Peter Block*

Group Participation Style Indicator

HOW DO YOU SEE YOURSELF IN GROUPS?

We spend much of our time in groups—all kinds of groups—work groups, social groups, professional groups, ad hoc groups, committees, boards, task forces, to name a few. Below are seven sets of words which are descriptive of ways people see themselves in groups. **Please rank order each set of words** in terms of how well each word describes **your behavior** in a group setting. **There are no right or wrong answers.**

Assign a different rank to each word, giving a 4 to the word which best describes your behavior; 3 to the word which is next most descriptive, 2 to the word which is next and 1 to the word which is least descriptive of your behavior in groups. The total for each row will be 10.

EXAMPLE: _2_ bulldog   _1_ pussycat   _3_ fox   _4_ eagle

1.   a____ conceptual   b____ caring   c____ creative   d____ methodical

2.   a____ supportive   b____ intuitive   c____ practical   d____ evaluative

3.   a____ analytical   b____ amiable   c____ innovative   d____ structured

4.   a____ insightful   b____ realistic   c____ theoretical   d____ wholistic

5.   a____ logical   b____ spontaneous   c____ experimenting   d____ thorough

6.   a____ considerate   b____ risk-taker   c____ decisive   d____ rational

7.   a____ change-oriented   b____ results-oriented   c____ excellence-oriented   d____ relationship-oriented

Russell D. Robinson, Ph.D., University of Wisconsin-Milwaukee

SCORING   Record your ranking number response in the appropriate blank.

	Influential Doer	Analytical Thinker	Affiliative Helper	Intuitive Innovator	
1.	d____	a____	b____	c____	= 10
2.	c____	d____	a____	b____	= 10
3.	d____	a____	b____	c____	= 10
4.	b____	c____	d____	a____	= 10
5.	d____	a____	b____	c____	= 10
6.	c____	d____	a____	b____	= 10
7.	b____	c____	d____	a____	= 10

GROUP PARTICIPATION
STYLE COLUMN TOTALS   ____   ____   ____   ____   = 70

Interpretation of Column Scores: Profile Rating:

23 - 28 = preferred style - very much like me   HIGH
17 - 22 = frequent style - often like me   HIGH
12 - 16 = occasional style - sometimes like me   LOW
 7 - 11 = least preferred style - rarely like me   LOW
 1 - 6 = residual capacity

TO DETERMINE PARTICIPATION STYLE HIGH/LOW PROFILE:

Below circle HIGH for style column score of 17 or higher;
circle LOW for style column score 16 or lower.

High / Low	High / Low	High / Low	High / Low
DOER	THINKER	HELPER	INNOVATOR

Russell D. Robinson, University of Wisconsin-Milwaukee

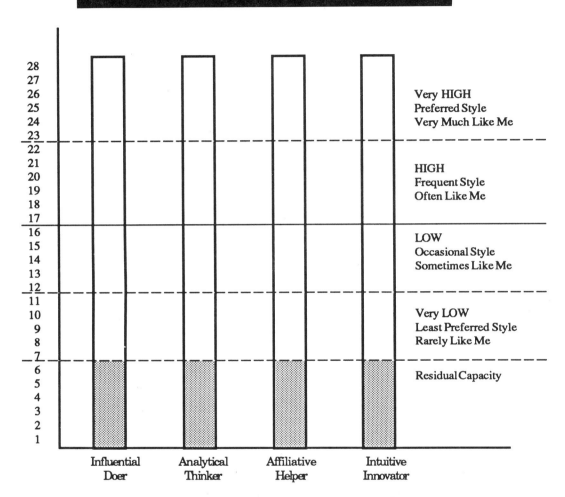

Robinson Group Participation Styles Profile

28				
27				
26				Very HIGH
25				Preferred Style
24				Very Much Like Me
23				
22				
21				HIGH
20				Frequent Style
19				Often Like Me
18				
17				
16				LOW
15				Occasional Style
14				Sometimes Like Me
13				
12				
11				Very LOW
10				Least Preferred Style
9				Rarely Like Me
8				
7				
6				Residual Capacity
5				
4				
3				
2				
1				

Influential Doer   Analytical Thinker   Affiliative Helper   Intuitive Innovator

For a graphic look at your profile, mark your score for each bar on the graph and complete the shading to show height of each bar for your profile.

Note: No one can score below seven in any Group Participation Style. This is symbolic of the fact that each of us has some degree of each style and thus the capacity to further develop that part of ourselves.

Russell D. Robinson, Ph.D., University of Wisconsin-Milwaukee

Robinson Leadership Style Profile Type Identifier

To determine your primary leadership style profile type, bring your high/low profile ratings for DOER, THINKER, HELPER, and INNOVATOR from the preceding score sheet and locate your combination on the matrix below. Underline your leader-ership profile type.

COMBINATIONS OF RELATIVELY HIGH, RELATIVELY LOW
GROUP PARTICIPATION STYLE ORIENTATIONS:

INFLUENTIAL DOER	ANALYTICAL THINKER	AFFILIATIVE HELPER	INTUITIVE INNOVATOR	LEADERSHIP STYLE PROFILE TYPE
High	High	High	High	Transformative Leader
High	High	High	Low	Management Team Leader
High	High	Low	High	Analytical Change Leader
High	Low	High	High	Relational Change Leader
High	High	Low	Low	Task Leader
High	Low	High	Low	Relational Leader
High	Low	Low	High	Initiating Change Leader
Low	High	High	High	Change Specialist
Low	High	High	Low	Staff Specialist
Low	High	Low	High	Problem Solving Specialist
Low	Low	High	High	Human Relations Specialist
Low	High	Low	Low	Task Specialist
Low	Low	High	Low	People Specialist
High	Low	Low	Low	Action Specialist
Low	Low	Low	High	Idea Specialist

Your primary leadership style profile type: _____

Secondary profile type (if any): _____

Note that any column "LOW" score based on 15 or 16 points indicates an "occasional style." Reconfigure your profile considering such column scores as **high**. The resulting profile, if different from your primary type, could be considered a secondary or occasional leadership style.

Note that any column "HIGH" score based on 23 or higher points is **very high** and indicates a "preferred style." Double circle that high to indicate that this represents a strong tendency.

Note that any column "LOW" score based on scores of 11 or below is **very low**. Double circle that low to indicate that this represents an area particularly needing development.

Russell D. Robinson, Ph.D., University of Wisconsin-Milwaukee

Robinson Transformative Leadership Skill Inventory

Please circle the appropriate scale value for each of the skills below in accord with what you feel represents your present competence in each skill.

Scale:	
5	I am very competent in this skill
4	I am quite competent in this skill
3	I have some competence in this skill
2	I have little competence in this skill
1	I have no competence in this skill
0	I don't know what this skill is

1. Advocating   5 4 3 2 1 0
2. Analyzing   5 4 3 2 1 0
3. Assessing Resources   5 4 3 2 1 0
4. Assigning Tasks   5 4 3 2 1 0
5. Brainstorming   5 4 3 2 1 0
6. Charting   5 4 3 2 1 0
7. Clarifying Issues   5 4 3 2 1 0
8. Communicating   5 4 3 2 1 0
9. Compromising   5 4 3 2 1 0
10. Controlling   5 4 3 2 1 0
11. Consensus Taking   5 4 3 2 1 0
12. Cooperating   5 4 3 2 1 0
13. Coordinating   5 4 3 2 1 0
14. Creating Ideas   5 4 3 2 1 0
15. Creative Adaptation   5 4 3 2 1 0
16. Creative Problem Solving 5 4 3 2 1 0
17. Critiquing   5 4 3 2 1 0
18. Critical Thinking   5 4 3 2 1 0
19. Data Collecting   5 4 3 2 1 0
20. Defining Problems   5 4 3 2 1 0
21. Delegating   5 4 3 2 1 0
22. Designing   5 4 3 2 1 0
23. Diagnosing   5 4 3 2 1 0
24. Dialogue   5 4 3 2 1 0
25. Directing   5 4 3 2 1 0
26. Elaborating   5 4 3 2 1 0
27. Encouraging   5 4 3 2 1 0
28. Enabling   5 4 3 2 1 0
29. Examining Assumptions   5 4 3 2 1 0
30. Expressing Group Feeling 5 4 3 2 1 0
31. Evaluating   5 4 3 2 1 0
32. Fact Finding   5 4 3 2 1 0
33. Following   5 4 3 2 1 0
34. Gate Keeping   5 4 3 2 1 0
35. Generating Alternatives 5 4 3 2 1 0
36. Goal Setting   5 4 3 2 1 0
37. Harmonizing   5 4 3 2 1 0
38. Imagining Solutions   5 4 3 2 1 0
39. Information Seeking   5 4 3 2 1 0
40. Initiating Action   5 4 3 2 1 0
41. Inquiry   5 4 3 2 1 0
42. Linking   5 4 3 2 1 0

43. Logical Thinking   5 4 3 2 1 0
44. Managing   5 4 3 2 1 0
45. Mediating   5 4 3 2 1 0
46. Moving Forward   5 4 3 2 1 0
47. Norm Setting   5 4 3 2 1 0
48. Organizing   5 4 3 2 1 0
49. Overseeing   5 4 3 2 1 0
50. Persuading   5 4 3 2 1 0
51. Planning   5 4 3 2 1 0
52. Prioritizing   5 4 3 2 1 0
53. Protecting Traditions   5 4 3 2 1 0
54. Rational Planning   5 4 3 2 1 0
55. Reconciling   5 4 3 2 1 0
56. Reflection   5 4 3 2 1 0
57. Reframing   5 4 3 2 1 0
58. Reinventing   5 4 3 2 1 0
59. Rethinking   5 4 3 2 1 0
60. Risking Action   5 4 3 2 1 0
61. Stating Objectives   5 4 3 2 1 0
62. Summarizing   5 4 3 2 1 0
63. Supervising   5 4 3 2 1 0
64. Supporting   5 4 3 2 1 0
65. Systems Thinking   5 4 3 2 1 0
66. Task Structuring   5 4 3 2 1 0
67. Teamworking   5 4 3 2 1 0
68. Tension Relieving   5 4 3 2 1 0
69. Testing Feasibility   5 4 3 2 1 0
70. Trouble-shooting   5 4 3 2 1 0
71. Using Statistical Tools 5 4 3 2 1 0
72. Visualizing   5 4 3 2 1 0

TRANSFORMATIVE LEADERSHIP INDEX:

Total of all circled values from above _____

289-360	You're on your way!
217-288	You're making strides!
145-216	Improve those skills!
73-144	Learn and practice, learn and practice!
0-72	Enormous underdeveloped potential!

Russell D. Robinson, Ph. D., University of Wisconsin-Milwaukee

Group Participation Style Leadership Skill Indexes

SCORING:

To determine leadership skill indexes for each individual group participation style, transfer your circled values (5-4-3-2-1-0) on the matrix below.

Locate the number for each item on the list below and record the scale value you allocated:

1. _____	2. _____	8. _____	5. _____
4. _____	3. _____	9. _____	14. _____
10. _____	6. _____	11. _____	15. _____
13. _____	7. _____	12. _____	16. _____
21. _____	17. _____	27. _____	18. _____
25. _____	19. _____	28. _____	22. _____
36. _____	20. _____	30. _____	24. _____
40. _____	23. _____	33. _____	29. _____
44. _____	26. _____	34. _____	35. _____
46. _____	31. _____	37. _____	38. _____
48. _____	32. _____	42. _____	41. _____
49. _____	39. _____	45. _____	56. _____
50. _____	43. _____	47. _____	57. _____
51. _____	54. _____	53. _____	58. _____
52. _____	61. _____	55. _____	59. _____
60. _____	62. _____	64. _____	65. _____
63. _____	69. _____	67. _____	70. _____
66. _____	71. _____	68. _____	72. _____
TOTALS _____	_____	_____	_____
Influential Doer	**Analytical Thinker**	**Affiliative Helper**	**Intuitive Innovator**

Interpreting your skill index for each participation style:

73-90	You perceive considerable skill strength in this participation style
55-72	Your perceived skills need some improvement in this participation style
37-54	Your perceived skills need much improvement in this participation style
0-36	An area ripe for skill development

Russell D. Robinson, Ph.D., University of Wisconsin-Milwaukee

Robinson Leadership Style Profile Data

Summary of Research and Findings

Following is summarized the research and findings with respect to the Group Participation Styles Indicator and Leadership Style Profile Type Identifier.

Group Participation Styles Indicator

The Group Participation Styles Indicator instrument "How Do You See Yourself in Groups?" contains twenty-eight words descriptive of ways people may see themselves behaving in a group setting. Respondents are asked to assign a rank to each word in seven series of four words representing different "styles."

The words were initially drawn from leadership, change, motivation, learning, and personality literature where descriptive words are commonly used as a vehicle to help people identify "styles," usually done by rank ordering contrasting words by forced choice. A large number of such words were identified and reduced to seven sets of four, and piloted with 90 respondents. In a number of cases, certain descriptive words were substituted when respondents frequently questioned the meaning of a word. For example, "passionate" in an earlier version was changed to "caring", "empathic" was changed to "amiable", and so on, until the instrument reached its present form.

The four styles are denominated **Influential Doer**, **Analytical Thinker**, **Affiliative Helper**, and **Intuitive Innovator**. The table below lists the seven descriptive words chosen to be compared across rows for ranking to identify each style.

TABLE I. DESCRIPTIVE WORDS TO IDENTIFY STYLES

INFLUENTIAL DOER	ANALYTICAL THINKER	AFFILIATIVE HELPER	INTUITIVE INNOVATOR
Results-oriented	Excellence-oriented	Relationship-oriented	Change-oriented
Decisive	Rational	Considerate	Risk-taker
Thorough	Logical	Spontaneous	Experimenting
Realistic	Theoretical	Wholistic	Insightful
Structured	Analytical	Amiable	Innovative
Practical	Evaluative	Supportive	Intuitive
Methodical	Conceptual	Caring	Creative

Forced rankings of 4, 3, 2, or 1 for the words in each row are intended to indicate a respondent's perception of the relative importance of each of these words as descriptive of "style." Each row must add up to 10. Total scores for a "style" column may range from a low of 7 to a high of 28.

Robinson Group Participation Styles Profile

For visual comparison purposes, column scores are plotted on the **"Robinson Group Participation Styles Profile."** Scores within each style can be viewed as very low (7-11), low (12-16), high (17-22), or very high (23-28). No respondent can receive a style score under 7, symbolic of the fact that every individual has at least a "residual" of each of the four styles.

Robinson Leadership Style Profile Type Identifier

Any column score of 17 or over in any group participation style is considered "High" and a score of 16 or under is considered "Low". The resulting column High or Low score ratings from the "Group Participation Styles Indicator" are transferred to the **"Robinson Leadership Style Profile Type Identifier"** which identifies for each respondent one of 15 possible combinations of Highs and Lows, excluding the possibility of Low-Low-Low-Low which the instrument does not permit.

A particular combination for each individual identifies a primary **"Leadership Style Profile Type."** The **"primary profile type"** represents an individual's preferred style of leadership. A **"secondary profile type"** may be identified by considering any "low" scores of 15 or 16 as "high" and reconfiguring the profile. The secondary style may or may not be different from the primary type, and represents an "occasional style."

Transformative Leader

An underlying assumption is that high (17+) scores in **all four** Group Participation Styles constitute an "ideal" leadership type called "Transformative Leader." As the total points for all Group Participation Styles together cannot exceed a total of 70, the instrument provides a very narrow "window" for designation of Transformative Leader as one's primary profile type. As one might expect, relatively few persons are so identified. But when the window is opened to include scores of 15 or higher, relatively more persons are designated Transformative Leader as their "secondary style."

231

Research Sample and Data Analysis

Data have been collected via a purposive sampling process from 973 adults engaged in adult and continuing education, workplace training or elementary and secondary education. The sample included those in administrative roles such as administrators, supervisors, principals, managers and directors, and those in non-administrative roles such as teachers, trainers, workers and adult students.

As is shown by Graph A, the population sample was relatively evenly distributed between administrative (48.6%) and non-administrative (51.4%) positions occupied and with respect to experience in roles, those with four or less years of experience (52.0%) as compared to those with five years or more experience (48.0%). In terms of age, the sample had a greater number in the 41 years or older group (57.9%) than in the 40 years or younger group (42.1%). With respect to gender, more than two-thirds of the group were females (68.4%) and less than one-third were males (31.6%).

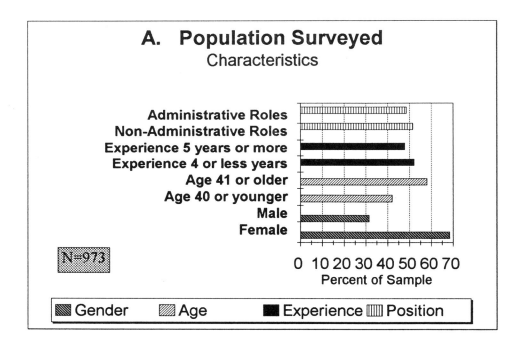

The data from 973 adults were analyzed using a variety of methods including frequencies, Multivariate Analysis of Variance (MANOVA), one way Analysis of Variance (ANOVA) and Chi-Square Test (Crosstabs). These analyses compared Leadership Style Profile Types or Group Participation Style subgroups (Doers, Thinkers, Helpers, Innovators) with respect to position, experience, age, and gender.

Data for 255 of the respondents were further analyzed using crosstabs to compare each of the 28 descriptive words used to identify Group Participation Style subgroups. For each of the 28 descriptors, Pearson Chi-square values were computed between high and low scores for each of the words to designate Doers, Thinkers, Helpers, and Innovators.

Results: Descriptor Words and Group Participation Styles

Table II summarizes the crosstabulation findings comparing high and low scores by showing Chi-square values for each descriptor constituting each Group Participation Style category.

TABLE II. PEARSON CHI-SQUARE VALUES FOR DESCRIPTOR WORDS BY GROUP PARTICIPATION STYLE GROUPS
(degrees of freedom = 3)   N = 255

Descriptors	DOERS	THINKERS	HELPERS	INNOVATORS
DOER Words				
Methodical	64.98875	7.51013	29.49371	43.30335
Practical	72.75284	12.64276	10.04698	28.93581
Structured	96.87111	5.24391	14.57563	45.35349
Realistic	77.98741	5.55531	4.18953	21.74553
Thorough	55.70771	8.74973	11.08235	41.95992
Decisive	24.92782	2.90266	19.07951	12.05116
Results-oriented	42.27691	3.33064	11.83379	10.92911
THINKER Words				
Conceptual	2.97985	55.15336	24.22839	9.19301
Evaluative	11.65786	32.15955	30.96456	4.52788
Analytical	7.81811	64.43662	17.24281	3.86284
Theoretical	4.84415	17.34573	20.38866	2.07403
Logical	17.45587	60.36601	10.65539	32.76493
Rational	22.64796	54.39838	15.81386	29.87665
Excellence-oriented	10.41563	33.58996	15.45359	11.62402

233

TABLE II continued

Descriptors	DOERS	THINKERS	HELPERS	INNOVATORS
HELPER Words				
Caring	10.86117	33.41742	94.59728	7.61503
Supportive	14.12863	20.72208	72.47861	1.26945
Amiable	9.74161	32.73741	65.94585	13.39975
Wholistic	24.70121	9.23832	15.68952	7.38578
Spontaneous	25.10625	71.76296	30.72763	15.4672
Considerate	11.86337	12.09969	80.91288	4.94281
Relationship-oriented	13.00668	19.93832	83.84158	3.01633
INNOVATOR Words				
Creative	28.32821	17.23445	3.60321	83.31083
Intuitive	46.80254	10.27507	0.80822	54.18487
Innovative	37.52472	19.69043	2.57857	104.03673
Insightful	26.24608	5.46124	5.66176	23.56473
Experimenting	46.06762	9.14928	8.15466	65.79751
Risk-taking	26.43239	23.77158	4.55591	81.66492
Change-oriented	19.8671	3.02161	8.59922	45.01372

The data indicate that, for each descriptor word, the highest values fall under the expected Doer, Thinker, Helper, or Innovator designation, with only four exceptions out of the 28 words.

"Theoretical" had a somewhat higher value for the category of Helpers than the expected higher value for the category of Thinkers; "wholistic" had a somewhat higher value for Doers than the expected higher value for the category of Helpers; the word "spontaneous" had a substantially higher value for Thinkers than the expected higher value for Helpers; and the word "insightful" had a somewhat higher value for Doers than the expected higher value for Innovators. Of the 112 Chi-square computations, 83% (all but 19) were statistically significant at $p < .05$ and 76% (85 out of the 112 computations) were statistically significant at $p < .01$ level.

Results: Group Participation Styles Score Variance

Table III shows the results of a multivariate analysis of variance (MANOVA) comparing gender, age, experience and position and their interactions on the four group participation style summary scores. MANOVA is a statistical technique for determining whether groups differ on more than one dependent variable simultaneously. It is quite similar to the t test and to analysis of variance, except that a MANOVA can be done to determine statistically significant differences on all the variables considered together. The MANOVA determines if the subgroups representing the four independent variables (position, experience, age, gender) differ significantly with respect to each of the four dependent variables (group participation style scores for Doer, Thinker, Helper, Innovator).

When all the variables were considered together, there were significant differences (at $p < .05$ level) with respect to the independent variable of gender, and the interaction of age and gender, of position, age and gender, and of position, experience, age and gender.

TABLE III. MANOVA. MULTIVARIATE TEST OF SIGNIFICANCE OF INTERACTIONS OF GENDER, AGE, EXPERIENCE, AND POSITION ON GROUP PARTICIPATION STYLE SUMMARY SCORES   N=973

Source of Variation	Hotellings Approx. F	Statistical Significance
Gender	9.56829	p = .000
Age	1.81992	
Experience	0.65771	
Position	0.42127	
Position x Gender	1.18835	
Position x Age	0.90551	
Position x Experience	0.49073	
Experience x Age	0.46134	
Experience x Gender	1.41886	
Age x Gender	2.61588	p = .034
Position x Experience x Age	0.77819	
Position x Experience x Gender	1.69912	
Position x Age x Gender	2.47006	p = .043
Experience x Age x Gender	1.10951	
Position x Experience x Age x Gender	2.50352	p = .041

The table below shows univariate F-Tests on each dependent variable, considering Doer, Thinker, Helper and Innovator separately. The tests indicate several significant differences (at p <.05 level).

TABLE IV. ANOVA. UNIVARIATE F-TESTS OF SIGNIFICANCE OF INTERACTIONS OF GENDER, AGE, EXPERIENCE, AND POSITION ON GROUP PARTICIPATION STYLE SCORES OF DOERS, THINKERS, HELPERS, INNOVATORS   Statistical significance (at p <.05) N=973

Source of Variation	DOERS	THINKERS	HELPERS	INNOVATORS
Gender Age Experience Position		p = .000	p = .000	
Position x Gender Position x Age Position x Experience Experience x Age Experience x Gender Age x Gender	p = .035	 p = .039 p = .023		 p = .004
Position x Experience x Age Position x Experience x Gender Position x Age x Gender Experience x Age x Gender		 p = .026		 p = .038 p = .014
Position x Experience x Age x Gender		p = .018		p = .009

For **Doers**, there was statistical significance in variance in two way interactions of position and gender. For **Thinkers**, there was statistical significance in the case of gender alone, in two way interactions of experience and gender, and age and gender, in three way interactions of position, experience and gender, and in four way interactions of position, experience, age, and gender. For **Helpers**, there was statistical significance in variance in the case of gender alone. For **Innovators**, there was statistical significance in variance in the case of two way interactions of age and gender, and in three way interactions of position, experience and gender, and position, age, and gender, and four way interactions of position, experience, age and gender.

The table below shows Chi-square values comparing the frequency of participation styles between administrative and non-administrative positions, less than four years and five or more years of experience, ages 40 years and younger and 41 years or older, and male and female for Doers, Thinkers, Helpers, and Innovators. Gender is the most important factor for each Group Participation Style, and statistically significant (at p <.05) for Thinkers, Helpers and Innovators.

TABLE V. CHI-SQUARE VALUES WITHIN CHARACTERISTICS AND GROUP PARTICIPATION STYLES Significance (at p <.05) N=973

	%	DOERS	THINKERS	HELPERS	INNOVATORS
POSITION		18.55724	19.06448	20.33075	14.32868
Administrative	48.6				
Non-administrative	51.4				
EXPERIENCE		19.56851	17.95737	18.03496	15.74348
4 years or less	52.0				
5 years or more	48.0				
AGE		21.78117	19.19315	27.49889	18.92724
40 and younger	42.1				
41 and older	57.9				
GENDER		33.04215	68.62717	41.53351	36.04005
Male	31.6				
Female	68.4	p = .080	p = .000	p = .005	p = .022

Results: Distribution of Group Participation Style Scores

Graph B on the following page shows the frequency distribution of scores for Influential Doer, Analytical Thinker, Affiliative Helper and Intuitive Innovator. Combining group participation style high scores of 17-22 and very high scores of 23-28, the largest number of "high scores" for all respondents were in the Helper style category with 67% percent of respondents scoring 17 or above. Doer scores of 17 or more were in second place (57%), Innovator scores in third place (54%) and the Thinker category with the lowest number of high scores (52%). Low score extremes (7-11) were in Helper and Thinker categories; the highest score extremes (23-28) in Helper scores.

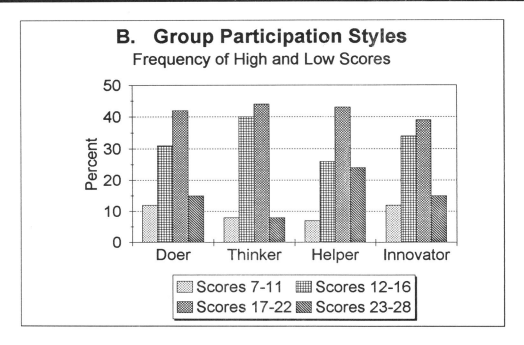

B. Group Participation Styles
Frequency of High and Low Scores

Graph C shows Group Participation Style Mean Scores for "high" Doers, Thinkers, Helpers and Innovators compared with overall distribution of mean scores for the sample. The graph shows composite Group Participation Style Profiles for each group.

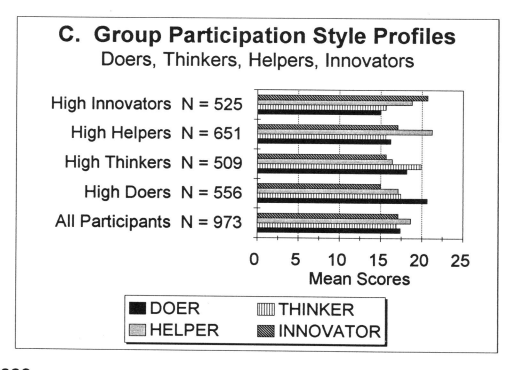

C. Group Participation Style Profiles
Doers, Thinkers, Helpers, Innovators

Results: Leadership Style Profile Types

Frequencies by Leadership Style Profile Types of 973 respondents are reported below.

TABLE VI.   Leadership Style Profile Types

LEADERSHIP STYLE PROFILE TYPE	NUMBER	PERCENT
Transformative Leader	11	1.1
Management Team Leader	121	12.4
Analytical Change Leader	60	6.2
Relational Change Leader	82	8.4
Task Leader	139	14.3
Relational Leader	95	9.8
Initiating Change Leader	35	3.6
Change Specialist	77	7.9
Staff Specialist	42	4.3
Problem Solving Specialist	55	5.7
Human Relations Specialist	195	20.1
Task Specialist	5	0.5
People Specialist	29	2.9
Action Specialist	13	1.3
Idea Specialist	15	1.5
Totals	973	100

By far the most frequent Leadership Style Profile Type was the Human Relations Specialist, one fifth of the sample (20.1%). Next most frequent was the Task Leader (14.3%), the Management Team Leader (12.4%), Relational Leader (9.8%), Relational Change Leader (8.4%), Change Specialist (7.9%), Analytical Change Leader (6.2%) and the Problem-solving Specialist (5.7%). Together these account for nearly 85% of persons surveyed.

239

The other fifteen percent included Staff Specialists (4.3%), Initiating Change Leaders (3.6%) and People Specialists (2.9%), and lower percentages for Task Specialists, Action Specialists, Idea Specialists and Transformative Leaders.

Crosstabulations were computed for each of the 15 Leadership Style Profile Types. The frequency counts of position, experience, age, and gender within each profile type were converted to percentages and a Chi-Square computed. The Pearson test yielded statistical significance (at $p<.01$, df = 14) for position (p = .00570), experience (p = .01896), and gender (p = .0005). All but age (p = .08658) proved significant.

Likelihood ratios were also computed with respect to the variables of position, experience, age and gender. The following graphs numbered from 1 to 15 present for each variable the degree to which a person with a particular leadership type would be more likely or less likely to be occupying an administrative or non-administrative position, have four years or less experience in the role or five years or more, be age 40 or younger or age 41 or older, and whether the individual would be more likely or less likely to be male or female.

In summary, the data indicate:

Transformative Leaders (11 persons [1.1%]) were more likely to be younger and have less experience.

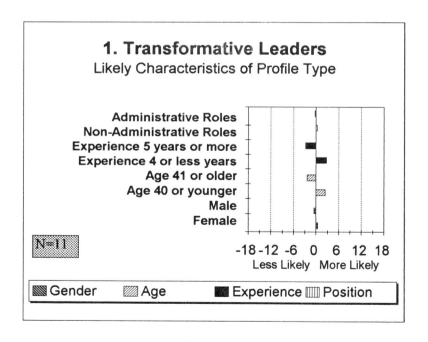

Management Team Leaders (121 persons [12.4%]), the third largest group in the study, were much more likely to be in non-administrative roles, to be have less experience, and to be younger.

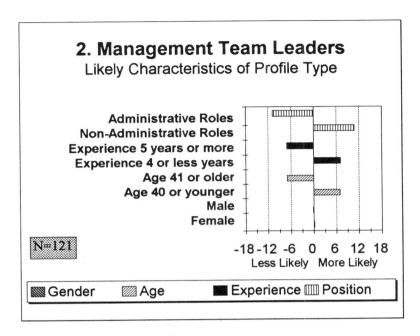

Analytical Change Leaders (60 persons [6.2%]) were more likely to be administrators and to be male, and much more likely to be more experienced and to be older.

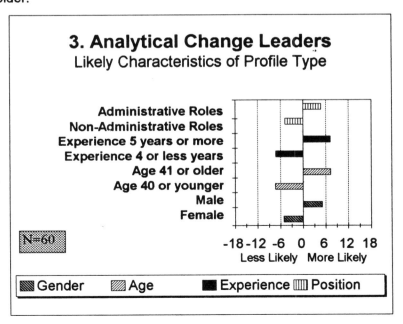

Relational Change Leaders (82 persons [9.8%]) were very much more likely to be female and much more like to have 5 or more years of experience and to be older.

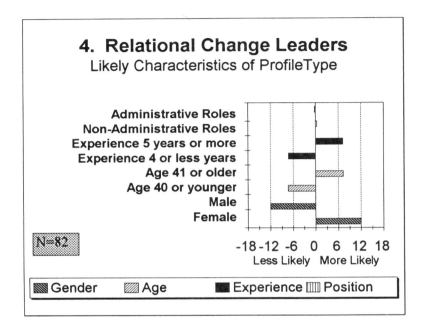

Task Leaders (139 persons [14.3%]), the second largest group in the study, were very much more likely to be male.

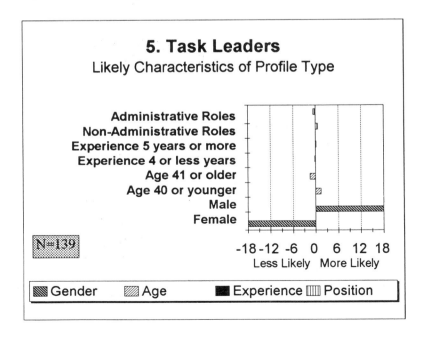

Relational Leaders (95 persons [9.8%]) were more likely to be found in administrative roles, more likely to be experienced and very much more likely to be female.

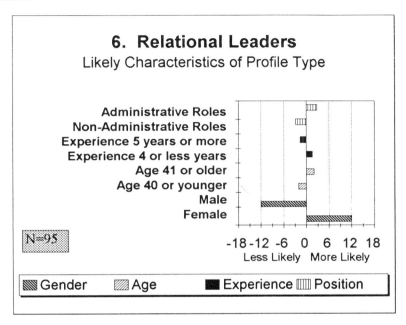

Initiating Change Leaders (35 persons [3.6%]) were more likely to be in administrative roles and to be female.

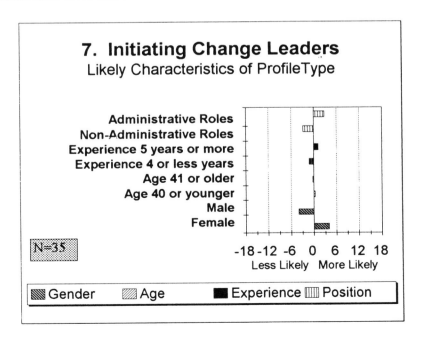

Change Specialists (77 persons [7.9%]) were more likely to be in non-administrative roles, to be older and to be male, and much more likely to have five years or more experience.

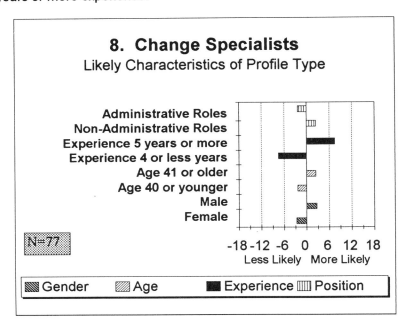

Staff Specialists (42 persons [4.3%]) were more likely to be younger, have less experience, and much more likely to be male.

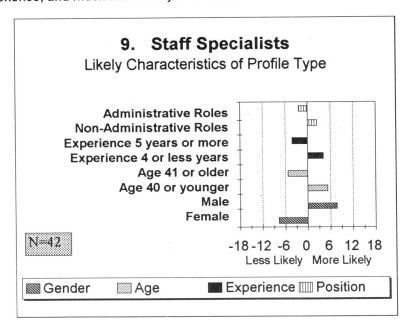

Problem Solving Specialists (55 persons [5.7%]) were more likely to be in administrative roles, to be more experienced, to be older and to be male.

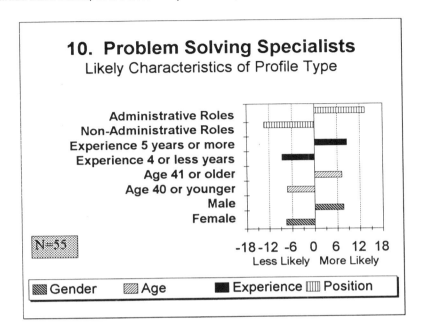

Human Relations Specialists (194 persons [20.1%]), the largest group in the study, were much more likely to be female, and to have four years or less experience, and more likely to be younger.

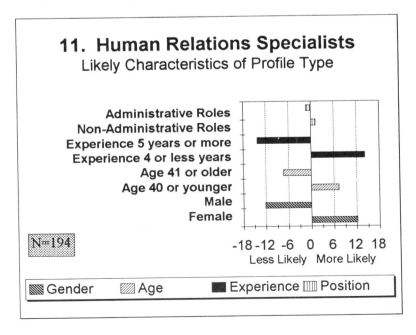

Task Specialists (5 persons [.5%]) were a little more likely to have more experience and to be older.

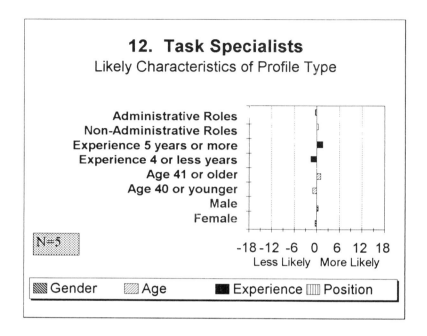

People Specialists (29 persons [2.9%]) were more likely to be in non-administrative roles, to be younger and to be female.

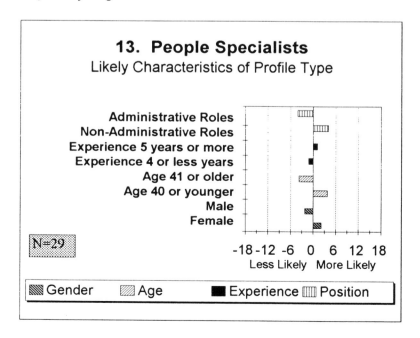

Action Specialists (13 persons [1.3%]) were a little more likely to be in administrative roles and have less experience and to be older.

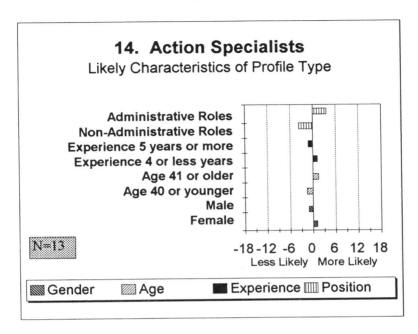

Idea Specialists (15 persons [1.5%]) were a little more likely to have less experience.

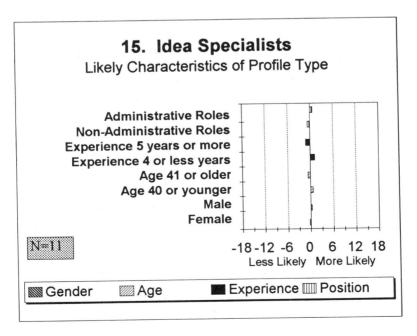

It is obvious that gender plays a major role with respect to group participation and leadership style. Womens' profiles compared to men show disproportionate numbers of Relational Change Leaders (high Doer, Helper, Innovator), Relational Leaders (high Doer, Helper), Initiating Change Leaders (high Doer, Innovator), Human Relations Specialists (high Helper, Innovator) and People Specialists (high Helper). Men are disproportionately Task Leaders (high Doer, Thnker), Analytical Change Leaders (high Doer, Thinker, Innovator), Change Specialists (high Thinker, Helper, Innovator), Staff Specialists (high Thinker, Helper), and Problem Solving Specialists (high Thinker, Innovator). Gender appears not to be relevant in relation to Transformative Leaders (high Doer, Thinker, Helper, Innovator), and Management Team Leaders (high Doer, Thinker, Helper).

Secondary Leadership Styles

Graphs D and E display the distribution of "secondary leadership style profiles" compared with the "primary leadership style profiles" reported in the data above. Secondary profiles are obtained by recalculating previous "low" scores of 15 or 16 for any group participation style as if they were "high". These new configurations represent "occasional styles" and suggest a potential for development. That is, the respondents are already relatively "closer" to "high" and presumably more "ready" to learn the leadership skills in their "occasional style" categories.

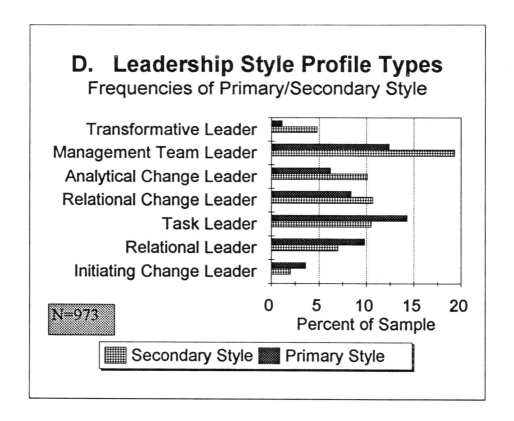

D. Leadership Style Profile Types
Frequencies of Primary/Secondary Style

N=973

248

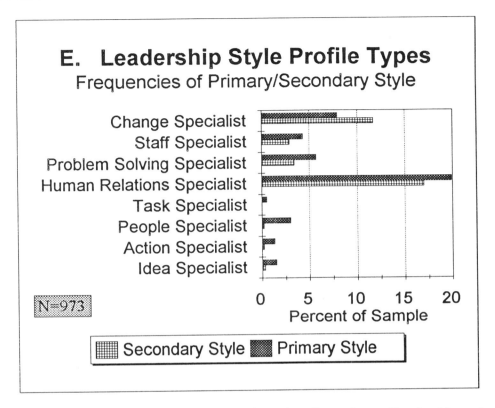

The prognosis is optimistic for developing other dimensions of leadership and learning additional leadership skills. Transformative Leaders (high Doer, Thinker, Helper, Innovator) increase when secondary occasional profiles are calculated. There are likewise increases in the percentage of Management Team Leaders (high Doer, Thinker, Helper), Analytical Change Leaders (high Doer, Thinker, Innovator), Relational Change Leaders (high Doer, Helper, Innovator) and Change Specialists (high Thinker, Helper, Innovator).

In contrast, in the secondary configuration, the proportions of Task Leaders (high Doer, Thinker), Relational Leaders (high Doer, Helper), Initiating Change Leaders (high Doer, Innovator), Human Relations Specialists (high Helper, Innovator), Staff Specialists (high Thinker, Helper), and Problem Solving Specialists (high Thinker, Innovator) all decrease as individuals add other dimensions and improve their balance. Task, People, Action and Idea Specialists all but "disappear."

These data suggest that there are many leaders who already have a predisposition to achieve greater balance and to strengthen additional leadership skills. They are open to shared vision, empowerment, shared decision making, creative change, team learning, and continuing skill development. They are ready to move toward transformative leadership.

249

Worksheets
activities for groups

Also see Transformative Leadership Instruments, 224-229.

1. Group Stem Sentences

Please complete these sentences:

1. When I enter a new group, I feel _____

   _____

   _____

2. When a group meeting begins, I _____

   _____

   _____

3. When I'm in a new group, I feel most comfortable when _____

   _____

   _____

4. When people remain silent, I feel _____

   _____

   _____

5. When someone does all the talking, I _____

   _____

   _____

6. I feel most productive when a leader _____

   _____

   _____

7. I feel annoyed when the leader _____

   _____

   _____

8. In a group, I am most afraid of _____

   _____

   _____

9. Those who really know me, think I am _____

   _____

   _____

251

2. Group Observation Guide

Things to look for:

Participation

Did all have opportunities to participate?
Were some excluded?
Was an effort made to draw people out?
Did a few dominate?

Leadership

Did a leader, as such emerge?
Was a leader designated?
Was leadership shared?
Was there any structuring of the group?

Roles

Who initiated ideas? Were they supported? By whom?
Did anyone block? Who helped push for decisions?
Was there an attempt to summarize or pull together ideas?

Decision Making

Were a lot of ideas suggested before the group began to reach a
    decision?
Did everyone agree to the decisions made?
Who helped influence the decisions of others?
What issues did the group seem to resolve? To not resolve?

Communication

Did people feel free to talk? Was there any interrupting?
Did people really listen to others?
Was there clarification of the points made?
Whom did people look at when they talked? Did they single out
    others, scan the group or not look at anyone?

Sensitivity

Were members sensitive to the needs and concerns of others?
What feelings did you see being expressed, either verbally or
    nonverbally?

252

3. Group Role Check Sheet

	NAME										
TASK	INITIATING										
	INFORMATION SEEKING										
	INFORMATION GIVING										
	CLARIFYING										
	EVALUATING										
	SETTING GOALS										
MAINTENANCE	GATE-KEEPING										
	ENCOURAGING										
	CONSENSUS SEEKING										
	TENSION RELIEVING										
	FOLLOWING/ AGREEING										
	HARMONIZING										
PERSONAL	RECOGNITION SEEKING										
	DOMINATING										
	DISTRACTING/ HORSING AROUND										
	BLOCKING										

4. Reaction Scale

First	*Second*

First

1. To what extent are your opinions and thoughts being solicited by the group? I feel:

   they are □   they are not □   undecided □

2. How satisfied do you feel with the amount and quality of your participation in moving toward a joint decision? I feel:

   satisfied □   not satisfied □   uncertain □

3. How much responsibility for making the decision work do you feel? I feel:

   responsible □   not responsible □   uncertain □

4. How committed do you feel to the decision your group is making? I feel:

   committed □   not committed □   uncertain □

5. How much frustration do you feel as the work on decision goes on? I feel:

   frustrated □   not frustrated □   uncertain □

6. How good is the decision your group is making? I feel:

   it is
   a good
   decision □   it is not
   a good
   decision □   uncertain □

Second

1. To what extent are your opinions and thoughts being solicited by the group? I feel:

   they are □   they are not □   undecided □

2. How satisfied do you feel with the amount and quality of your participation in moving toward a joint decision? I feel:

   satisfied □   not satisfied □   uncertain □

3. How much responsibility for making the decision work do you feel? I feel:

   responsible □   not responsible □   uncertain □

4. How committed do you feel to the decision your group is making? I feel:

   committed □   not committed □   uncertain □

5. How much frustration do you feel as the work on decision goes on? I feel:

   frustrated □   not frustrated □   uncertain □

6. How good is the decision your group is making? I feel:

   it is
   a good
   decision □   it is not
   a good
   decision □   uncertain □

5. Attitudes About Leadership

Leaders who wish to examine their own attitudes may find a guide in the following list of statements. Even among the most effective leaders there will be some disagreement in their attitudes and philosophy. Here are some questions which other leaders have had to face. Check the answer which you feel applies to each statement.

After checking the list, meet in sub-groups of 4 to compare responses. Where you are in disagreement or unsure, the sub-group may change statements so that they can agree.

1. The most important factor in the group's effectiveness is the ability of each member to make a maximum contribution.
    Agree/Unsure/Disagree

2. The most important factor in the group's effectiveness is the wisdom of the leader.
    Agree/Unsure/Disagree

3. Goals set by the total group in the long run will be the best for the group.
    Agree/Unsure/Disagree

4. Often the leader knows better than the group what goals the group should achieve.
    Agree/Unsure/Disagree

5. The most effective group is the one in which each member feels free to lead.
    Agree/Unsure/Disagree

6. All groups need a single leader.
    Agree/Unsure/Disagree

7. The leader must retain some authority over the group.
    Agree/Unsure/Disagree

8. Authority is rightly the property of the total group.
    Agree/Unsure/Disagree

9. The leader loses effectiveness if his/her ideas are challenged too often.
    Agree/Unsure/Disagree

10. An effective group is one whose members are always free to challenge the leader.
    Agree/Unsure/Disagree

11. A leader should try to minimize status differences between him/herself and the group.
    Agree/Unsure/Disagree

12. A leader should have more status and prestige than group members.
    Agree/Unsure/Disagree

13. Most people are too uninformed to make a contribution to a group discussion.
    Agree/Unsure/Disagree

14. A leader should welcome dependence on him/her and use it to teach the group.
    Agree/Unsure/Disagree

15. A leader should hold on to power if he/she uses it wisely and justly.
    Agree/Unsure/Disagree

255

6. Exercise in Group Feedback

Group Participant Feedback Sheet

DIRECTIONS: For each participant, including yourself, write in two major assets and liabilities in regard to personality. These will be read aloud.

PARTICIPANT	ASSETS	LIABILITIES

7.   Exercise in Self-Knowledge

Self-Knowledge and Tally Sheet:

DIRECTIONS: In the spaces below list the major assets and liabilities of your personality. Then place a check mark in front of those aspects of yourself which you have revealed to the participants of the group so far. Next use Worksheet XII to provide feedback to other group participants. When the leader has collected the feedback sheets and reads them aloud, you may use the "Others" column to tally those perceptions of you held by other group participants.

ASSETS

SELF	OTHERS

LIABILITIES

SELF	OTHERS

8. Workplace Motivation Opinionnaire

Directions: The following statements have seven possible responses.

Strongly Agree	Agree	Slightly Agree	Don't Know	Slightly Disagree	Disagree	Strongly Disagree
+3	+2	+1	0	-1	-2	-3

Please mark one of the seven responses by circling the number that corresponds to the response that fits your opinion. For example: If you "Strongly Agree " circle the number "+3." Complete every item.
You have about 10 minutes to do so.

1. Special wage increases should be given to employees who do their jobs very well.   +3 +2 +1 0 -l -2 -3

2. Better job descriptions would be helpful so that employees will know exactly what is expected of them.   +3 +2 +1 0 -l -2 - 3

3. Employees need to be reminded that their jobs are dependent on the company's ability to compete effectively.   +3 +2 +1 0 -l -2 -3

4. A supervisor should give a good deal of attention to the physical working conditions of his employees.   +3 +2 +1 0 -l -2 -3

5. The supervisor ought to work hard to develop a friendly working atmosphere among his/her employees   +3 +2 +1 0 -l -2 - 3

6. individual recognition for above-standard performance means a lot to employees.   +3 +2 +1 0 -l -2 -3

7. Indifferent supervision can often bruise feelings. +3 +2 +1 0 -l -2 -3

8. Employees want to feel that their real skills and capacities are put to use on their jobs.   +3 +2 +1 0 -l -2 -3

9. The company retirement benefits and stock programs are important factors in keeping employees on their jobs.   +3 +2 +1 0 -l -2 -3

10. Almost every job can be made more stimulating and challenging.
+3 +2 +1 0 -l -2 -3

11. Many employees want to give their best in everything they do.
+3 +2 +1 0 -l -2 -3

12. Management could show more interest in the employees by sponsoring social events after hours.   +3 +2 +l 0 -l -2 -3

(continued)

13. Pride in one's work is actually an important reward. +3 +2 +1 0 -I -2 -3

14. Employees want to be able to think of themselves as "the best" at their own jobs.   +3 +2 +1 0 -I -2 -3

15. The quality of the relationships in the informal work group is quite important.   + 3 +2 + I 0 - I -2 -3

16. Individual incentive bonuses would improve the performance of employees. +3 +2 +1 0 - I -2 -3

17. Visibility with upper management is important to employees. +3 +2 +1 0 -I -2 -3

18. Employees generally like to schedule their own work and to make job-related decisions with a minimum of supervision.   +3 +2 +1 0 -I -2 -3

19. Job security is important to employees. +3 +2 +1 0 -I -2 -3

20. Having good equipment to work with is important to employees. +3 +2 +1 0 -I -2 -3

SCORING:

1. Transfer the numbers from the statements above to the appropriate places in the chart below:

Self-actualization	Self-esteem	Social	Security	Physiological
10. ___	6. ___	5. ___	2. ___	1. ___
11. ___	8. ___	7. ___	3. ___	4. ___
13. ___	14. ___	12. ___	9. ___	16. ___
18. ___	17. ___	15. ___	19. ___	20. ___
Total ___	Total ___	Total ___	Total ___	Total ___

2. Circle your **total** scores in the chart below for each area of needs motivation.

Self-actualization	-12	-10	-8	-6	-4	-2	0	+2	+4	+6	+8	+10	+12
Self-esteem		-12	-10	-8	-6	-4	-2	0	+2	+4	+6	+8	+10	+12
Social		-12	-10	-8	-6	-4	-2	0	+2	+4	+6	+8	+10	+12
Security		-12	-10	-8	-6	-4	-2	0	+2	+4	+6	+8	+10	+12
Physiological		-12	-10	-8	-6	-4	-2	0	+2	+4	+6	+8	+10	+12

Once you have completed this chart you can see the relative strength of your use of each of these areas of needs motivation. 'There is of course no "right" answer. What is right for you is what matches the actual needs of your employees and that, of course, is specific to each situation and each individual. In general, however, the "experts" tell us that today's employees are best motivated by efforts in the areas of Social Needs and Self-esteem.

9. Active Listening

Read each of these statements. Decode the feeling (in one or several words; some statements may contain more than one feeling.) How would you respond as an active listener?

> *Example: Sender:* "I don't know what is wrong. I can't figure it out. Maybe I should just quit trying." *(stumped; discouraged; tempted to give up.)* Possible response: "You're feeling discouraged, huh?" or "You're really stumped on how to solve this one."

1. "Oh, boy, only ten more days until my vacation."

2. "I don't know how I'm going to untangle this messy problem."

3. "I'll never be as good as Jim. I practice and practice and I don't improve."

4. "My boss gives me too much work to do. I can never get it all done. What'll I do?"

5. "Damn it! Why can't I get accurate reports out of that department?"

6. "Do you think I'm doing this report right? Will it be good enough?"

7. "I'm sorry, I wasn't listening to you. I guess my mind is occupied with a problem at home with my son, Gregg. He's all screwed up."

8. "Go away; leave me alone. I don't want to talk to you or anybody else. You don't care what happens to me anyway."

9. "For a while I was doing OK, but now I'm worse than before. I try hard, but it doesn't help. What's the use?"

10. "Please, don't ask about that now."

11. "I thought the meeting today accomplished nothing!"

12. "I think I know what to do, but maybe it's not right. I always seem to do the wrong thing. What do you think I should do, keep working or go back to school?"

10. I-Messages

For each situation, examine the "you-message" and then write an "I-message" in the space provided.

1.   You are working on an important project. A co-worker keeps interrupting. "You shouldn't ever interrupt someone when you see he is busy."

2.   Jane doesn't answer letters promptly. "You're hired to get those letters out. Do it. Don't procrastinate."

3.   Pete forgot to show up for an appointment. You had rearranged your schedule to accommodate him. "Pete, that was thoughtless and inconsiderate not to keep the appointment."

4.   Bill, a subordinate, repeatedly interrupts you and other group members at staff meetings, seriously reducing effectiveness of the group. "For heavens' sake, Bill, let other people have their say before you make your points. Don't talk so much!"

5.   A committee chairperson fails to get a report in on time for the board meeting. "Everyone else got the reports in. The least you could do is to do the same."

6.   Frank volunteers to do jobs but often doesn't follow through. "You say you'll do it, but you never do."

7.   A secretary is late for work three days in a row. You are angry. "You're late again! Don't you think of anybody but yourself?"

8.   Your boss has asked you to stay late to get a report out. You had other plans. "You should have asked me earlier so I could have changed my plans."

9.   Your boss doesn't tell you things you need to know. "You never tell me anything. How do you expect me to know what's going on around here?"

11. Transactions

Identify the following responses as P *(Parent),* A *(Adult) or* C *(Child):*

Response to:

— seeing a piece of modern art:
_____ Good grief! What's it supposed to be?
_____ That costs $350, according to the price tag.
_____ Oh, what a pretty color!

— a request for an office report:
_____ No matter what I do, I can't please Mr. Smith.
_____ I know Mr. Smith needs these by five o'clock.
_____ Mr. Smith is not cut out to be a supervisor.

— rock music:
_____ It's hard for me to think or talk when the music is so loud.
_____ What horrible stuff kids listen to today!
_____ That makes me want to dance.

— a request for the time:
_____ You're always in such a hurry!
_____ Why do you always ask me?
_____ It is eleven o'clock.

— a request to take the car in for service:
_____ I have the wash to do and you expect me to take the car in?
_____ How about tomorrow? I have plans for today.
_____ You never think about anybody but yourself.

— a request of spouse to use the car to visit sister:
_____ Gee, you never want to talk with me.
_____ At today's gas prices, you want to drive over there?
_____ OK, you may need to get some gas.

— a request by boss to do a job:
_____ If you organized your work better, you wouldn't give this to me at the last minute.
_____ I have a few more minutes with this and then I'll get to it immediately.
_____ I can't ever get anything done before you give me something else.

— a late arrival at the office:
_____ Poor thing looks as if she hadn't slept a wink.
_____ If she doesn't make up her time, the other employees will be dissatisfied.
_____ I sure wish I could take time off for fun.

12. Conflict Stem Sentences

Please complete the following sentences. Discuss.

1. Conflict is disruptive in an organization because

2. Conflict can be helpful when

3. When conflict develops, I

4. Communication is difficult in conflict situations because

5. In a conflict situation, I am most likely to try to resolve it by

13. How You Resolve Conflicts

The proverbs listed below can be thought of as descriptions of some of the different strategies for resolving conflicts. Proverbs state traditional wisdom, and these proverbs reflect traditional wisdom for resolving conflicts. Read each of the proverbs carefully. Using the following scale, indicate how typical each proverb is of your actions in a conflict.

5 = very typical of the way I act in a conflict
4 = frequently typical of the way I act in a conflict
3 = sometimes typical of the way I act in a conflict
2 = seldom typical of the way I act in a conflict
1 = never typical of the way I act in a conflict

_____ 1. It is easier to refrain than to retreat from a quarrel.
_____ 2. If you cannot make a person think as you do, make him or her do as you think,
_____ 3. Soft words win hard hearts.
_____ 4. You scratch my back, I'll scratch yours.
_____ 5. Come now and let us reason together.
_____ 6. When two quarrel, the person who keeps silent first is the most praiseworthy.
_____ 7. Might overcomes right.
_____ 8. Smooth words make smooth ways.
_____ 9. Better half a loaf than no bread at all.
_____ 10. Truth lies in knowledge, not in majority opinion.
_____ 11. He who fights and runs away lives to fight another day.
_____ 12. He bath conquered well that bath made his enemies flee.
_____ 13. Kill your enemies with kindness.
_____ 14. A fair exchange brings no quarrel.
_____ 15. No person has the final answer but every person has a piece to contribute.
_____ 16. Stay away from people who disagree with you.
_____ 17. Fields are won by those who believe in winning.
_____ 18. Kind words are worth much and cost little.
_____ 19. Tit for tat is fair play.
_____ 20. Only the person who is willing to give up his or her monopoly on truth can ever profit from the truths that others hold.
_____ 21. Avoid quarrelsome people as they will only make your life miserable.
_____ 22. A person who will not flee will make others flee.
_____ 23. Soft words ensure harmony.

(continued)

_____ 24. One gift for another makes good friends.
_____ 25. Bring your conflicts into the open and face them directly; only then will the best solution be discovered.
_____ 26. The best way of handling conflicts is to avoid them.
_____ 27. Put your foot down where you mean to stand.
_____ 28. Gentleness will triumph over anger
_____ 29. Getting part of what you want is better than not getting anything at all.
_____ 30. Frankness, honesty, and trust will move mountains.
_____ 31. There is nothing so important you have to fight for it.
_____ 32. There are two kinds of people in the world, the winners and the losers.
_____ 33. When one hits you with a stone, hit him or her with a piece of cotton.
_____ 34. When both give in halfway, a fair settlement is achieved,
_____ 35. By digging and digging, the truth is discovered.

SCORING:

Avoiding	Competing	Accommodating	Compromising	Collaborating
__ 1.	__ 2.	__ 3.	__ 4.	__ 5.
__ 6.	__ 7.	__ 8.	__ 9.	__10.
__11.	__12.	__13.	__14.	__15.
__16.	__17.	__18.	__19.	__20.
__21.	__22.	__23.	__24.	__25.
__26.	__27.	__28.	__29.	__30.
__31.	__32.	__33.	__34.	__35.
___Total	___Total	___Total	___Total	___Total

The higher the total score for each conflict strategy, the more frequently you tend to use that strategy. The lower the total score for each conflict strategy, the less frequently you tend to use that strategy.

14. Leadership Style

The following statements are grouped in pairs. Allocate ten points between each pair (0 to one and 10 to other; 5 and 5; 3 and 7; etc.) There is no right or wrong answer.

1. a) The leader should direct and control the members, leading them to the proper decision. The members should acknowledge the leader's authority.   a)_____

    b) The group is owned by the members. All members, with the leader's assistance, should contribute to its effectiveness.   b)_____

2. c) The group is responsible, with occasional and appropriate help from the leader, for reaching a decision.   c)_____

    d) The leader focuses his/her attention on the task to be accomplished. The leader brings the group back from any diverse wandering.   d)_____

3. e) The leader performs all of the functions needed to arrive at the proper decision.   e)_____

    f) Decisions are the product of full group participation. The leader is a servant and helper to the group.   f)_____

4. g) The leader sets limits and uses rules of order to keep the discussion within strict limits set by the agenda.   g)_____

    h) Members of the group should be encouraged and helped to take responsibility for its productivity.   h)_____

5. i) Feelings, emotions and conflicts are recognized by the members and the leader as legitimate items demanding serious attention.   i)_____

    j) The leader keeps the group logically thinking and objective, avoiding emotional responses which will disrupt group work.   j)_____

6. k) Disruptive behavior in the group must be faced and solved within the group and by the group.   k)_____

    l) The leader should handle a disruptive member's behavior by talking to him/her away from the group.   l)_____

7. m) The group task at hand is primary. The varying needs of individuals are secondary.   m)_____

    n) Needs, feeling and purposes of all members should be recognized so that the group can work effectively.   n)_____

(continued)

8. o) The leader is the focal point of group work. She/he needs the greatest responsibility and power to lead the group.   o)_____

    p) Member contributions are the focal point of group work. Responsibilities and power are equally distributed.   p)_____

9. q) The leader is the servant of the group and should flex with the needs of the members. Group members welcome the opportunity to share in the leading of the group.   q)_____

    r) The leader should maintain a power position. Leaders are leaders because their competence and prestige have been recognized. Most group members seem to welcome a strong leader who can exert control and provide safety.   r)_____

10. s) The leader should make all decisions. She/he should stand up for personal ideas, opinions and attitudes, even if it sometimes results in member withdrawal.   s)_____

    t) The group, including the leader, should search for workable, acceptable decisions. Consensus is used to coordinate ideas, opinions and attitudes.   t)_____

SCORING INSTRUCTIONS

Add up the points for the following letters: Points

b) _____

c) _____

f) _____

h) _____

i) _____

k) _____

n) _____

p) _____

q) _____

t) _____

Grand Total for 'S' score: _____

Key:

The total points are your 'S' score, for "Shared Leadership."   100%

Subtract your 'S' score from 100 and you will have your 'T' score. 'T' stands for "Traditional Leadership."

('S' score) _____

('T' score) _____

15. Change Stem Sentences

Please complete the following sentences. Discuss.

1. The trouble with organizations today is

2.   When I think about my role in any organization, I

3.   I think change today is

4.   If there is one change that is really needed, it is

5.   Change would be a lot easier if

6.   People resist change because

7.   My responsibility in bringing about change is

16. Problem Analysis

Select a significant problem in your back-home situation that you would like to change (and that you would be willing to discuss with another person here).

Problem Specification

1. How would you describe the problem?

2. Who are the people (in addition to yourself) involved in the problem?

3. What other factors relate to the problem?

4. What specifically would you like to change in that situation?

Forces Identification

5. *Driving Forces* (forces pushing for the change you favor)

6. *Restraining Forces* (forces resisting the change you favor)

17. Problem Solving

Following completion of Worksheet IX, develop a plan for solving the problem.

- **Generating Alternate Solutions**

1. Whom will you involve in generating solutions to the problem?

2. How will you involve him/her/them?

3. What alternate solutions do you see as available?

- **Evaluating the Alternate Solutions**

4. What are the advantages/disadvantages, the costs/benefits of the alternate solutions?

5. Which alternative solutions meet the needs of all parties concerned?

- **Choosing a Solution**

6. Which solution is mutually acceptable?

- **Implementing the Solution**
7. How will the solution be implemented? Who does what by when?

- **Follow-Up**
8. What is your plan for follow-up?

18. Dialogue Skill

Answer the following questions to evaluate your dialogue skill.

1. Did I see the dialogue as an opportunity for giving and receiving rather than for discussion or decision making?

2. Did I express myself in personal terms using "I" and not "we" and did I speak from my own personal experience?

3. Did I work through the question and issue rather than seek a "resolution"?

4. Did I give each person space/time to speak with words and silence?

5. Did I try to suspend my assumptions and to allow others to question them?

6. Did I find a balance between advocacy (presenting my own ideas/experience) and inquiry (exploring others' ideas/experiences)?

7. Did I see disagreement as an opportunity to learn and as a sign that this is a place where we can dig deeper?

8. Did I pay attention to my inattention and see why I was not focusing?

9. Did I remain self aware so that I could consciously use my feelings and perceptions as a resource?

10. Did I find myself inferring meaning?

    imposing my own value judgments?

    trying to debate?

    generalizing?

11. What did I learn about my listening and learning?

19. Ground Rules for Consensus

Object: to reach group consensus in making a decision.

1. Do not vote, trade, average, flip a coin, etc.

2. No individual group member should give in only to reach agreement.

3. You should not simply argue for your own decision but approach this task using reason and logic.

4. Disagreements can be resolved by facts.

5. Conflict can lead to understanding and creativity if it does not make group members feel threatened or defensive.

20. Ground Rules for Creative Problem Solving

Object: for group to come up with creative ideas to solve a problem.

1. Adopt a questioning attitude.

2. Establish an environment of acceptance in which ideas are considered before being judged.

3. Brainstorm ideas without evaluation.

4. Examine the problem from new angles; try stating it in atypical ways.

5. Break the problem up into its components and list as many alternatives as possible for each component; combine the alternatives to create new solutions.

21. Bricks Problem

Your group has just been stranded without provisions on a deserted island. In your search for supplies, you and your fellow members locate a little food and two thousand bricks. In discussing the situation, the group determines that rescue probably will not occur for at least two weeks and that the food is insufficient to support everyone for that period. Therefore, the members decide that the task of immediate importance is to generate creative ways of using the bricks to increase chances for survival.

Discussion following exercise:

1. What method did your group use to generate ideas? What was helpful about this method? What was not helpful?
2. How was your group's approach "creative"?
3. Did everyone in your group participate equally? If not, why did some members participate more than others? What effect did the members' levels of participation have on the group's ability to solve the problem creatively?
4. How might this activity relate to problem solving at work? at home?
5. What might be a first step toward incorporating creative problem solving into your back-home situation?

22. New Van Decision

You are a TV technician for a large TV and Stereo Store. Your job is to fix broken televisions. Repairmen must present a good store image to customers, as well as competently repair TV's. The manager of the repair department is an ex-repairman. Each morning, the manager meets with the crew at the store to assign work for the day. Each repairman works alone and ordinarily does several jobs in a day. Recently the manager has regarded the crew as a "team" and has been referring decisions to them, particularly decisions about which they have direct information. Replacement of vans has been postponed some years, even though maintenance costs have increased and the prospect is that the new van authorized this year will be the only new van for the next two years. The manager has turned to his crew to determine who gets to use the new van. The repairmen drive "their own" vans to various locations in the city to do repair work. Each of them takes pride in the van's appearance. Repair vans are "status symbols" for the crew and each person likes to keep his/her assigned van in good condition.

Some facts about the crew and their vans:

Crew Person	Years with the store	Van assigned
John	12 years; 10 as manager	Manager
Mike	14 years	2 year old Dodge
Steve	9 years	4 year old Chevrolet
Shannon	5 years	3 year old Ford
Nancy	4 years	5 year old Ford
Rick	1 year	6 year old Dodge

Most of the crew drives in the city, but Steve and Shannon cover the jobs in the suburbs. The manager has called a meeting of the team to decide who gets the new van. In playing your role, accept the facts as given. Let your feelings develop in accordance with the events that occur while role playing. When facts or events arise which are not covered by the roles, make up things that are consistent with the way it might be in a real-life situation.

Questions for discussion:

1. What decision making method role did the manager promote?
2. How did you feel about the team process? Was it fair?
3. Did the final solution benefit you? How?
4. How would you describe the team activity; as conflict or cooperation? Why?
5. How can you relate this case problem to your own organization? What have you learned from it?

23. Group Growth Evaluation

Directions: In front of each of the items below there are two blank spaces. Rate your group on the characteristic as the group was **initially** and as it is **now**. Use a seven-point scale, where 7 is "very much" and 1 is "very little".

Initially   Now

_____ _____ 1. I am treated as a human being rather than Just another group member.

_____ _____ 2. I feel close to the members of this group.

_____ _____ 3. There is cooperation and teamwork present in this group.

_____ _____ 4. Membership in this group is aiding my personal growth development.

_____ _____ 5. I have trust and confidence in the other members of the group.

_____ _____ 6. Members of this group display supportive behavior toward each other.

_____ _____ 7. I get a sense of accomplishment as a result of membership in this group.

_____ _____ 8. I am willing to share information with other members of the groups.

_____ _____ 9. I feel free to discuss important personal matters with group members.

_____ _____ 10. This group uses integrative, constructive methods in problem-solving rather than a win-lose approach.

_____ _____ 11. As a member of this group, I am able to deal promptly and well with important group problems.

_____ _____ 12. The activities of this group reflect a constructive integration of the needs and desires of its members.

_____ _____ 13. My needs and desires are reflected in the activities of this group.

_____ _____ 14. I feel that there is a sense of real group responsibility for getting a job done.

275

24. Group Climate Inventory

Directions: Think about how your fellow group members normally behave toward you. In the parentheses in front of the items below place the number corresponding to your perceptions of the group as a whole, using the following scale.

5 They can **always** be counted on to behave this way .
4 I **typically** would expect them to behave this way.
3 I would **usually** expect them to behave this way.
2 They would **seldom** behave this way.
1 They would **rarely** behave this way.
0 I would **never** expect them to behave this way.

I would expect my fellow group members to.....

1. (   ) level with me.

2. (   ) get the drift of what I am trying to say.

3. (   )   interrupt or ignore my comments.

4. (   ) accept me for what I am.

5. (   ) feel free to let me know when I "bug" them.

6. (   ) misconstrue things I say and do.

7. (   ) be interested in me.

8. (   )   provide an atmosphere where I can be myself.

9. (   ) keep things to themselves to spare my feelings.

10. (   ) perceive what kind of person I really am.

11. (   ) include me in what's going on.

12. (   ) act "judgmental" with me.

13. (   ) be completely frank with me.

14. (   ) recognize readily when something is bothering me.

15. (   ) respect me as a person, apart from my skills or status.

16. (   ) ridicule me or disapprove if I show my peculiarities.

For scoring reverse the scores for statements 3, 6, 9, 12, and 16.

25. Team Functioning Evaluation

Below are ten characteristics of well-functioning teams.

Please indicate the functioning of your team with respect to each of these characteristics on a scale of 1 to 4 as follows:

4 = excellent   3 = good   2 = fair   1 = poor

1. **Purpose -** Members proudly share a sense of why the team exists and are invested in accomplishing its mission.   4 3 2 1

2. **Priorities -** Members know what needs to be done next, by whom, and by when to achieve team goals.   4 3 2 1

3. **Roles -** Members know their roles in getting tasks done and when to allow a more skillful member to do a certain task.   4 3 2 1

4. **Decisions -** Authority and decision-making lines are clearly understood.   4 3 2 1

5. **Conflict -** Conflict is dealt with openly and is considered important to decision-making and personal growth.   4 3 2 1

6. **Personal traits -** Members feel their unique personalities are appreciated and well utilized.   4 3 2 1

7. **Risk -** Members are able to share risky ideas and feel supported by the team rather than feel criticized or sniped at.   4 3 2 1

8. **Effectiveness -** Members find team meetings efficient and productive and look forward to this time together.   4 3 2 1

9. **Success -** Members know clearly when the team has met with success and share in this equally and proudly.   4 3 2 1

10. **Training -** Opportunities for feedback and updating skills are provided and taken advantage of by team members.   4 3 2 1

After completing this form, team members compare and discuss their evaluations.

277

26.   Team Effectiveness Scale

Indicate your assessment of your team and way it functions by circling the number on each scale below that you feel is most descriptive of your team.

1. Goals and Objectives

There is a lack of commonly understood goals and objectives.

Team members understand and agree on goals and objectives

1   2   3   4   5   6   7   8   9

2. Utilization of Resources

All member resources are not recognized and/or utilized.

Member resources are fully recognized and utilized.

1   2   3   4   5   6   7   8   9

3. Trust and Conflict

There is little trust among members, and conflict is evident.

There is a high degree of trust among members, and conflict is dealt with openly and worked through.

1   2   3   4   5   6   7   8   9

4. Leadership

One person dominates, and leadership roles are not carried out or shared.

There is full participation in leadership; leadership roles are shared by members.

1   2   3   4   5   6   7   8   9

5. Control and Procedures

There is little control, and there is a lack of procedures to guide team functioning.

There are effective procedures to guide team functioning; team members support these procedures and regulate themselves.

1   2   3   4   5   6   7   8   9

Bibliography
for reference and further study

Adams, J. *Effective Leadership for Men and Women.* New York: Alex Publishing Co., 1985

Allessandra, T., O'Connor, M., with Van Dyke, J. *People Smarts.* San Diego: Pfeiffer and Co., 1994.

Allport, Gordon W., *Becoming.* New Haven: Yale University Press, 1955.

Apps, Jerold W.. *Leadership for the Emerging Age - Transforming Practice in Continuing Education.* San Francisco: Jossey-Bass, 1994.

Apps, Jerold W. *Mastering the Teaching of Adults.* Malabar, FL: Krieger/LERN, 1991.

Argyris, Chris. *Knowledge for Action: A Guide to Overcoming Bariers to Organizational Change.* San Francisco: Jossey-Bass, 1993.

Argyris, Chris. *Overcoming Organizational Defenses.* NY: Prentice-Hall, 1990.

Argyris, Chris. *Reasoning, Learning and Action: Individual and Organizational.* San Francisco: Jossey-Bass, 1982.

Argyris, Chris, Putnam, R. and Smith, D. *Action Science.* San Francisco: Jossey-Bass, 1988.

Argyris, Chris and Schon, Donald. *Theory in Practice.* San Francisco: Jossey-Bass, 1988.

Austin, H. S., and Leland, C. *Women of Influence, Women of Vision: A Cross-Generational Study of Leaders and Social Change.* San Francisco: Jossey-Bass, 1991.

Bales, Robert F. "Task Roles and Social Roles in Problem-Solving Groups" in *Readings in Social Psychology* (3rd edition). N. Maccoby (ed). New York: Holt, Rinehart & Winston, 1958.

Bandler, Richard and Grinder, John. *Frogs into Princes: Neuro-Linguistic Programming.* Moab, Utah: Real People Press, 1979.

Bard, Ray, Bell, C. R., Stephen, L., Webster, L. *The Trainer's Professional Development Handbook.* San Francisco: Jossey-Bass, 1987.

Baron, Robert S., Kerr, Norbert L. and Miller, Norman. *Group Process, Group Decision, Group Action.* Pacific Grove, CA: Brooks/Cole Publishing, 1992.

Bass, Bernard M. *Leadership and Performance Beyond Expectations.* New York: The Free Press, 1985.

Bass, Bernard M. *Bass and Stogdill's Handbook of Leadership* (3rd ed.) New York: Free Press, 1990.

Belenky, Mary Field and others. *Women 's Ways of Knowing.* New York: Basic Books, 1986.

Bennis, Warren. *On Becoming a Leader.* Reading, MA: Addison-Wesley, 1989.

Bennis, Warren. *Why Leaders Can't Lead: The Unconscious Conspiracy Continues.* San Francisco: Jossey-Bass Publishers, 1988.

Bennis, Warren, Benne, Kenneth D. and Chin, Robert. *The Planning of Change.* (4th ad.). NewYork: Holt, Rinehart, and Winston, 1985.

Bennis, Warren, and Nanus, Burt. *Leaders: The Strategies for Taking Charge.* New York: Harper and Row, 1985.

Berne, Eric. *Games People Play.* New York: Grove Press, 1964.

Berne, Eric. *The Structure and Dynamics of Organizations and Groups.* New York, Grove Press, 1963.

Berne, Eric. *What Do You Say After You Say Hello.* New York: Grove Press, 1972.

Bion, W. R. *Experiences in Groups.* New York: Basic Books, 1961.

Blake, Robert R. and Mouton, Jane S. *The Managerial Grid III, (3rd edition).* Houston: Gulf, 1984.

Blanchard, Kenneth and Johnson, Spencer. *One Minute Management.* New York: Morrow, 1982.

Block, Peter. *The Empowered Manager: Positive Political Skills at Work.* San Francisco: Jossey-Bass, 1990.

Block, Peter. *Stewardship.* San Francisco: Jossey-Bass, 1993.

Boccialetti, Gene. *It Takes Two: Managing Yourself When Working with Bosses and Other Authority Figures.* San Francisco: Jossey-Bass, 1995.

Bohm, David. *Unfolding Meaning.* Loveland, CO: Foundation House, 1985.

Bohm, David. *Wholeness and the Implicate Order.* London: Ark Paperbacks, 1980.

Bolman, Lee G. and Deal, Terrence E. *Leading with Soul: An Uncommon Journey of Spirit.* San Francisco: Jossey-Bass, 1995.

Bolman, Lee G. and Deal, Terrence E. *Reframing Organizations: Artistry, Choice and Leadership.* San Francisco: Jossey-Bass, 1991.

Boulding, Kenneth E. "The Universe as a General System." Behavioral Science, 22, pp. 299-306, 1977.

Bower, Sharon Anthony and Bower, Gordon H. *Asserting Yourself.* Menlo Park: Addison-Wesley, 1976.

Bradford, Leland P. *Group Development.* (Second Edition) LaJolla: University Associates, 1978.

Brammer, Lawrence M. *The Helping Relationship.* Englewood Cliffs: Prentice Hall, 1973.

Brassard, Michael. *The Memory Jogger: A Pocket Guide of Tools for Continuous Improvement.* Methuen, MA: GOAL/QPC, 1988.

Brassard, Michael. *The Memory Jogger Plus+: Featuring the Seven Management and Planning Tools.* Methuen, MA: GOAL/QPC, 1989.

Brookfield, Stephen D. *Developing Critical Thinkers: Challenging Adults to Explore Alternative Ways of Thinking and Acting.* San Francisco: Jossey-Bass, 1988.

Brookfield, Stephen D. *The Skillful Teacher.* San Francisco: Jossey-Bass, 1990.

Brookfield, Stephen D. *Understanding and Facilitating Adult Learning.* San Francisco: Jossey-Bass, 1987.

Brinkerhoff, Robert O. and Gill, Stephen J. *The Learning Alliance: Systems Thinking in Human Resource Development.* San Francisco: Jossey-Bass, 1994.

Bunker, Barbara Benedict, Rubin, Jeffrey Z. and Associates. *Conflict, Cooperation, and Justice.* San Francisco: Jossey-Bass, 1995.

Burns, James MacGregor. *Leadership.* New York: Harper and Row, 1978.

Burrell, G. and Morgan, G. *Sociological Paradigms and Organizational Analysis.* London: Heinemann, 1979.

Burton, John. *Conflict Resolution and Prevention.* New York: St. Martin's Press, 1990.

Bush, Robert A. Baruch and Folger, Joseph P. *The Promise of Mediation: Responding to Conflict Through Empowerment and Recognition.* San Francisco: Jossey-Bass, 1994.

Capra, Fritjof, Steindl-Rast, David, and Madison, Thomas. *Belonging to the Universe.* San Francisco: Harper, 1991.

Capra, Fritjof. *The Tao of Physics.* New York: Bantam Books, 1991.

Cartwright, D. and Zander, A. *Group Dynamics: Research and Theory* (2nd edition). Evanston, IL: Row, Peterson & Co., 1960.

Champy, James. *Reengineering Management: The Mandate for New Leadership.* New York: Harper, 1994.

Christensen, C. R., Garvin, D. A., Sweet, A. (eds) *Education for Judgment: The Artistry of Discussion Leadership.* Boston: Harvard Business School Press, 1991.

Clark, Miriam B., and Freeman. F. H. *Leadership Education 1990: A Source Book.* Greensboro, NC: Center for Creative Leadership, 1990.

Cleveland, Harlan. *The Knowledge Executive: Leadership in an Information Society.* New York: Truman Talley Books, 1985.

Conklin, Robert. *How to Get People To Do Things.* Chicago: Contemporary Books, 1979.

Corey, Marianne Schneider, and Corey, Gerald. Groups Process and Practice (4th ed.) Pacific Grove, CA: Brooks/Cole Publishing Co., 1992.

Covey, Stephen R. *The 7 Habits of Highly Effective People.* NY: Fireside, 1989.

Covey, Stephen R. *Principle-Centered Leadership.* New York: Simon & Schuster, 1991.

Crosby, Phillip. *Leading: The Art of Becoming an Executive.* New York: McGraw-Hill, 1990.

Dalziel, Murray M. and Schoonover, Stephen C. *Changing Ways: A Practical Tool for Implementing Change Within Organizations.* New York: American Management Association, 1988.

Deal, Terrence E. and Peterson, Kent D. *The Leadership Paradox: Balancing Logic and Artistry in Schools.* San Francisco: Jossey-Bass, 1994.

De Bono, Edward. *Serious Creativity: Using the Power of Lateral Thinking to Create New Ideas.* HarperBusiness, 1992.

Delbesq, Andre, VandeVen, Andrew H.,and Gustafson, David H. *Group Techniques for Program Planning, a Guide to Nominal Group and Delphi Processes.* Glenview, Ill.: Scott, Foresman, 1975.

Deming, W. Edwards. *Out of the Crisis.* Cambridge: MIT Center for Advanced Engineering, 1982.

DePree, Max. *Leadership Is an Art.* New York: Doubleday/Currency, 1989.

DePree, Max. *Leadership Jazz.* New York: Doubleday, 1992.

Dolan, W. P. *Restructuring Our Schjools: A Primer on Systematic Change.* Kansas City: Systems and Organizations, 1994.

Drucker, Peter F. *The Changing World of the Executive.* New York: Times Books, 1985.

282

Drucker, Peter F. *Innovation and Entrepreneurship Practices and Principles*. New York: Harper and Row, 1986.

Drucker, Peter F. *Managing in Turbulent Times.* NY: Harper and Row, 1980.

Drucker, Peter F. *Managing the Future.* New York: Dutton, 1992.

Drucker, Peter F. *The New Realities: In Government and Politics - In Economics and Business - In Society and World View.* New York: Harper & Row, 1990.

Dyer, Wayne W. *The Sky's the Limit.* New York: Pocket Books,1980.

Dyer, Wayne W. *Your Erroneous Zones.* New York: Funk & Wagnalls,1976.

Ferguson, M. *The Aquarian Conspiracy.* Los Angeles: Tarcher, 1980.

Fiedler, Fred E. and Chemers, Martin M. *Improving Leadership Effectiveness: the Leader Match Concept.* (2nd ed.) New York: Wiley Press, 1984.

Filley, Alan C. *The Compleat Manager: What Works When.* Green Briar Press, 1985.

Filley, Alan C. *Interpersonal Conflict Resolution.* Glenview, Ill.: Scott, Foresman, 1975.

Fisher, B. A. and Ellis, E. G. *Small Group Decision Making: Communication and the Group Process* (3rd ed.) New York: McGraw-Hill, 1990.

Fisher, James C. and Cole, Kathleen M. *Leadership and Management of Volunteer Programs: A Guide for Administrators.* San Francisco: Jossey-Bass, 1993.

Fisher, Roger and Brown, Scott. *Getting Together: Building Relationships as We Negotiate.* NY: Penguin Books, 1988.

Fisher, Roger and William Ury, *Getting to Yes: Negotiating Agreement Without Giving In.* Boston: Houghton Mifflin,1981.

Forsyth, Donelson R. *An Introduction to Group Dynamics.* Monterey, Calif.: Brooks/Cole Publishing Co., 1983.

Fox, William M. *Effective Group Problem Solving: How to Broaden Participation, Improve Decision Making, and Increase Commitment.* San Francisco: Jossey-Bass, 1987.

Frankl, Viktor. *Man's Search for Meaning.* Boston: Beacon Press, 1959.

Francis, Dave, and Young, Don. *Improving Work Groups: A Practical Guide for Team Building.* San Diego: Pfeiffer and Co., 1992.

French, John R., and Raven, Bertram. "The Bases of Social Power," in Cartwright and Zander (eds) *Group Dynamics* (2nd edition). Evanston, IL: Row, Peterson, 1960.

French, Wendell L. and Bell, Cecil H. Jr. *Organization Development: Behavioral Science Interventions for Organizational Improvement.* (Fifth Edition) Englewood Cliffs: Prentice Hall, 1995.

Fritz, Robert. *Creating.* NY: Fawcett-Collumbine, 1991.

Fritz, Robert. *The Path of Least Resistance.* NY: Fawcett-Collumbine, 1989.

Fullan, Michael G. *The New Meaning of Educational Change.* New York: Teacher's College Press, 1991.

Gardner, John W. *On Leadership.* New York: The Free Press, 1990.

Gardner, John W. *Self-Renewal.* New York: Norton, 1981.

Getzels, Jacob W. "Administration as a Social Process" in *Administrative Theory of Education,* A. Halpin (ed) New York: Macmillan, 1958.

Gilligan, Carol. *In a Different Voice: Psychological Theory and Women's Development.* Cambridge: Harvard University, 1982.

Ginnott, Haim G. *Teacher and Child .* New York: Avon, 1972.

Glasser, William. *Control Theory: A New Explanation of How We Control Our Lives.* New York: Harper and Row, 1984.

Glasser, William. *The Quality School: Managing Students Without Coercion.* NY: Harper and Row, 1990.

Glasser, William. *Reality Therapy.* New York: Harper & Row, 1965.

Gleick, J. *Chaos: Making a New Science.* New York: Viking, 1987.

Glickman, Carl D. *Renewing America's Schools: A Guide for School-based Action.* San Francisco: Jossey-Bass, 1993.

Goodall, H. L. *Small Group Communication in Organizations* (2nd ed.). Iowa: W. C. Brown, 1990.

Gordon, Thomas. *Group Centered Leadership.* Boston: Houghton Mifflin, 1955.

Gordon, Thomas. *Leader Effectiveness Training: The No-Lose Way to Release the Production Potential of People.* New York: David McKay Co., 1978.

Graham, Morris A. and Lebaron, Melvin J. *The Horizontal Revolution: Guiding the Teaming Takeover.* San Francisco: Jossey-Bass, 1994.

Gray, John. *Men are from Mars, Women are from Venus.* New York: Harper-Collins, 1992.

284

Greenleaf, Robert K. *Servant Leadership.* New York: Paulist Press, 1977.

Gregorc, Anthony. *An Adult's Guide to Style.* Maynard, MA: Gabrial Systems, 1982.

Grenier, Larry E. *Consulting to Management.* Englewood Cliffs: Prentice-Hall, 1983.

Gutteridge, Thomas G., Leibowitz, Zandy B. and Shore, Jane E. *Organizational Career Development: Benchmarks for Building a World-Class Workplace.* Jossey-Bass, 1993.

Hagberg, J. O. *Real Power: Stages of Personal Power in Organizations.* San Francisco: Harper Collins, 1984.

Hampton, David R. and C. E. Summer, R. A. Webber. *Organizational Behavior and the Practice of Management.* Glenview, IL: Scott, Foresman and Co., 1987.

Handy, Charles. *The Age of Unreason.* Boston: Harvard Business School, 1990.

Hanson, E. Mark. *Educational Administration and Organizational Behavior* (3rd ed.) Boston: Allyn and Bacon, 1991.

Harman, Willis and Hormann. *Creative Work: The Constructive Role of Business in a Transforming Society.* Indianapolis, IN: Knowledge Systems, 1990.

Harman, W. *Global Mind Change.* Indianapolis: Knowledge Systems, Inc., 1988.

Harper, Charles L. *Exploring Social Change* (second edition). Prentice Hall, 1993.

Harris, B. *Improving Staff Performance through In-service Education.* Boston: Allyn & Bacon, 1980.

Harris, Thomas A. *I'm OK, You're OK: A Practical Guide to Transactional Analysis.* New York: Harper and Row, 1967.

Harshman, Carl L. and Phillips, Steven L. *Teaming Up: Achieving Organizational Transformation.* Pfeiffer and Company, 1994.

Havelock, Ronald G. *A Change Agent's Guide to Innovation in Education.* Englewood Cliffs: Educational Technology Publications, 1973.

Havelock, Ronald G. *Planning for Innovation through Dissemination and Utilization.* Ann Arbor: Institute for Social Research, University of Michigan, 1971.

Heider, John. *The Tao of Leadership.* New York: Bantam Books, 1985.

Helgeson, S. *The Female Advantage: Women's Ways of Leadership.* New York: Doubleday, 1990.

Hemphill, John K. *Leader Behavior Description.* Columbus: Ohio State University, 1950.

Herman, Stanley. *A Force of Ones: Reclaiming Individual Power in a Time of Teams, Work Groups, and Other Crowds.* San Francisco: Jossey-Bass, 1994.

Herman, Stanley. *The Tao at Work on Leading and Following.* San Francisco: Jossey-Bass, 1994.

Herrmann, Ned. *The Creative Brain.* Lake Lure, NC: Brain Books, 1988.

Hersey, Paul and Ken Blanchard. *Management of Organizational Behavior.* (Sixth Edition) New York: Prentice Hall, 1993.

Herzberg, Frederick, and others. *The Motivation to Work.* New York: John Wiley, 1967.

Hickman, Craig R. and Silva, M. A. *Creating Excellence: Managing the Corporate Culture. Strategy and Change in the New Age.* New American Library, 1984.

Hirokawa, R. Y. "Communication and Group Decision-making Efficacy" in *Small Group Communication: A Reader.* Iowa: W. C. Brown, 1992.

Hoffer, Eric. *The Ordeal of Change.* New York: Harper & Row, 1963.

Hoffer, Eric. *The True Believer.* New York: Harper and Bros., 1951.

Hudson, F. M. *The Adult Years: Mastering the Art of Self-Renewal.* San Francisco: Jossey-Bass, 1991.

Imaia, Masaaki. *Kaizen, The Key to Japan 's Competitive Success.* New York: Random House, 1986.

Imparato, Nicholas and Harari, Oren. *Jumping the Curve: Innovation and Strategic Choice in an Age of Transition.* San Francisco: Jossey-Bass, 1994.

Ishikawa, Kaoru. *What is Total Quality Control?: The Japanese Way.* New York: Prentice Hall, 1985.

Jacobson, Stephen L. and Conway, James A. *Education Leadership in an Age of Reform.* New York: Longman, 1990.

Jaffe, Dennis T., Scott, Cynthia D., and Tobe, Glenn R. *Rekindling Commitment: How to Revitalize Yourself, Your Work, and Your Organization.* San Francisco: Jossey-Bass, 1994.

James, Muriel. *The OK Boss.* Menlo Park: Addison-Wesley, 1975.

James, Muriel and Dorothy Jongeward. *Born to Win: Transactional Analysis with Gestalt Experiments.* Menlo Park: Addison-Wesley Publishing Co., 1971.

Janov, Jill. *The Inventive Organization: Hope and Daring at Work.* San Francisco: Jossey-Bass, 1994.

Johnson, David W. *Reaching Out.* Englewood Cliffs: Prentice-Hall, 1972.

Johnson, David W. and Johnson, Frank P. *Joining Together: Group Theory and Group Skills.* Englewood Cliffs: Prentice-Hall, 1982.

Johnson, David W. and Johnson, Roger T. *Leading the Cooperative School.* Edina, MN: Interaction Book Co., 1989.

Jourard, Sidney M. *The Transparent Self* New York: Van Nostrand Reinhold Co. 1971.

Jung, Carl G. *Psychological Types.* New Jersey: Princeton University Press, 1976.

Juran, Joseph M. *Juran on Planning for Quality.* New York: Free Press, 1988.

Kanter, Rosabeth Moss, *The Change Masters: Innovation and Entrepreneurship in the American Corporation.* New York: Simon and Schuster, 1983.

Katzenbach, Jon R. and Smith, Douglas K. *The Wisdom of Teams: Creating the High-Performance Organization.* Harvard Business School Press, 1993.

Kelly, James N. and Gouillart, Francis J. *Transforming the Organizations.* New York: McGraw-Hill, 1995.

Kelly, Robert. *The Power of Followership: How to Create Leaders People Want to Follow and Followers Who Lead Themselves.* New York: Doubleday, 1992.

Kemp, C. Gratton, *Perspectives on the Group Process.* Boston: Houghton-Mifflin, 1970.

Kirkpatrick, D. L. *How to Manage Change Effectively.* San Francisco: Jossey-Bass, 1985.

Knowles, Malcolm S. and Knowles, Hulda. *Introduction to Group Dynamics.* New York: Association Press, 1959.

Knox, A. B. *Adult Development and Learning: A Handbook on Individual Growth and Competence in the Adult Years.* San Francisco: Jossey-Bass, 1977.

Knox, A. B. *Helping Adults Learn: A Guide to Planning, Implementing, and Conducting Programs.* San Francisco: Jossey-Bass, 1986.

Knowles, Malcolm. *The Modern Practice of Adult Education.* Chicago: Follett, 1980.

Knox, A. B. *Adult Development and Learning.* San Francisco: Jossey-Bass, 1977.

Knox, A. B. *Helping Adults Learn: A Guide to Planning, Implementing and Conducting Programs.* San Francisco: Jossey-Bass, 1986.

Kolb, David A., Rubin, I. M. and McIntyre J. M. *Experiential Learning.* New Jersey: Prentice-Hall, 1984.

Kolb, David A. *Learning Style Inventory*. Boston: McBer & Co., 1981.

Kolb, Deborah M. and Associates. *When Talk Works: Profiles of Mediators*. San Francisco: Jossey-Bass, 1994.

Kotter, John P. *A Force for Change - How Leadership Differs From Management*. New York: The Free Press, 1990.

Kotter, John P. *The Leadership Factor*. New York: Free Press, 1988.

Kottler, Jeffrey. *Beyond Blame: A New Way of Resolving Conflicts in Relationships*. San Francisco: Jossey-Bass, 1994.

Kouzes, James M. and Posner, Barry Z. *Credibility: How Leaders Gain and Lose It, Why People Demand It*. San Francisco: Jossey-Bass, 1993.

Kouzes, James M. and Posner, Barry Z. *The Leadership Challenge*. San Francisco: Jossey-Bass, 1990.

Kuhn, Thomas. *The Structure of Scientific Revolutions*. Chicago: University of Chicago Press, 1970.

Lakein, Alan. *How to Get Control of Your Time and Your Life*. New York: Signet, 1973.

Laud, George, and Jarmon, Beth. *Breakpoint and Beyond: Mastering the Future Today*. New York: Harper Business, 1992.

Lax, D. A., and Sebenius, J. K. *The Manager as Negotiator*. New York: Free Press, 1986.

Leavitt, Harold J. *Managerial Psychology*. Chicago: University of Chicago Press, 1964.

Lieberman, Ann and Miller, Lynne. *Staff Development for Education in the 1990's*. New York: Teacher's College Press, 1991.

Lippitt, Ronald, Watson, Jeanne, Westley, Bruce. *Dynamics of Planned Change*. New York: Harcourt & Brace, 1958.

Luft, Joseph. *Group Processes*. Palto Alto, Calif.: National Press, 1963.

Lunenburg, Fred C. and Ornstein, Allan C. *Educational Administration: Concepts and Practices*. Belmont, CA: Wadsworth Publishing Co., 1991.

Lynch, D. *Your High-Performance Brain: An Operator's Manual*. Englewood Cliffs, NJ: Prentice-Hall, 1984.

Manz, C. C. and H. P. Sims. *SuperLeadership: Leading Others to Lead Themselves*. New York: Prentice-Hall, 1989.

Margerison, Charles and McCann, Dick. *Team Management*. London: Mercury, 1990.

Maslow, Abraham H. *Toward a Psychology of Being*. Princeton: Van Nostrand Co., 1968.

McClelland, David C. *The Achievement Motive*. New York: Appleton-Century-Crafts, 1953.

McClelland, David C. *The Achieving Society*. Princeton, NJ: D. Van Nostrand Co., 1967.

McGregor, Douglas. *The Human Side of Enterprise*. New York: McGraw-Hill, 1960.

Merriam, Sharon B. and Caffarella, Rosmary S. *Learning in Adulthood*. San Francisco: Jossey-Bass, 1991.

Merrill, David W. and Reid, Roger H. *Style Awareness Text*. Denver: Personnel Predictions and Research, Inc., 1976.

Miles, Matthew B. *Learning to Work in Groups*. New York: Teachers College, 1959.

Mink, Oscar G., Esterhuysen, Pieter W., Mink, Barbara P., and Owen, Keith Q. *Change at Work: A Comprehensive Management Process for Transforming Organizations*. San Francisco: Jossey-Bass, 1993.

Mink, Oscar G., Mink, Barbara P., Downes, Elizabeth A. and Owen, Keith Q. *Open Organizations: A Model for Effectiveness, Renewal, and Intelligent Change*. San Francisco: Jossey-Bass, 1994.

Mintzberg, H. *The Nature of Managerial Work*. New York: HarperCollins, 1973.

Mintzberg, H. *The Structuring of Organizations*. Englewood Cliffs, NJ: Prentice-Hall, 1983.

Moran, Robert T., Harris, Philip R., and Stripp, William G. *Developing the Global Organization*. Gulf Publishing, 1993.

Morrison, Ann M. *The New Leaders: Guidelines for Leadership Diversity in America*. San Francisco: Jossey-Bass, 1992.

Nadler, David A., Shaw, R. B., Walton, A. E. *Discontinuous Change: Leading Organizational Transformation*. San Francisco: Jossey-Bass, 1994.

Nadler, Gerald and Hibino, Shozo. *Breakthrough Thinking: The Seven Principles of Creative Problem Solving* (Revised Second Edition). Prima, 1994.

Naisbitt, John and Aburdene, Patricia. *Megatrends 2000: Ten New Directions for the 1990's*. New York: William Morrow, 1990.

Nanus, Burt. *The Leader's Edge*. Chicago: Contemporary Books, 1989.

Nanus, Burt. *Visionary Leadership: Creating a compelling Sense of Direction for Your Organization*. San Francisco: Jossey-Bass, 1992.

Napier, Rodney W. and Gershenfeld, Matti K. *Groups: Theory and Experience.* Fifth Edition, Boston: Houghton-Mifflin, 1993.

National Training Laboratories, *Leadership in Action.* Selected Readings Series Two, 1951.

Newstrom, John W., and Scannell, Edward E. *Games Trainers Play.* New York: McGraw-Hill, 1980.

Nielsen, Duke. *Partnering with Employees: A Practical System for Building Empowered Relationships.* San Francisco: Jossey-Bass, 1993.

Nirenberg, John. *The Living Organization: Transforming Teams into Workplace Communities.* Pfeiffer/Business One Irwin, 1993.

Odiorne, George. *The Change Resisters: How They Prevent Progress and What Managers Can Do About Them.* New York: Prentice-Hall, 1981.

O'Hara-Devereaux, Mary and Johansen, Robert. *Globalwork: Bridging Distance, Culture, and Time.* San Francisco: Jossey-Bass, 1994.

Orlich, D. C. *Staff Development.* Boston: Allyn & Bacon, 1989.

Osborne, David and Gaebler, T. *Reinventing Government: How the Entrepreneurial Spirit is Transforming the Public Sector.* Reading, MA: Addison-Wesley, 1992.

O'Toole, James. *Leading Change: Overcoming the Ideology of Comfort and the Tyranny of Custom.* San Francisco: Jossey-Bass, 1995.

Owen, H. *Riding the Tiger: Doing Business in a Transforming World.* Potomac, MD: Abbott Publishing, 1991.

Owens, Robert G. *Organizational Behavior in Education.* Third Edition. Englewood Cliffs: Prentice-Hall, 1987.

Palmer, P. *The Active Life: A Spirituality of Work, Creativity, and Caring.* New York: HarperCollins, 1990.

Parker, Glenn M. *Cross-Functional Teams: Working with Allies, Enemies, and Other Strangers.* San Francisco: Jossey-Bass, 1994.

Pascale, R. T. *Managing on the Edge.* New York: Simon & Schuster, 1990.

Peck, M. Scott. *The Different Drum: Community Making and Peace.* New York: Simon and Schuster, 1987.

Peck, M. Scott. *The Road Less Traveled: A New Psychology of Love, Traditional Values and Spiritual Growth.* Simon and Schuster, 1978.

Perelman, Lewis J. *School's Out: A Radical New Formula for the Revitalization of American's Educational System.* New York: Avon, 1992.

Peters, Tom. *Liberation Management: Necessary Disorganization for the Nanosecond Nineties.* New York: Fawcett Columbine, 1992..

Peters, Tom. *Thriving on Chaos: Handbook for a Management Revolution.* New York: Harper, 1987.

Peters, Thomas J. and Austin, Nancy K. *A Passion for Excellence - The Leadership Difference.* New York: Random House, 1985.

Peters, Thomas J. and R. H. Waterman, Jr. *In Search of Excellence.* New York: Harper and Row, 1982.

Pfeiffer, J. William and John E . Jones. *A Hand book of Structured Experiences for Human Relations Training.* Volumes I, II, III, IV, V, VI, VII, VIII, IX, X. San Diego: Pfeiffer and Company, 1969-1988.

Pfeiffer, J. William. *The Annual Handbooks for Group Facilitators.* San Diego: Pfeiffer and Company, 1972-1994.

Phillips, Steven L. *The Team-Building Source Book.* San Diego: University Associates, 1989.

Pinchot, Gifford and Pinchot, Elizabeth. *The End of Bureaucracy and the Rise of the Intelligent Organization.* San Francisco: Berrett-Koehler, 1993.

Portnoy, Robert A. *Leadership.* Englewood Cliffs: Prentice-Hall, 1986.

Quinn, R. E. *Beyond Rational Management: Mastering the Paradoxes and Competing Demands of High Performance.* San Francisco: Jossey-Bass, 1988.

Redding, John C. *Strategic Readiness: The Making of the Learning Organization.* San Francisco: Jossey-Bass, 1994.

Robinson, Russell D. *Group Dynamics for Student Activities,* Reston, Va.: National Association of Secondary School Principals, 1977.

Robinson, Russell D. "Group Transactional Mode and Community Client Focus" in *Redefining the Discipline of Adult Education* (Boyd and Apps). Jossey-Bass, 1980.

Robinson, Russell D. *An Introduction to Helping Adults Learn and Change. Revised Edition.* West Bend, WI: Omnibook Co., 1994.

Robinson, Russell D. *Teaching the Scriptures: A Study Guide for Bible Students and Teachers.* Sixth Edition, Revised. Milwaukee: Bible Study Press, 1993.

Rogers, Carl. *On Becoming a Person.* Boston: Houghton-Mifflin, 1961.

Rogers, Everett M. *Diffusion of Innovations,* Fourth Edition. New York: Free Press, 1995.

Rosener, J. B. "Ways Women Lead" *Harvard Business Review,* Nov.-Dec., 1990., pp. 119-125.

Ross, Gerald, and Kay, Michael. *Toppling the Pyramids: Redefining the Ways Companies are Run.* Time Books, 1994.

Ross, Murray. *New Understandings of Leadership.* New York: Association Press, 1957.

Rowan, Roy. *The Intuitive Manager.* NY: Berkeley Books, 1987

Russell, Peter and Evans, Roger. *The Creative Manager: Finding Inner Vision and Wisdom in Uncertain Times.* San Francisco: Jossey-Bass, 1992.

Ryan, Kathleen D. and Oestreich, Danniel K. *Driving Fear Out of the Workplace.* San Francisco: Jossey-Bass, 1991.

Sarason, Seymour. *The Predictable Failure of Educational Reform.* San Francisco: Jossey-Bass, 1990.

Satir, Virginia. *Peoplemaking.* Palo Alto: Science and Behavior Books, 1972.

Scannell, Edward E. and Newstrom, John W. *More Games Trainers Play: Experiential Learning Exercises.* New York: McGraw-Hill, 1993.

Scannell, Edward E. and Newstrom, John W. *Still More Games Trainers Play. Experiential Learning Exercises.* New York: McGraw-Hill, 1991.

Schein, Edgar. *Organizational Culture and Leadership.* San Francisco: Jossey-Bass, 1985.

Schlechty, Phillip. Schools for the Twenty-first Century. San Francisco: Jossey-Bass, 1990.

Schmidt, John W. "The Leader's Role in Strategic Planning" in Simerly, R. *Strategic Planning and Leadership in Continuing Education.* San Francisco: Jossey-Bass, 1987.

Schmidt, Warren H. and Finnigan, J. P. *TQManager: A Practical Guide for Managing in a Total Quality Organization.* San Francisco: Jossey-Bass, 1993.

Schmuck, R. A. and Runkel, P.J. *Handbook of Organizational Development in Schools (4th ed).* New York: Prospect Heights, IL: Waveland Press, 1994.

Scholtes, Peter R. *The Team Handbook: How to Use Teams to Improve Quality.* Madison: Joiner, 1988.

Schon, Donald A. *Educating the Reflective Practitioner: Toward a New Design for Teaching and Learning in the Professions.* San Francisco: Jossey-Bass, 1990.

Schon, Donald A. *The Reflective Practitioner: How Professionals Think in Action.* New York: Basic Books, 1983.

Schumann, Paul and others. *Innovate! Straight Path to Quality, Customer Delight, and Competitive Advantage.* McGraw-Hill, 1994.

Schutz, Will. *The Human Element: Productivity, Self-Esteem, and the Bottom Line.* San Francisco: Jossey-Bass, 1994.

Schwarz, Roger M. *The Skilled Facilitator: Practical Wisdom for Developing Effective Groups.* San Francisco: Jossey-Bass, 1994.

Seashore, Stanley E. (ed.) *Assessing Organization Change.* New York: Wiley, 1983.

Senge, Peter M. *The Fifth Discipline: The Art & Practice of The Learning Organization.* New York: Doubleday, 1990.

Senge, Peter M. and others. *The Fifth Discipline Fieldbook: Strategies and Tools for Building a Learning Organization.* New York: Doubleday, 1994.

Sergiovanni, T. J. *Building Community in Schools.* San Francisco: Jossey-Bass, 1994.

Sergiovanni, T. J. *Moral Leadership.* San Francisco: Jossey-Bass, 1992.

Sergionvanni, T. J. *Value-Added Leadership: How to Get Extraordinary Performance in Schools.* San Diego: Harcourt Brace Jovanovich, 1990.

Simerly, Robert G. and Associates. *Strategic Planning and Leadership in Continuing Education.* San Francisco: Jossey-Bass, 1987.

Simon, Sidney B. and others. *Values Clarification.* New York: Hart Publishing Co., 1972.

Sims, Henry P., Jr., Giola, Dennis A. and associates. *The Thinking Organization: Dynamics of Organizational Social Cooperation.* San Francisco: Jossey-Bass, 1986.

Smith, Phyl and Kearny, Lynn. *Creating Workplaces Where People Can Think.* San Francisco: Jossey-Bass, 1994.

Srivastva, S., Cooperrider, D. L., and Associates. *Appreciative Management and Leadership: The Power of Positive Thought and Action in Organizations.* San Francisco: Jossey-Bass, 1990.

Steiner, George A. *Strategic Planning.* New York: Free Press, 1979.

Steiner, George A. and Miner, J. B. *Management Policy and Strategy.* New York: Macmillan, 1982.

Stogdill, R. M. *Handbook of Leadership.* New York: The Free Press, 1974.

293

Tagliere, Daniel A. *How to Meet, Think, and Work to Consensus*. San Diego: Pfeiffer and Co., 1993.

Tannen, Deborah. *You Just Don't Understand: Men and Women in Conversation*. NY: Ballantine Books, 1990.

Tannenbaum, Robert and Schmidt, Warren H. "How to Choose a Leadership Pattern" *Harvard Business Review*, March-April, 1958.

Taylor, Jack Wilson. *How to Select and Develop Leaders*. New York: McGraw-Hill, 1962.

Theobald, Robert. *The Rapids of Change. Social Entrepreneurship in Turbulent Times*. Indianapolis: Knowledge Systems, 1987.

Thelen, Herbert A. *Dynamics of Groups at Work*. Chicago: The University of Chicago Press, 1954.

Thompson, Scott D. (ed) *School Leadership: A Blueprint for Change*. Newberry Park, CA: Corwin Press, 1991.

Thousand, J. S., Villa, R., and Nevin, A. I. Creativity and Collaborative Learning. Paul H. Brooks, 1994.

Tichy, Noel M. and Sherman, Stratford. *Control Your Destiny or Someone Else Will*. New York: Doubleday, 1993.

Tichy, Noel M. and Devanna, Mary Anne. *The Transformational Leader*. New York: John Wiley, 1990.

Tores, Cresencio. *The Tao of Teams: A Guide to Team Success*. San Diego: Pfeiffer and Company, 1994.

Vaill, P. B. *Managing as a Performing Art: New Ideas for a World of Chaotic Change*. San Francisco: Jossey-Bass, 1989.

Verderber, Rudolph E. *Working Together: Fundamentals of Decision Making*. Belmont, California: Wadsworth Pub. Co., 1982.

Von Bertalanffy, L. *General System Theory*. New York: Braziller, 1949.

Vroom, Victor H. and Jago, Arthur G. *The New Leadership: Managing Participation and Organization*. Englewood Cliffs: Prentice-Hall, 1989.

Walton, Mary. *The Deming Management Method*. NY: Dodd, Mead and Co., 1986.

Warschaw, Tessa. *Winning by Negotiation*, New York: Berkley Books, 1980.

Watkins, Karen E. and Marsick, Victoria. *Sculpting the Learning Organization: Lessons in the Art and Science of Systems Change*. San Francisco: Jossey-Bass, 1993.

Wasley, P. A. *Teachers Who Lead.* New York: Teacher's College Press, 1991.

Wellins, Richard S., Byham, W. D., and Dixon, G. R. *Inside Teams: How 200 World-class Organizations are Winning Through Teamwork.* San Francisco: Jossey-Bass, 1994.

Wheelan, Susan A. *Group Processes: A Developmental Perspective.* Boston: Allyn and Bacon, 1994.

Wiener, N. *The Human Use of Human Beings: Cybernetics and Society.* New York: Avon Books, 1967.

Wilson, Jeanne M. and George, Jill A. *Team Leader's Survival Guide.* Development Dimensions International, 1994.

Wheatley, Margaret J. *Leadership and the New Science: Learning About Organizations from an Orderly Universe.* San Francisco: Berrett-Koehler Publishers, 1992.

Wlodkowski, Raymond J. *Enhancing Adult Motivation to Learn: A Guide to Improving Instruction and Increasing Learner Achievement.* San Francisco: Jossey-Bass, 1985.

Yeomans, William. *1000 Things You Never Learned in Business School.* NY: Penguin, 1985.

Yukl, Gary A. *Leadership in Organizations,* Second Edition. Englewood Cliffs: Prentice-Hall, 1989.

Zaltman, G., Florio, D. H., Sikorski, L. A. *Dynamic Educational Change.* New York: Free Press, 1977.

Zander, Alvin. *The Purposes of Groups and Organizations.* San Francisco: Jossey-Bass, 1985.

Zander, Alvin. *Making Groups Effective* (2nd edition). San Francisco: Jossey-Bass, 1994.

> He has achieved success who has lived well,
>   laughed often and loved much;
> Who has gained the respect of intelligent men
>   and the love of little children;
> Who has filled his niche and accomplished his
>   task;
> Who has left the world better than he found it,
>   whether by an improved poppy, a perfect poem,
>   or a rescued soul;
> Who has never lacked appreciation of earth's
>   beauty or failed to express it;
> Who has always looked for the best in others
>   and given the best he had;
> Whose life was an inspiration; whose memory
>   a benediction.
>
> -Wallace Bruce Amsbary

Index of Names

Index of Subjects

·Professor Russell D. Robinson was named professor emeritus in the Department of Administrative Leadership at the University of Wisconsin-Milwaukee in 1994. A native of Wisconsin, he joined the UWM faculty in 1963. He earned his B.S. (1950), M.S. (1961) and Ph.D. (1963) degrees at the University of Wisconsin, Madison. He became a member of the University of Wisconsin faculty in 1950. Prior to coming to Milwaukee, Dr. Robinson spent ten years with University Extension as youth agent for Waukesha County, primarily involved in leadership development. His youth leadership work won him national recognition and a three year Kellogg fellowship in the National Extension Center for Advanced Study.

For his first five years at UWM he was on a joint appointment with University Extension, first as a state youth development specialist and later as an urban community programs specialist. He resigned his half-time Extension assignment in 1968 and since then devoted full time to the adult education graduate program which he initiated and developed at UWM. Since the program began in 1966, more than 700 have been awarded master's degrees, and fifteen completed Ph.D. degrees under his direction. From 1978 to 1982 he served as chairperson of the Department of Administrative Leadership. From 1990, he has headed IDEAL, the Institute for the Development of Effective Administrative Leadership.

Dr. Robinson has been active in professional adult education groups, having served as a member of the Executive Committee of the Adult Education Association of the USA, chairman of the National Council of Affiliate Adult Education Organizations, chairman of the Commission on Adult Education Research for the United States and Canada, secretary-treasurer of the Commission of Professors of Adult Education, president of the Wisconsin Association for Adult and Continuing Education, chairman of the Wisconsin Adult Educator Lyceum, and president of the Milwaukee Council for Adult Learning.

In 1974 he was the recipient of the Distinguished Service Award given by the Milwaukee Council for "outstanding leadership, inspired teaching, and service to the community in adult education." In 1985 he received the Wisconsin Association's "Adult Educator of the Year" award for leadership, and the same year received a national leadership award from the American Association for chairing the national conference. In 1991 he received the "President's Award" from the Wisconsin Association for Adult and Continuing Education for "in recognition of 33 years of superb ledership and commitment to excellence in Wisconsin adult and continuing education."

He is a practitioner as well as professor of adult education, regularly teaching non-credit adult courses and in-service workshops in leadership, group dynamics, planned change, human relations, adult learning, and program development to groups of adult educators including administrators, teachers, clergy, nurses, and others. In 1977 the Milwaukee Council awarded him its Recognition of Achievement Award for his conducting more than 40 workshops for nurses. He has participated in a variety of community and state boards and committees. His service has included the Board of Future Milwaukee, the Milwaukee Inter-Institutional Committee for Higher Education Title I Programs, the Education Advisory Committee of the Mental Health Association of Milwaukee County, the Milwaukee Advisory Committee on Basic Adult Education, the International Cooperative Training Center Advisory Committee, the Wisconsin Recreation Leaders' Laboratory, the Advisory Committee of the Planned Parenthood Center for Training in Family Planning, and others.

For five years he directed Project Understanding, a program of civic education aimed at reducing prejudice and encouraging action on social issues. The program, sponsored by the National Conference of Christians and Jews and other groups, was twice offered on television with more than 8,000 persons formally enrolled in viewing-discussion groups. In 1969, Dr. Robinson was awarded the WTMJ-TV Public Service Award for "distinguished service to the community through broadcasting." He is an active layman in his church and a student of Bible and Church history. His book, Teaching the Scriptures: A Study Guide for Bible Students and Teachers, is now in its sixth edition.

He has written for such professional journals as Adult Education, Adult Leadership, and Journal of Extension. In addition to An Introduction to Dynamics of Group Leadership and Organizational Change, he is author of the text, An Introduction to Helping Adults Learn and Change, the pamphlet, Group Dynamics for Student Activities, and a chapter in Redefining the Discipline of Adult Education one of the Handbook Series of Adult Education.

To obtain books by Russell D. Robinson, Ph.D.:

⫸ ***An Introduction to
Dynamics of Group Leadership
and Organizational Change***

❏ ***An Introduction to
Helping Adults Learn and Change***

➥ Order from:
Omnibook Company
1171 Decorah Rd
West Bend, WI   53095-9509
Telephone: (414) 675-2760
FAX: (414) 675-2340

To obtain information about workshops, other inquiries:

➥ Contact:
Leadership Dynamics
9017 N. 70th Street
Milwaukee, WI   53223-2113
Telephone and FAX (414) 354-3504

304